MEN FROM THE MINISTRY

HOW BRITAIN SAVED ITS HERITAGE

SIMON THURLEY

YALE UNIVERSITY PRESS

NEW HAVEN AND LONDON

Designed by Emily Lees
Printed in Great Britain by T J International Ltd, Padstow, Cornwall

Library of Congress Cataloging-in-Publication Data

Thurley, Simon, 1962–
Men from the ministry : how Britain saved its heritage / Simon Thurley.
pages cm
Includes bibliographical references and index.
ISBN 978–0–300–19572–9 (cl : alk. paper)
1. Historic buildings – Conservation and restoration – Great Britain – History.
2. Historic sites – Conservation and restoration – Great Britain – History.
3. Great Britain – Antiquities – Collection and preservation – History.
4. Great Britain – Officials and employees. 5. Great Britain. Dept. of Ancient Monuments
and Historic Buildings – History. 6. Great Britain. Dept. of Ancient Monuments and Historic
Buildings – History. I. Title.
DA655.T48 2013
363.6'90941 – dc23
2013006721

A catalogue record for this book is available from the British Library

MEN FROM THE MINISTRY

CONTENTS

This book is the product of a research project I set up in 2012. Its purpose was to consult the many thousands of files in the English Heritage Archives to write the history of the Ancient Monuments Department of the Office of Works, its predecessors and successor bodies. My assistant, Becky Clark, has led the work in a masterly way, supervising two outstanding English Heritage researchers seconded to my office, Sebastian Fry and Nick Chapple. Among the three of them, they have made sense of a huge quantity of material, bringing alive the people and places that are core to the story of heritage protection in Britain. It would have been impossible to write this book were it not for them, and in many senses it is their book as much as mine. They were helped at an early stage by Harry Leech and Sally Bruce-Lockhart. Their comprehensive reports, prepared as the base research for this book, can be accessed in full online at www.english-heritage.org.uk.

For an organisation that deals with history everyday, English Heritage is surprisingly uninterested in its own ancestry. But, once we started to consult our colleagues, we found that dozens, maybe scores of them, past and present, had undertaken work on the subject. I am grateful in particular to Jeremy Ashbee, Roger Bowdler, Jonathan Coad, Keith Emerick, Emily Gee, Julian Holder, Edward Impey, Anna Keay, Deborah Lamb, Ian Leith, Nick Molyneaux, Andrew Saint, Michael Thompson, Michael Turner and Charles Wagner. I am also very grateful to our expert editorial team who read and commented on each of these chapters, correcting and improving them as they went: Jeremy Ashbee, Roger Bowdler, Steven Brindle, Emily Gee,

Edward Impey, Richard Morrice, Andrew Saint, Paul Stamper and Michael Turner. Professor Sir David Cannadine was kind enough to provide some excellent early advice. Professor Michael Port read and commented on the first four chapters and Merlin Waterson read and made some very helpful comments on chapter Thirteen. The Chair of English Heritage, Baroness Andrews, has supported this project throughout, and has also acted as expert referee, making many helpful comments. Needless to say the faults that remain are mine alone.

The librarians at the English Heritage Library at Swindon have been brilliant. Some of the library is directly inherited from the original Office of Works Library at Storeys Gate, and it has been a thrill to consult books inscribed by people who feature in this book. The English Heritage Archives and Photographic teams have also done sterling work, furnishing the rare and fascinating images in this book.

Today I am told that there are more than 400 different job types at English Heritage, a fact that would have astonished the first Ancient Monuments Inspector, General Pitt-Rivers. All of them contribute equally to the important work that goes on. But most of these jobs have become necessary only in the last thirty years. Before then, the Inspectors of Ancient Monuments and Historic Buildings had to be everything, do everything and know everything. So this book is dedicated to those special men and women from the Ministry, the Inspectorate past and present, and in particular, from my personal point of view, to Michael Green, the first Inspector I knew, who launched me on the most fascinating and enjoyable of careers.

> The work I am going to describe is the united effort of a small body of
> archaeologists and architects belonging to that great anonymous society,
> the Civil Service. Mute, modest and meritorious, they are, in these
> present times, the authentic successors of those monastic orders whose
> relics they study to preserve. Their deserts are known only to their
> heads of departments: they live in obscurity and die in poverty.[1]

It was in this way that, in 1931, Sir Charles Peers, Chief Inspector of Ancient
Monuments, described the employees of the Ancient Monuments Department of the Office of Works, the subject of this book. The Ancient Monuments Department was the smallest section within the smallest office in
Whitehall, yet its story is a remarkable one – and one that has not been
told before.

On the one hand this is strange, for the people who served in it, and the
ministers who were responsible for it, had a big role in making the country
in which we live today. On the other hand, it is no surprise. Governments
and civil servants rarely get the credit for anything they do and the history of Britain's conservation movement is no exception. Dozens of books
and articles have been written about the Society of Antiquaries, the Society
for the Protection of Ancient Buildings, the National Trust, the Georgian
Group, the Victorian Society, the Twentieth Century Society, the Ancient
Monuments Society and the Council of British Archaeology – deservedly
so, since their history is interesting and important, and perhaps all the more
important because they were established through voluntary effort without
the help or say-so of the State. But nobody has bothered to write about the
history of the one official body that the Government charged with what is
called 'preservation'.

This book is not that history, although I hope that one day it will be written. It is, however, about those who worked in Government to save Britain's historic places during the late nineteenth and twentieth centuries. The men from the Ministry who people this book had a closely defined role in what they called 'preservation'. This book follows those responsibilities and does not attempt to cover in detail the important parallel role of planning in protecting historic places; this has been extensively chronicled elsewhere. It ends when responsibility passed from ministers to an arm's-length body, English Heritage. So in essence this book attempts to put the men and women from the Ministry back into the heart of the story of conservation, where they belong.

What was their achievement? It was, I think, twofold. First, they accumulated the greatest national collection of monuments and historic buildings ever assembled: 880 of them acquired, in the main, between 1913 and 1978 to illustrate the nation's history. These were restored, researched and presented to a public, almost seventeen million of whom visited in 2012. Then they made an even bigger and more ambitious collection, a series of lists of places that were of outstanding national importance; by being on the list, these would acquire the protection of the State. There are now around 532,000 listed and scheduled places in Britain, places that give people pride, delight and beauty. Neither collection was ever going to be perfect. They did not get everything they wanted, nor certainly saved everything they wanted to save, but these collections, now in the custodianship of the three devolved bodies – English Heritage, Cadw and Historic Scotland – are truly monumental.

Most of the men from the Ministry who appear in this book were architects, archaeologists and historians, but they, as well as the administrative civil servants with whom they worked so closely, were also bureaucrats. The decisions they made, and the reasons for them, are covered in a magnificent series of minutely detailed files held by their national successor bodies, English Heritage, Cadw and Historic Scotland, and in The National Archives. The primary sources for this book are the unpublished, and never before researched, files of English Heritage, supplemented by the English files from The National Archives. We have not consulted the extensive archives for Scotland or Wales. In 1989 a large number of English files were incinerated in error, leaving some big gaps in the narrative. But the material is still extensive enough to tell a story that has not been told before.

I write in early 2013, the centenary of the Ancient Monuments Act of 1913. This anniversary provides the opportunity, and the excuse, to rescue the Ancient Monuments Department from obscurity, but what will this achieve? Obviously, I hope that it will be an important contribution to an understanding of how our people in the last century thought about the past, about history and archaeology; I also hope it will explain how and why they protected places and what they wanted to achieve. Working for politicians, sometimes much is done; at other times energy, brilliance and resources are needlessly and wastefully thrown away. Up until now the achievements of these men have been anonymous and unrecorded. I hope that this book will add a new dimension to our current understanding and provide a rich seam for future research.

But there is also a deeper purpose. The ministers responsible for what we today call our historic environment, the First Commissioners of Works and subsequently Ministers of Works and then the Environment, were often deeply committed to saving imperilled places of great beauty and antiquity. They recognised the intrinsic value of these places and their value to society. Some even recognised their value to the voters. In recent years, particularly the years either side of the millennium, that sense of value has been lost. While contemporary artistic expression is fervently admired, there has been a turning away from the remarkable achievements of the past – at least among the political and opinion-forming liberal elite in London.

When I became Director of the Museum of London in 1996, I was asked to make a film for the 'Faith Zone' in the Millennium Dome. This extraordinary and striking building bizarrely came to symbolise the nadir of appreciation of Britain's history and heritage. Its zones were free from the accumulated debris of what were seen as colonialism, xenophobia, national triumphalism, oppression and class war. My film ended up being criticised for not giving enough emphasis to pagan beliefs. Fortunately, this *fin-de-siècle* loss of cultural value attached to Britain's history and historic environment is a phase that has passed, like so many others. The triumphant celebration of British history and heritage that accompanied the opening of the London Olympic Games in 2012 marked the full turning of a circle. Unlike the Dome, it depicted a country comfortable with its historical roots, both the good parts and the bad.

Yet there is still a job to be done. When, in 2010, the new Conservative-Liberal Democrat coalition had to make massive cuts, ministers turned to the part of the National Heritage Collection in the care of English Heritage. Could it be given away, sold or dismembered in some way? Surely this was just a collection of old buildings randomly assembled that could be casually dispersed? These discussions made me feel acutely that, despite nearly a century of heroic collecting backed by political will and determination, the National Heritage Collection was not perceived as having the same cultural weight as other collections. While the British Museum, the National Gallery and the South Kensington Museums are all recognised as being part of the cultural fabric of the nation, the bodies that look after the greatest, largest and most ambitious of all the national collections are somehow not seen in the same light. The men from the Ministry, and their successors, in Cadw, Historic Scotland and English Heritage, are rarely seen as cultural champions curating the great outdoor museum of the nation's history. They are, in Charles Peers's words, 'part of the great anonymous society'. I hope that this book will draw attention to the extraordinary achievements of these people, both then and now – achievements that have fundamentally shaped a sense of our own history and identity and secured for us a country that is still rich in beauty and interest.

Their job is not over. Today, the successors of the men from the Ministry still have to make difficult choices about what will be regarded as special in the future and have to work out how to protect it. They do that in a historical context that stretches back into the 1880s. When Charles Peers accepted his RIBA Gold Medal in April 1933, he said:

> I stand here as representative not of myself, but of a cause and an enthusiasm which has been carrying on now for some generations, and will continue for many generations after we have gone . . . I am the last man in the world, standing here, to suggest that all that has been done will exceed in merit all that will be done. I am certain there will be things in the time to come which will test the skill of some far-off successor of mine, when he has to deal with the magnificent masterpieces of the Early Concrete Period. He will be just as enthusiastic in preserving its probably decaying remains as I have been in any of my works.

As that far-off successor, I believe that the complex issues we face deserve to be better understood and better appreciated, and I hope that what follows will help that to be the case.

I

SEEKING THE 'OLDEN TIME':
POPULAR ENTHUSIASM FOR HISTORY IN THE
NINETEENTH CENTURY

'Sir', wrote the anonymous M.D.K. to *The Times* on 26 August 1881,

> Permit me to draw the attention of those who are interested in the pres-
> ervation of ancient monuments to the present state of things at Furness
> Abbey. I was present in the ruins for three hours this Thursday afternoon
> last, and was extremely shocked at the spectacle I witnessed. The place was
> filled with a rough and noisy crowd of excursionists, and large numbers
> of children, apparently under no control, were climbing in and out of the
> beautiful sedilia and over the sculptured capitals of the fallen pillars, which
> lie on the ground in the ancient Chapter-house, to the extreme danger
> and, I fear, destruction of most exquisitely carved work.[1]

M.D.K.'s experience of Furness Abbey was not isolated or unusual. Since
the 1830s a trip to an ancient monument had been regarded by people of
all classes as a good day out, because in the half-century that followed the
Battle of Waterloo in 1815 the average Briton's perception of history was
transformed.

This rise in popular appreciation of the past had deep roots in English
culture. In the sixteenth and seventeenth centuries a few lone antiquaries
like John Leland (1503–1552) and Sir William Dugdale (1605–1686) began to
recognise the unique value and interest of the monuments of the past. They
described and wrote histories of what they saw, partly from a realisation that

much of it was threatened with destruction. By the early eighteenth century antiquarianism and the study of the past were becoming more widespread, so much so as to lead to the foundation of the Society of Antiquaries of London, which first met in 1707–8.

The Society was important in promoting the idea that medieval ruins should be preserved as cultural monuments. The year after its foundation came the first recorded set-piece debate (or rather, row) over the preservation of a historic structure: Sir John Vanbrugh, building Blenheim Palace for the 1st Duke of Marlborough, was struck by the beauty of the medieval Woodstock Manor and urged its preservation as a picturesque feature. His pleas were swept aside by his great adversary, Sarah, Duchess of Marlborough, and the old manor was totally destroyed.

Vanbrugh was not a lone voice. The Georgian upper classes increasingly took interest in ancient monuments. The Continental Grand Tour also stimulated the idea of cultural tourism at home, while a rising appreciation of landscape and the picturesque encouraged people to see medieval ruins as beautiful and evocative. Landscape and topographical art were increasingly popular, and the makers of prints and engravings turned to their local monuments as subject matter.

For these kinds of reasons, a number of ruins in similar situations to Woodstock Manor were saved. The abbeys of Rievaulx and Roche in Yorkshire and Old Wardour Castle in Wiltshire were close enough to the new houses of their aristocratic owners to be incorporated into extensive landscaped parks. Less fortunate owners built sham castles and ruins to adorn their new landscapes. Horace Walpole (1717–1797), the writer and aesthete who promoted a revival of Gothic architecture through the development of his own home, Strawberry Hill House at Twickenham, would have warmly approved. In the late eighteenth century the Gothic style, or a cosmetic version of it, was an increasingly fashionable choice for country houses and interiors. So medieval architecture was becoming valued, in certain circumstances, for visual and picturesque reasons: how far it was appreciated for its historical value is rather more of a moot point. For in the Georgian age true antiquarianism was still a minority hobby: cartoonists like Thomas Rowlandson could still present antiquaries as eccentric figures of fun.[2]

Thus it is fair to say that an interest in ancient monuments was the preserve of the elite. In the mid-nineteenth century a variety of factors, including patriotism, historical novels, railways and the rise of middle-class tour-

The entrance to the chapter house of Furness Abbey was fenced off by the time this photograph was taken in 1898 – possibly because of the 'noisy crowds of excursionists'. Reproduced by permission of English Heritage

ism, conspired to bring an appreciation of the past and its monuments to altogether wider audiences. In 1814 Sir Walter Scott (1771–1832) published his first novel, *Waverley; or, 'Tis Sixty Years Since*. He was already a successful and well-known poet, but this book marked a turning point, not only in his career but also in the way that people experienced the past. *Waverley* was the first of twenty-three novels that Scott wrote in the thirteen years before 1827. Only three were set in his lifetime; each of the others took place in different periods of the past. What proved to be so powerful about Scott's writing was its realism; his novels were rooted in historical events, set in existing historic places and contained brilliantly described historical figures. They were also full of historical information, making the past tangible and realistic in a way it had never been before.[3]

The locations in which Scott's novels were set quickly became places of pilgrimage. At Ashby de la Zouch, in Leicestershire, the Scott effect was ruthlessly exploited by the locals. The great tournament in *Ivanhoe* (1819) is set at the castle, and its craggy ruins became a tourist magnet. After finding saline springs at his Moira Colliery 3 miles away, the castle's owner, the Marquess of Hastings, decided to pipe the water to Ashby, where he built the Ivanhoe Baths, a complex in the Greek Revival style, with a façade more than 200 feet long. Nearby was a big new hotel, the Royal, designed to accommodate those who came for the romance of the castle and the effects of the spring water. Kenilworth in Warwickshire, made famous by Scott's novel of the same name, published in 1821, was likewise transformed. The trickle of people who had come to view the ivy-clad ruins in the eighteenth century turned into a flood. Amongst their number were Queen Victoria, who visited in 1858, and the novelists Charles Dickens and Henry James. The popularity of the castle encouraged greater care for the ruins; gradually, ivy was torn down, trees felled and fallen masonry removed. The Revd E. H. Knowles, a local antiquarian, made a careful study of the castle, cleared of accretions; he published an account of what he found in 1872 as *The Castle of Kenilworth*.[4]

Scott's imagination inspired two generations of writers, some of whom enjoyed considerable success. In the late 1830s and 1840s William Harrison Ainsworth (1805–1882), sometime business partner of Charles Dickens, wrote a series of historical novels that enjoyed huge popularity. *The Tower of London* (1840), *Old St Paul's* (1841) and *Windsor Castle* (1843) combined detailed and acute architectural descriptions with an imaginative version of history. Hugely successful, *The Tower* went into its sixth edition within five years, and was translated into French, Spanish, German and Dutch.

From the 1820s these historical novels were brought alive by advances in print technology, including, in 1822, the introduction of steel engraving, which allowed tens of thousands of quality impressions from a single plate. Both Harrison Ainsworth's *The Tower of London* and *Windsor Castle* were illustrated by George Cruikshank (1792–1878), who mixed spectral figures with carefully observed architectural depictions. Some engravings, such as *Queen Jane's First Night in the Tower*, convey more vividly than Ainsworth's mediocre text the full Gothic horror of the stories. From 1827 it became possible to integrate woodcuts into the text, unleashing a deluge of popular books and magazines at a more popular level. The exhaustingly prolific writer and publisher Charles Knight (1791–1873) was perhaps the most successful at exploiting this new technology. Between 1832 and 1845 he was the publisher of the *Penny Magazine,* which at its peak sold 200,000 copies a

Queen Jane's First Night in the Tower, by George Cruickshank from Harrison
Ainsworth's *The Tower of London: A Historical Romance* (1840). Here Lady Jane Grey
stumbles across a carelessly abandoned executioner's axe in St John's Chapel in the White
Tower. © Heritage Images

week and may have been read by a million people. Favourite subjects were
the ruins of castles and abbeys and famous historical sites like the Tower of
London, which were covered in depth.[5]

The *Penny Magazine*'s chief rival, the weekly *Saturday Magazine*, was also
interested in historic sites. In 1840 it secured the publishing of the plates
from Joseph Nash's *Mansions of England in the Olden Time*. The first volume

of Nash's book came out in 1839, to be followed by two more by 1849. The plates illustrated views of Tudor and early Stuart country houses with groups of authentically dressed characters. These illustrations presented for the first time, in an accessible format, tangible images of life in the 'Olden Time' that people had got to know through novels and magazines.

Nash's plates reflected and contributed to a noticeable shift in interest in popular literature from the ruins of medieval sites, prominent in the 1830s, to a greater interest in Tudor and Stuart buildings and ruins in the 1840s. Symbolic of this shift was the intense interest taken in Shakespeare's birthplace in Stratford-upon-Avon. In 1835 a committee had been formed to preserve his tomb in Holy Trinity Church. In 1838 the indefatigable Charles Knight began issuing a popular edition of Shakespeare's works, and in 1843 he published a very successful biography. When the house widely believed to be Shakespeare's birthplace was put up for sale in 1847, Knight was in the forefront of a campaign to save it as a visitor attraction.[6]

This close connection between romantic perceptions of the past and historic sites was increasingly reinforced by travel books, guides and itineraries.

Bolsover Castle, Derbyshire: 'The Hall in the Little Castle', from Joseph Nash, *The Mansions of England in the Olden Time*, 1840 volume, pl. VI. The Little Castle was unfurnished at the time this image was made. Reproduced by permission of English Heritage

William Howitt (1792–1879) was a writer, journalist, poet and social reformer who wrote three successful books singing the praises of the English countryside: *The Rural Life of England* (1838), *The Boy's Country-Book* (1839) and *Visits to Remarkable Places* (2 vols, 1840–2). He had a strong belief in encouraging tourism by road and rail as a means of personal improvement, and *Visits to Remarkable Places*, part history, part travelogue and part guide, vividly describes historic places such as Stratford-upon-Avon and Hampton Court.[7]

Others were producing books that were meant to be used as guides in the field. William Beattie (1793–1875), a Scottish physician and poet, published *The Castles and Abbeys of England* in 1842. He told his readers: 'Hitherto the grand objection to works of this description has been their expense which has confined the circulation of picturesque antiquarian works to the opulent classes of society. The great recommendation of the present work is its unprecedented cheapness.' He claimed that it was only a twentieth of the cost of any previous similar publication. The text, accompanied by 250 engravings, could be followed room by room by visitors to eight castles and abbeys open to the public.

In 1862, with his wife Mary, William Howitt took the art a stage further by publishing *Ruined Abbeys and Castles of Great Britain*. This was a pioneering work, the first substantial guidebook to ruined historical sites to be illustrated by photographs, covering seventeen different places across Great Britain. Almost immediately extracts were published so that visitors to Yorkshire and the Welsh and Scottish borders could take smaller, area-focused, volumes with them. In 1864 a second series was published that included a further sixteen ruined sites. The Howitts believed that these remains 'stand amid the fair landscapes of England as if meant only to stud them with gems of additional loveliness'; Britain, we learn, is alone in having 'such numbers of graceful skeletons and fractured bones of the once proud forms of papal greatness'.

Visiting historic sites was not a new phenomenon after the Napoleonic Wars, but it did become a more intensive one. War had shut off the Continent to tourists, and stimulated a domestic tourist boom. The development of turnpikes from the seventeenth century had already opened up the countryside to the better off, and touring ancient sites and ruins, map and guidebook in hand, had become an enthusiastic pastime. After the wars, however, leisure tourism became a feature of many more people's lives. As well as having Sunday as a 'rest' day, from the mid-1840s it became common to get a half-day on Saturdays, then a full weekend, and by the end of the

Carisbrooke Castle, from William and Mary Howitt's book *Ruined Abbeys and Castles of Great Britain* (1862). Each of the twenty-seven plates features individuals or groups of tourists enjoying the ruins. These were not empty haunting remains, but lively, populated tourist attractions. Reproduced by permission of English Heritage

century many manual workers had an annual week-long holiday and clerical workers might have two.

Before the coming of the railways, tourists had ventured out by foot, coach and boat. In the early 1830s railway companies began offering excursion trains, chartered services taking groups on leisure trips. The Great Exhibition (1851) provided a huge stimulus to the rail excursion, since hundreds of thousands came to London on such services. At first, most excursion trains ran only on Sundays, but soon they ran on weekdays too. In 1872 the Midland Railway provided third-class carriages on all trains and two years later amalgamated the third and second classes to create more space for the cheapest tickets. The consequences were astonishing – an increase on the line of four million passenger journeys a year. Rail travel now became a means of mass conveyance, and access became much easier for working-class people, with more small stations in the countryside.[8] Many rail services took people to the seaside, but visits to historical sites remained very popular. Trips were often organised through tourist societies. The York Society, for instance, was busy arranging rail outings to 'historical relics of bygone ages' with the purpose of 'making us better able to understand and appreciate the manners and mode of life of our Norman and Saxon forefathers'. In 1878 they spent a happy day at Conisbrough Castle and Roche Abbey, despite the fact that the line from York to Doncaster was blocked by a broken-down locomotive.[9]

The tourist societies provided fun days out, but the huge number of county archaeological societies, founded from the 1840s, had a more serious purpose. They brought together leisured and well-off men (mainly) who were seized by the fashionable interest in medieval churches, ruins and Roman and prehistoric remains. Those founded in the decade after 1845 included county societies in Northamptonshire, Lincolnshire, Norfolk, Sussex, Bedfordshire and Buckinghamshire, and outings were an important part of their activities.[10] The Revd Richard Harris Barham (1788–1845), who wrote a hugely popular satirical saga, *The Ingoldsby Legends* (1837–43), under the pen name Thomas Ingoldsby, was one of the first to satirise the middle-class enthusiasm for visiting and studying ruined sites in *The Spectre of Tappington*. One wet morning a house party set off for a picnic in the picturesque ruins of Bolsover Abbey. One of their number, Mr Simpkinson, a distinguished member of an antiquarian society, started to lecture the party on the ruins' history: 'Bolsover Priory', he said, 'was founded in the reign of King Henry the Sixth, about the beginning of the eleventh century. Hugh de Bolsover had accompanied that monarch to the Holy Land, in the expedition undertaken by way of penance for the murder of his young nephews in the Tower.' The other guests listened to this nonsense, spellbound, while his romantically inclined daughter communed with 'a gothic window of the Saxon order'.[11]

The ruins of the fictional Bolsover Abbey were open free for the enjoyment of Thomas Ingoldsby's party, but increasingly historic places were becoming visitor attractions at which an entrance fee was charged. John Bloom, vicar of Castle Acre in Norfolk, for instance, described visitors freely picnicking in the ruins of the Norman priory there in 1843. By the time the railway arrived at King's Lynn and Swaffham later in the decade, the priory was a regular and popular excursion, so much so that its owner, the Earl of Leicester, needed to make special arrangements for tourists. By the late 1880s

The custodian's house and garden at Castle Acre Priory, Norfolk, in 1900. The prior's lodging, in which the custodian lived, was later stripped out and opened to the public by the Office of Works. Reproduced by permission of English Heritage

there was a full-time caretaker who charged an admission fee of sixpence per visitor, and by 1908 he was selling an official guidebook.[12]

Cleeve Abbey in Somerset was likewise made available to the public by the coming of the railway. In 1855 attention was being drawn to the ruins by the Somerset Archaeological and Natural History Society (itself established in 1848). Two substantial articles published in its journal demonstrated the importance and quality of the remains that were, at the time, being used as a farmstead. As a consequence, the buildings were bought by an enlightened local landlord, George Fownes Luttrell (1828–1910) of Dunster Castle, who was an enthusiast for the Middle Ages and had commissioned Anthony Salvin (1799–1881) to renovate Dunster for him. He was also busy with tourism, having invested heavily in the development of Minehead as a seaside resort. This included bringing the railway to the town, which led, in 1874, to a branch line to Washford, close to Cleeve. The following year Luttrell leased Cleeve to one Mr Tarr, who was given the responsibility of opening the ruins to the public at a charge of twopence a head. Surviving visitors' books

Cleeve Abbey, Somerset, *circa* 1860. At this date the custodian was Charles H. Clapp, a police constable. His daughter, who was born at the abbey, was named Cleevena in its honour. Reproduced by permission of English Heritage

from around 1900 show that the charge had risen to one shilling by then, and that people were coming from as far away as Inverness, Bombay and the West Indies. But visitor numbers were modest: in the first six months of 1900 only 740 called.[13]

Kenilworth Castle has already been mentioned. When the novelist Henry James visited in the 1870s he found it swarming with visitors 'like a startled hive'. By 1883 there was a full-time porter stationed in a wooden hut and adults were charged threepence and children a penny. It seems that the owner, the Earl of Clarendon, used the charge as a means of regulating access rather than turning a profit, because admission fees were donated to the poor folk of Kenilworth, an altruistic gesture since the castle was in poor condition and the earl was forced to spend considerable sums on repairing it.[14]

A handful of major country house owners charged entrance fees for visitors, but it was mainly as a means of visitor control. Cobham Hall, Kent (from as early as the 1830s), and Blenheim Palace, Oxfordshire (from 1856), both levied charges for this reason. Charges at Wilton, Wiltshire (from around 1870), and Eaton Hall, Cheshire (from 1854), were, like those at Kenilworth, given to charity.[15]

Despite the widespread efforts of private individuals, by 1840 it was the Government that was by far the largest and most successful operator of historic visitor attractions. Three of the most famous historic sights in London were controlled by national institutions:[16] by virtue of the established church, Westminster Abbey and St Paul's Cathedral were effectively national monuments, as was the Tower of London, run by the Board of Ordnance. Westminster Abbey had long charged admission for visitors who were not attending a service. Vergers, minor canons, lay clerks and organists all either charged for access to the areas for which they were responsible or expected a heavy tip for imparting information. It was an expensive day out. St Paul's had charged visitors to climb the dome and see the views of London since the eighteenth century, but after 1797 it began to receive a series of monuments to war heroes, becoming a serious rival to the abbey as a historic attraction and national pantheon. Twopence was the official entrance charge, but visitors had to buy subsidiary tickets if they wished to see more than the nave, as at Westminster Abbey. Various campaigns were run against the two institutions in an attempt to get them to drop charges, but in vain.

The Tower of London had been opened to paying visitors for even longer than the two churches. The royal collection of exotic animals, the menagerie,

The interior of the New Horse Armoury at the Tower of London showing the Line of Kings, the first major interpretive display paid for by the Government in a historic building in England. The Armoury was demolished and the displays relocated in 1883. Reproduced by permission of English Heritage

had been its oldest attraction, but this had been moved to Regent's Park after a lion was accused of biting a soldier in 1835. A guidebook of 1754 shows that there were standardised charges levied to see the attractions: sixpence for the menagerie, a shilling for the crown jewels and twopence for the Spanish Armoury. Gradually, from the early nineteenth century, traditional offices and functions, such as the mint, began to move out of the Tower and tourism began to assume a greater importance. In 1825 work started on building an exhibition hall to contain the Tower's great collection of historic armour. The main display was a reworking of the seventeenth-century 'Line of Kings', now wearing armour appropriate to their date, and was hailed as 'the only collection in Europe truly and historically arranged'. Samuel Rush Meyrick (1783–1848), the pioneering historian of arms and armour who had arranged the armoury at Sir Walter Scott's house at Abbotsford, and for George IV at Windsor Castle, advised. This was an important and pioneering venture, the first purpose-built permanent exhibition building at a national historic monument in England. The New Horse Armoury was funded by

The Jewel House at the Tower of London – the first and only purpose-built home for the Crown Jewels opened in 1841. Within, the Regalia were arranged under a large dome of glass and iron.

the Board of Ordnance, in response to overwhelming public interest, particularly in the Tudor and Stuart pieces, the largest part of the collection, which were for visitors most expressive of the 'Olden Time'.

The Crown Jewels had been an attraction since 1669, when the Martin Tower was converted into a repository for Charles II's new regalia. This was never just a store since its primary purpose was to display the artefacts to the public. It was hugely successful and popular, but by the early nineteenth century hopelessly inadequate, being described by one visitor as 'a dismal hole resembling the cell of the condemned'. As a result it was decided that a new jewel house be built to the south of the Martin Tower and the jewels were moved there in 1841. Like the New Horse Armoury this was effectively a purpose-built museum constructed by the Office of Woods and Works, which had responsibility for the royal aspects of the Tower. It was not a great success. Too little thought had been given to balancing security arrangements with the needs of visitors, and despite several modifications the jewels were moved, in 1869, to the Wakefield Tower, where they remained for nearly a century.[17]

Thanks to Walter Scott, who featured the Tower in two of his novels, to Harrison Ainsworth, and later to William Hepworth Dixon, who wrote a very successful history in 1869–70, people believed that the Tower was constructed for incarceration, torture and execution; was filled with deep, dark dungeons; and was haunted by the tragic spirits of the condemned. Guidebooks to the Tower and to London picked up the theme and most focused on the Tower's victims. History painters such as Paul Delaroche reinforced aristocratic and royal tragedy in lurid paintings like the *Execution of Lady Jane Grey* (1833: London, National Gallery) and *The Princes in the Tower* (1830; several versions). These transformed perceptions of the Tower, which moved from being a collection of individual experiences, rather like a modern theme park, into a historic monument where medieval architecture was no longer an incidental backdrop, but part of the main event. Visitor numbers surged,[18] and by 1851 a purpose-built ticket office was constructed at the western entrance with public lavatories and a tearoom. The first authorised guide to the Tower of London was first published in 1886, written by W. J. Loftie.[19]

Hampton Court Palace had been part of the tourist's itinerary since the reign of Queen Elizabeth I, and a tip to the palace keeper almost always en-

The western entrance of the Tower viewed from the Wharf in 1934, showing the ticket office and refreshment room of 1851, the first Government-funded, purpose-built, tourist infrastructure in England. © Royal Armouries

sured a guided tour. After the court left for the last time in 1737 a standard charge of a shilling was levied, but this was not a formal arrangement such as existed at the Tower. Hampton Court came to be opened to the public on a more regular basis thanks to the activities of the Parliamentary Select Committee on 'The Arts and Their Connection to Manufactures', set up in 1836. This led Queen Victoria, who had only just come to the throne, to open the palace to the public for free in 1837.[20]

The Office of Works was to be responsible for opening the palace from Saturday to Thursday, with Fridays being reserved for cleaning. In addition to a housekeeper, a superintendent, two assistants and a porter were appointed to stand duty in the state apartments. The following year two new assistants were appointed and by the 1850s there were nine attendants in all.[21] A discerning American visitor to the palace in 1856 remarked: 'Soldiers were standing sentinel at the exterior gateways, and at the various doors of the palace; but they admitted everybody without question, and without fee', and noted: 'The English Government does well to keep it up, and to admit the people freely to it.'[22] The numbers of visitors were substantial in 1839, 115,971 people in all. In the following years numbers rose steeply, to 147,740 in 1841 and up to 176,000 in 1843. Thereafter the numbers reached a plateau until 1851, the Great Exhibition year, when they rose to a colossal 350,848 before subsiding back to the 170,000 or so of the 1840s.[23]

It soon became clear that privies must be provided for visitors. Although this had been suggested in December 1837 it took two years to persuade Grace and Favour residents, who still occupied most of the palace, that an old round game larder could be converted for the purpose. Other conveniences were gradually added for visitors, including drinking fountains in the gardens and, in winter, warming stoves in the apartments.[24] For this new generation of visitors, a series of guidebooks was rapidly provided. In 1839 Edward Jesse published the first edition of *A Summer's Day at Hampton Court*,[25] and in 1841 Henry Cole published *A Handbook to Hampton Court*. Because Cole was a Government employee, his book had to be written under the pseudonym of Felix Summerly. Both guides were in a pocket-sized format conveniently designed for use in the state apartments, and both were illustrated with a choice selection of engravings. Cole continued his interest in Hampton Court and published another guidebook in 1842, giving the opening times of other attractions in and around London.

Government commitment to Hampton Court and the Tower had been stimulated by the coming to power of the reforming Whig government in 1832, which put political will behind liberal attitudes to mass education. Increasingly, pressure was brought to bear to make access to great public assets free: at the Tower there had been cries for free access since the 1820s. John Bayley (d. 1869), the Tower of London's first historian, argued that 'The Armouries, and other places of public attraction in the Tower, are supported by the public purse, and, as national institutions, the people should, under proper restrictions, have access to them, free of those enormous expenses which every one is now obliged to incur.' Moreover, he argued, 'in other countries we find no impositions laid on admittance to national institutions, and why should England thus descend from her pre-eminence amongst nations?'[26]

Bayley's arguments were ahead of their time in 1821, but by the 1840s there was a clear sense that the Tower of London was a *national* monument and that this implied some ownership by the public. Harrison Ainsworth in his historical romance *The Tower of London* (1840) appealed for more parts of the building to be open to the public, since they were 'the property of the nation, and should be open to national inspection'.[27] Inspection of such places, believed Charles Knight, writing the sections on the Tower in his six-volume part-series *London*, strengthened society, because 'The more people are conversant with our national antiquities, and have an abiding historical knowledge impressed upon them by associations which all can understand, the more will the foundations of this fabric be strengthened.'[28]

A series of Parliamentary Select Committees aired these views and others, with the result that in the years around 1840 four out of five national monuments made significant concessions to public access. The British Museum extended its opening times and printed guides; the admission charge to the Tower was dropped to sixpence; charges were abolished at Westminster Abbey for all but the tombs; and the shilling at Hampton Court was abolished. Only St Paul's Cathedral stubbornly retained its charges. The following year a Select Committee was convened on National Monuments and Works of Art under the chairmanship of the radical reforming Scottish MP Joseph Hume. Hampton Court was considered as the prime example of the beneficial effects of free access. The committee noted that 'the number of visitors has also greatly increased; and the propriety of their demeanour has fully warranted this accommodation'.[29] William Howitt went further and saw the opening of Hampton Court free to the public as

Shakespeare's birthplace in Stratford-upon-Avon, *circa* 1850. Bought by a trust at auction in 1847, the house was immediately a tourist attraction. The gentlemen outside were probably some of the 2,500 tourists that annually visited the house in the 1850s. By 1900 it had 30,000 visitors a year. © The Francis Frith Photographic Collection

the first step towards the national appropriation of public property. It is long since it was said, 'The king has got his own again', and it is now fitting that the people should have their own again. Of all the palaces, the towers, the abbeys, and cathedrals, which have been raised with the wealth and ostensibly for the benefit of the people, none till lately have been freely open to the footsteps of the multitude.[30]

Howitt's view of national patrimony was not confined to national monuments; in his opinion, there was no part of the English landscape 'in which you do not become aware that there some portion of our national glory has originated. The very coachman as you traverse the highways continually points out to you spots made sacred by men and their acts. There, say they, was born, or lived, Milton or Shakespeare, Locke or Bacon, Pope or Dryden.' The countryside studded with monuments was thus a sort of national property.[31] These were minority views, but it was only a few years later that Charles Knight campaigned for the Government or some 'public society' to purchase Shakespeare's birthplace in Stratford-upon-Avon as a national monument. Lord Morpeth, First Commissioner of Woods and Forests, responded that 'members of the Government are disposed to think that the acquisition of so interesting a property pertains still more to the people of England than the Government'. The 'people' bought it after a national appeal and the press recorded, perhaps for the first time, a 'national monument having been secured for the nation'.[32]

By the 1880s romantic interest in the 'Olden Time' had given birth to the idea that the great historical monuments of England were part of a national patrimony and that access to them should be allowed by their owners. Hundreds of owners did so and millions of people visited. In this the most successful and popular participant was the State through the agency of Her Majesty's Office of Works. And it is to the Office of Works that we must now turn.

2

THE OFFICE OF WORKS

The Office of Works was established in the fourteenth century to build and maintain Crown property. Its activities had gradually expanded and, by the early nineteenth century, they were wide and various. Building contracts are notoriously difficult to control, and throughout its long history the Office was regularly wracked by financial scandal and structural reform was frequently thought to be the solution. It survived, however, in various forms, and indeed the functions of the original Office of Works, after many vicissitudes, began to fragment only in 1972 with the creation of the Property Services Agency. In the twenty-first century its historical roles are divided between dozens of organisations.[1]

In 1832 the Office of Works became a division of the Office of Woods and Forests: the combined organisation became known as the Office of Woods and Works. In 1851 it was reconstituted as what was effectively a department of public building under full parliamentary control.[2] The notion of the Office having a board was retained, and this gave rise to its political head (the minister) being called First Commissioner and the administrative head (in today's parlance Permanent Secretary) being called Secretary. Sir George Murray (1849–1936), Permanent Secretary to the Treasury, thought that the post of First Commissioner of Works 'is almost the most interesting place in the public service. But in the matter of administration and particularly of finance there is a good deal of work of a rather sombre sort.'[3] It was, indeed, very interesting, but contentious. First Commissioners regularly clashed with the Treasury over the cost of public works and with

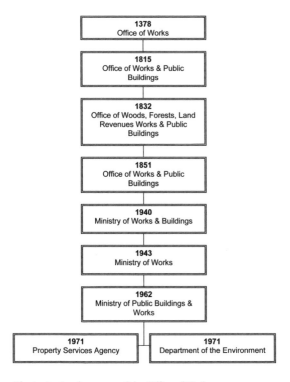

1378
Office of Works

1815
Office of Works & Public Buildings

1832
Office of Woods, Forests, Land Revenues Works & Public Buildings

1851
Office of Works & Public Buildings

1940
Ministry of Works & Buildings

1943
Ministry of Works

1962
Ministry of Public Buildings & Works

1971	1971
Property Services Agency	Department of the Environment

The institutional ancestry of the Office of Works.

MPs, architects and the public over their design. Central to the role, however, was the close interface with the royal family because the Office retained responsibility for works at royal palaces and for royal ceremonial (coronations, funerals, etc.).

When Lionel Earle (1866–1948) was first appointed to the post of Permanent Secretary in 1912, King George v told him that he was always available to be consulted on any matter and, as Earle later recalled, 'during my twenty years of office, I have availed myself of his kindness on many occasions, and these interviews have solved many difficult problems'.[4] Regular contact with the monarch affected the sort of people appointed as First Commissioner and Secretary. Both were generally recruited from a narrow circle of aristocratic families known to the royal family; and those from outside were required to have impeccable savoir-faire. The unlikely consequence of this was that, although First Commissioner was a relatively minor Government post, it enjoyed high prestige. In fact, from George Shaw Lefevre's tenure of the post in 1891 (with only one short interlude), it came with a seat in the Cabinet. The Office of Works thus had disproportionate political influence.

An important feature of the Office of Works was that, since it was responsible for the historic estate of the Crown, it had more experience of historic buildings and monuments than any other body. It also, as has been seen, acquired the task of running the largest tourist attractions in the land. To this latter responsibility it brought special skills, and the opening of Hampton Court to the public in 1837 tested these to the maximum.

In 1837 the Office was faced with a problem. Hampton Court was indelibly associated with Cardinal Wolsey, Henry VIII and Anne Boleyn, with Elizabeth I and with Charles I's captivity there by Oliver Cromwell. But the palace that visitors saw bore none of the romance that these historical characters promised. The buildings had been mothballed for a century – given over to Grace and Favour residences and altered in an entirely pragmatic way. The great Tudor elevations did not look Tudor – they were peppered with Georgian sash windows and chimney stacks. The most important Tudor interiors, especially the Great Hall, were not open to the public. Hampton Court was a big disappointment to people brought up on the *Waverley Novels* and Joseph Nash's *Mansions of England in the Olden Time*.

The surveyor of the Office of Woods and Works with responsibility for the Hampton Court district was Edward Jesse (1780–1868), a naturalist and sometime antiquarian. His approach to Hampton Court was influenced by his admiration of Jeffry Wyatville's Gothic remodelling of Windsor Castle and his close friendship with the Revd John Mitford, editor of the antiquarian journal the *Gentleman's Magazine* (1834–50). From the first he gained an understanding of the transformational power of restoration on the imagination, from the second the necessity to justify his restorations by historical precedent.

His first task was to create, out of the barren stone-lined Tudor great hall, an interior that looked as if it belonged in Nash's book. Between 1838 and 1845 it was hung with tapestry, armour, flags and coats of arms; the ceiling was painted and the windows filled with stained glass by Thomas Willement. The resultant show was one of the most important, and most visited, romantic interiors of the nineteenth century. His friend reviewed it in the *Gentleman's Magazine* calling it 'probably the finest and most brilliantly embellished building in Europe'.

The Great Hall, Hampton Court, after Edward Jesse's restoration. A brilliant re-creation of the 'Olden Time' designed to fulfill the expectations of visitors in the 1840s.
Reproduced by permission of English Heritage

For the outside of the palace Jesse turned to the architect Edward Blore (1787–1879), who had started his career drawing medieval buildings to illustrate county and building histories including Sir Walter Scott's *Antiquities of Scotland* (1819–26). This gave him probably the most thorough knowledge of Tudor architecture of any living designer and won him the commission to design a new wing at Lambeth Palace for the Archbishop of Canterbury. This

The Tower of London from the western approaches in detail in a drawing of 1826 by J. Tugmam, showing how the romantic medieval expectations of visitors were dashed by the encrustations of the seventeenth and eighteenth centuries. After Salvin's work the main tower was once again visible. © Museum of London

efficiently executed piece gained him the confidence of the Office of Woods and Works and a commission from Jesse to rid the west front of Hampton Court of its Georgian accretions. His work transformed the appearance of the building, fulfilling the expectations of hundreds of thousands of visitors. Charles Knight enthused: 'The whole front is fast growing harmonious and picturesque.' It is down to Blore and his assistant William Southcote Inman (1798–1879) that Hampton Court today looks remotely Tudor.[5]

The problems were, if anything, more severe at the Tower of London. Visitors who had been captivated by Harrison Ainsworth's book with its alluring illustrations by George Cruikshank were disappointed by the reality of the dilapidated fortress, where many of the most 'exciting' historical locations were closed off. The Constable of the Tower, the Duke of Wellington (in post 1826–52), was, at heart, against visitors, and saw the fortress primarily as a military emplacement. Just before the duke's death in 1852, in response to the Great Exhibition, there was an extraordinary surge in visitors. Many of the 233,000 tourists wanted to see inside the Beauchamp Tower, which was filled with graffiti left by sixteenth- and seventeenth-century prisoners. Cruikshank had invented a masterly scene showing the interrogation of Lady Jane Grey there, and Ainsworth had suggested that it be opened to the public. In April 1851 the architect Anthony Salvin (1799–1881) was consulted about letting the public in. Salvin had already been used by the Office for the repair of the castles of Newark, Caernarfon and Carisbrooke.[6] His work had been praised and his control of the costs had been robust. After Wellington's death Salvin demolished the later accretions around the Beauchamp Tower and removed internal partitions, exposing the historic graffiti. Medievalised windows and battlements were inserted and the building was made accessible to the public.[7]

In 1855 the Prince Consort came to see Salvin's work and asked for a comprehensive programme of restoration. Over the next eleven years Salvin restored the Salt Tower, the White Tower, St Thomas's Tower, the Wakefield Tower and more. The appearance of the fortress was transformed: brick facing was replaced with stone, sashes with lancets, and flat parapets with crenellations.[8]

Perhaps even more dramatic in its effects, and certainly more visible to legislators, was the work commissioned by the Office of Works at Westminster Abbey. Since it was built, the abbey's chapter house had been considered to be a government responsibility, it having been used for a succession of secular purposes, latterly as the record office for the Exchequer fitted with cupboards and bookcases. In 1864, at the instigation of the abbey's surveyor George Gilbert Scott (1811–1878), Dean Stanley petitioned the Prime Minister, William Gladstone, to fund the restoration of the building back to its medieval form. Gladstone, a devout and cultivated High Church Anglican, agreed, and the Office of Works was instructed to progress matters with a vote of £25,000 to hand.

The architect was Scott, who, as the most expert of all the Gothic Revival architects, had made a very careful study of the building and proposed a radical restoration. All the external stonework was replaced and a steeply pitched conical roof added, based on the chapter house at Salisbury Cathedral; inside, an entirely new vault was constructed supported by an elegant central pillar. The effects of the work, completed in 1871, were dramatic, redefining views of the abbey from the south and transforming the hugely important interior. Work completed, the Office of Works installed a 'policeman' or custodian and asked the dean to make the chapter house available to the public.[9]

In the matter of restoration of ancient sites and monuments, then, the Office of Works came to be seen as the natural focus for Government activity. But some felt that the State's involvement in safeguarding sites of national importance should go further. Ever since the French had set up the Commission des Monuments Historiques in 1837, there had been calls for a similar arrangement in England. During the 1841 Parliamentary Select Committee hearing on National Monuments and Works of Art, evidence was given by the antiquary and topographer John Britton (1771–1857), who argued that a commission of experts be established by the Government to advise on the repair and preservation of national monuments. He believed that if such a committee had existed sites such as the prehistoric stone circle at Avebury, which had been badly damaged by thoughtless action, would have been better protected. One of the tasks of the commission might be to 'publish cheap guides and short descriptions of the various buildings and objects of antiquity in the country'. MPs liked the idea and referred it to the Board of Woods and Works.

The First Commissioner, the Conservative Henry Pelham-Clinton, Lord Lincoln (1811–1864), viewed the proposal with caution, but was concerned enough to seek the advice of the antiquary Philip Bliss (1787–1857), Registrar of Oxford University, and of the Cambridge professor Robert Willis (1800–1875), who was a leading authority on medieval architecture. Their suggestions, collated by Edward Blore, a witness at the Select Committee of 1841, do not survive. But going by Blore's earlier evidence to the committee it is likely that neglect as well as over-restoration of monuments was sternly condemned. Lincoln passed the advice to his friend, the Prime Minister Sir Robert Peel.

The commission, however, was not progressed so Britton elicited the support of the Irish MP Thomas Wyse (1791–1862). Wyse, an educational reformer and historian, had sat on the sister committee to that on National Monuments, which was considering fine art. In 1845 he was persuaded to move a motion for the establishment of a 'Museum of National Antiquities in conjunction with a Commission for the conservation of National Monuments'. The idea was killed by Henry Goulburn (1784–1856), Chancellor of the Exchequer, who described in some detail the evils of such commissions: 'they got into the hands of individuals who, having themselves peculiar tastes of their own on the subject of art, and being succeeded again by others, perhaps, whose tastes differed from theirs, produced this result – should bad taste prevail – that bad taste was perpetuated by such Commissions.'[10] Despite this put-down, later that year Lord Lincoln's successor, George Howard, Lord Morpeth (1802–1864), did ask Blore to draw up some rules for the conservation of monuments in the care of the Woods and Works. Blore, with the help of the antiquarian draftsman William Twopenny, drew up guidelines that emphasised the dangers of 'injudicious repairs conducted with well meant but ill judged zeal' and emphasised the importance of properly qualified and informed practitioners producing clear drawings properly archived.[11] As far as is known, the rules were never adopted.

The idea of some sort of commission to protect national monuments was revived in 1868, under First Commissioner Austen Henry Layard (1817–1894). Layard was a wealthy adventurer who, on his travels, had become an accomplished archaeologist, uncovering the great palaces at Nimrud in the mid-1840s and bringing spectacular spoils back to the British Museum. In 1851 he became an MP and was appointed First Commissioner in Gladstone's government of 1868, presumably because it was thought that his artistic credentials would have a beneficial effect on the quality of public building. He approached the task with enthusiasm, and amongst other innovations turned his attention to the protection of church monuments and 'others of a national and archaeological character'. He wrote to the Society of Antiquaries in February 1869 asking them to compile a list of 'Regal and other historical Tombs or Monuments ... as in their opinion would be desirable to place under the protection and supervision of the Government, with a view to their proper custody and preservation'.

Thirty-eight Fellows of the Society of Antiquaries were mobilised, including many distinguished names such as the expert on medieval fortification, G.T. Clark (1809–1898), and the antiquary John Gough Nichols (1806–1873). They provided a long list out of which 531 monuments were chosen. The list was significant in that it was deliberately not a work of antiquarian curiosity. Rigorous editing had ensured that it comprised only monuments to people 'commemorated as actors in the great drama of our national history'. It was proudly submitted to the Office of Works in June 1871. Layard, however, had rapidly become disillusioned with his job as First Commissioner and thought it 'little better than that of a clerk in the Treasury'. Gladstone was fed up with him too and sacked him, sending him to Madrid as minister to keep him quiet. His successor, Acton Ayrton (1816–1886), was an entirely different proposition. A radical Liberal MP, he was recklessly determined on cost cutting and told the Antiquaries that Layard had acted without Treasury authority and that there was no intention of taking the matter further. Though the Antiquaries did eventually see their report laid before Parliament, the matter rested there.

Although the Office of Works was becoming the acknowledged governmental focus for protecting historic monuments, this did not save it from criticism when it came to works it was undertaking on its own buildings.

Indeed, during the last three decades of the nineteenth century the Office of Works frequently found itself hailed not as the expert saviour of ancient buildings but condemned as the ignorant destroyer of them.

The Office's opponent and critic was the Society for the Protection of Ancient Buildings founded in 1877 by William Morris (1834–1896). The SPAB had been founded to campaign against the over-restoration of historic buildings, in particular churches, and was, from the start, an efficient, well-run and well-funded pressure group. As time went on its principal committees, particularly its Restoration Committee, were filled with expert and capable people with time, zeal and contacts. While most of their energy was directed to the protection of churches, prominent buildings in the care of the Office of Works were firmly in their sights.[12]

On the other side was A. B. Freeman-Mitford (1837–1916), appointed Secretary to the Board of Works in 1874.[13] Bertram Mitford (as he liked to be known) came from an aristocratic background, was educated at Eton and Christ Church, Oxford, and was a friend of the Prince of Wales. Mitford not only had the pedigree for the job, he also had the energy and the imagination. A series of glamorous postings in the Foreign Office had sent him all over the world and he had a deep love of history and the arts. Mitford was an admirer of Salvin's work at the Tower, but the impetus had gone out of the restoration programme there after the death of the Prince Consort in 1861. In 1876 Mitford became determined to restart it and turned his attention to the defences to the east of the Wakefield Tower, an area blighted by large storehouses and offices. The Lieutenant Governor of the Tower had complained in 1866 of 'the monstrous warehouses and store offices which disfigure the river front of the Tower . . . in the decorative style of the great gin-palaces of London'; these, in the words of Mitford, hid 'our noblest national monument from the river as if it had been... a thing of shame'. It is hard not to have sympathy with this view: the eighteenth-century Ordnance Office was too big and in the wrong place. Fortunately for Mitford it was also falling down. To repair it would be more expensive than to start afresh, and so demolition was agreed.[14]

By the late 1870s Salvin was too old and ill to continue at the Tower and the in-house Office of Works architect, John Taylor (1833–1912), took over the work of restoration. Salvin's restorations had been relatively modest and were seen as part of opening up the Tower to visitors. But the mood had changed by the 1870s. Not only were Taylor's works on a much larger scale, but also the SPAB had begun to challenge restorations of ancient buildings. Taylor's proposal was to demolish the Ordnance Office and the other buildings along the line of the inner curtain between the Wakefield and Salt towers and reconstruct what he thought the inner defences had originally looked like. The SPAB was appalled and wrote to Mitford saying that they opposed the demolition of the old Record House next to the Wakefield Tower and that any reproduction medieval defences would be 'mischievous, illusory and ridiculous'.

Demolition went ahead, and as it did so Taylor produced a justification that was passed to the SPAB by the First Commissioner. But the SPAB Restoration Committee did not accept it and after another site inspection reiterated their opposition. The SPAB lost the argument and Taylor demolished the record office, built a new curtain wall on an alignment that bore no relation to its medieval predecessor, and took his knighthood. Thackeray Turner (1853–1937), the SPAB secretary, wrote to the Office of Works crossly

The former Ordnance Office at the Tower of London in a photograph of 1882. It was built in 1777 and 1792 and heightened in 1853–4. It completely obscured views of the White Tower from the river and became a symbol of the loss of the Tower's medieval character © Royal Armouries

predicting that in a few years the *raison d'être* of the SPAB would be 'so generally received by educated people that the notion of building a medieval tower to show what England was like in the thirteenth century will finally be given up and in place of it a respect for genuine remains of former times will prevail'.[15]

At Hampton Court work was less assertive and far-reaching. Ernest Law (1854–1930), the palace's historian, described Mitford as presiding over

> a gradual ridding of the palace ... of several unsightly excrescences which had been allowed to build up and disfigure its appearance in former days; while of equal importance were the replacing of shabbily executed modern repairs by work in harmony with the old and the renewal of all decayed ornamental features, in a style and manner adhering as closely as possible to that of the past, great care being taken, neither to destroy the smallest portion of the old work or to mar the antique aspect of the palace, by sham and unnecessary restoration.[16]

Mitford's architect was John Lessels (1833–1914), who had been appointed to the Office's Windsor district in 1860 and who had worked on the restoration of Windsor Castle. On his retirement the Board wrote to him saying that he had 'an archaeological knowledge and discrimination and an artistic sympathy which have enabled them [the Board] to deal with questions of maintenance, of alteration, or of restoration in a manner which they believe has met with general approval'.[17] In 1880 he turned to the Great Gatehouse on the west front of Hampton Court, which had been viciously truncated in the eighteenth century. Lessels subtly redesigned its elevation to make it look less plain and replaced various Tudor features to give the palace entrance more dignity. This included most spectacularly the restoration of a massive stone vault in the carriageway, completed, in the presence of Mitford and his guests, in January 1882.

In 1890 Lessels was asked to replace the draughty eighteenth-century leaded casements in the Chapel Royal. It was agreed that he should use the single surviving Tudor window that had been blocked up around 1700 as a model. On 23 October 1893 Thackeray Turner, of the SPAB, wrote objecting to the proposed replacement of what he called Wren's windows and suggesting that this and other 'ill advised works' had damaged the building in recent years. By the time Turner's letter was received it was too late. The masonry was cut and the finances committed.[18]

Lessels's work at Hampton Court was, by the standards of the age, scholarly and, in fact, representative of the increasing care taken by the Office of Works over restoration. A more telling contrast is that between the approaches of the Office of Works and the War Office at Edinburgh Castle. The Office of Works had been given increased responsibility for Edinburgh in 1877, but the War Office was still in charge. In 1885 the millionaire publisher William Nelson had offered to pay for the restoration of the Great Hall, the Portcullis Gate and St Margaret's Chapel. The first two were in the care of the War Office; the chapel was under the Office of Works. Nelson and his own architect, Hippolyte Jean Blanc, recreated the Portcullis Gate as the 'Argyle Tower' in the style of King David II in the belief that it stood on the site of a tower built in his reign. Work in the Great Hall paid a little more regard to the structural evidence, but was still a romantic reconstruction of a lost interior.

Nelson and Blanc wanted to undertake a similar thoroughgoing restoration of the ancient St Margaret's Chapel, enriching it with new Romanesque detail; but the Office of Works was entirely against this. Lord Napier, retired from diplomatic service and a champion of restoration, wrote to Blanc in early 1886:

> I have heard from Mr. Nelson of the difficulties that have occurred about the chapel. I do not at all agree with the views of the London Office ... I consider it quite legitimate to remove every portion of the external building of the seventeenth and eighteenth century and to replace that building with ecclesiastical work of the earliest and rudest Norman type ...

The Office of Works stood firm and the chapel remained unrestored.[19]

It was perhaps because of these disagreements that when cries for a national supervisory body to protect ancient monuments were made, it was frequently envisaged as being an independent commission and not part of the Office of Works. William Morris's address at the SPAB's Annual General Meeting of 1879 demanded a public tribunal that could regulate proposals to alter 'Public and National Monuments' and these, presumably, included monuments in the care of the State. In 1882 James Bryce, the historian and radical MP for Tower Hamlets, added his voice to the call for a Commission for Historic Monuments. By this stage, however, something was actually being done. The Liberal MP for Maidstone, Sir John Lubbock, was attempting to get a bill passed that would establish just such a body to protect ancient monuments.

3

THE 'MONUMENTALLY ANCIENT' ACT OF 1882

THE BIRTH OF MODERN ARCHAEOLOGY

Despite the concerns of the SPAB, of campaigns for a commission or a Government inspectorate, and the interests of the Office of Works, concern about the destruction of privately owned monuments focused at first, not on buildings, but on prehistoric and Roman remains. Since the 1740s antiquaries had been outraged by the acts of landowners who had defaced monuments such as Avebury and Stonehenge. During the later eighteenth century the development of the turnpikes and the absorption of new land for agriculture led to the crunching up of megaliths for road stone and the ploughing out of long barrows. Voices were raised against this vandalism, but they were the faint cries of men with obscure and rarefied interests. It was the birth of a more scientific approach to archaeology in the 1850s and 1860s that began to raise the status of what we would now call archaeological remains.

Up until this point the Society of Antiquaries had been not much concerned with scientific archaeology, especially prehistory; most of its members were interested in medieval art and architecture. For this reason the British Archaeological Association was founded in 1843 and the Archaeological Institute the following year to try and establish archaeology more seriously and to provide a popular forum for it. The Ethnographical Society was also founded in 1843 with what would now be considered archaeological interests. During the 1860s these societies became much more focused on prehistory. A small group of men led the field including Augustus Lane Fox (better known by his later name General Pitt-Rivers),[1] Augustus Wollaston Franks, Assistant Keeper of Medieval Antiquities at the British Museum, and the banker, politician and scientific writer Sir John Lubbock, later Lord Avebury (1834–1913).[2]

Lubbock was intellectually omnivorous and physically hyperactive. He sat on more committees and was president of more bodies than any other contemporary. He collected radical causes as avidly as his friend Pitt-Rivers collected ethnographical specimens. Reforming became his profession: bank holidays, shop opening hours, the bankers' clearing house, registration of dentists and the transportation of rare birds' feathers all came within his gaze. Thirty bills passed into law through his energies.

As a child Lubbock had been taught natural history by Charles Darwin and had been one of a generation of young men interested in science whose worldview had been changed in 1859 by the publication of Darwin's *On the Origin of Species by Means of Natural Selection*. The ideas in this book were behind a series of field trips Lubbock was to make to study prehistoric remains, tangible evidence, he thought, for the origins of man. Most significantly for the purposes here, Lubbock became interested in Denmark, where archaeology not only enjoyed a greater status but where remains were also given formalised legal protection. Lubbock learnt Danish so that he could understand their methods properly and on two visits in 1861 and 1863 became convinced that Britain needed a royal conservator of national antiquities on the Danish model, because 'We cannot put Stonehenge or the Wansdyke into a Museum – all the more reason why we should watch over them where they are.'[3]

Lubbock inherited his father's baronetcy in 1865 and decided, to the horror of his scientific friends and sponsors, to enter politics. He was eventually, in 1870, elected Liberal MP for Maidstone, from which moment he was determined to introduce a Private Member's Bill for a national protection system along Danish lines.[4] Before he had got very far, however, he was confronted by a plea for help to save one of England's most important prehistoric sites. In 1871 he was contacted by the rector of Avebury, who was appalled that parts of the monument had been bought by a building society and sold in plots for the construction of new cottages. Lubbock paid off the cottagers and bought land some distance away for their new homes. The same year he and fellow archaeologist Colonel Lane Fox were called to another threatened site, Dyke Hills at Dorchester, Oxfordshire, where, though Lubbock's chequebook stayed in his pocket, work was voluntarily (and temporarily) stopped by the landowner.[5]

John Lubbock commissioned a series of paintings from Ernest Griset (1844–1907) to show what prehistoric life might have been like. Here is an imagined reconstruction of a prehistoric village site atop a lake. Archaeological remains of so-called Swiss Lake Villages may have inspired the painting. Reproduced by kind permission of the Lubbock family

LUBBOCK'S BILL

These incidents, and others, reinforced Lubbock's determination to win legal protection for British monuments. His measure was, unlike Layard's exactly contemporary initiative (above, p. 31), narrowly focused on prehistory, with the provision to apply the act to Roman and Saxon remains if necessary. The plan was to establish a National Monuments Commission funded by the Treasury that would acquire rights over a list of archaeological sites by agreement. If one of these were at risk of mutilation, notice would be served to the Commission, which would either have to agree to the damage or purchase the monument. Owners had a right of appeal against purchase. Attached to the bill was a schedule of monuments proposed for protection.[6]

Lubbock did not even get the support of the Society of Antiquaries. He asked them to help draft the list of English monuments to be attached to his bill but, because they were engaged on Layard's scheme, backed by the Office of Works (above, p. 31), which looked as if it would have a greater chance of success, they declined. So Lubbock's English schedule was compiled by a committee of archaeologists chosen by Lubbock; it was then sent to the

Society of Antiquaries, who asked A. W. Franks to approve it. The complete list included a single Roman site and one later site (Old Sarum); otherwise, it was composed entirely of prehistoric remains. Lubbock had deliberately excluded medieval remains on the ground that they were expensive and complicated to repair.

Lubbock's bill enjoyed a mild degree of support in the press. Referring to the 1874 bill, for instance, *The Times* remarked: 'the monumental history of the land has been for so many ages defaced at pleasure by the caprice or carelessness of any ignorant landowner or occupier, it will be a great thing to have it in any shape recognised by law that national monuments are really monuments of national concern'. But three days later the same paper noted that the bill had been 'Ruthlessly exterminated'.[7] In 1877 *The Times* wrote that the bill was likely to be 'as roughly treated as the monuments that it seeks to preserve'. Indeed it was, and in 1880 Lubbock got his schedule published as a book with an archaeological description of each site including dimensions, sketches and reconstructions. The appendices included a roll of shame listing those who had voted against his bill and a section demolishing the arguments of particular MPs who had spoken out against it.[8]

A lively reconstruction of the 'Vallum' at Avebury including a cast of thousands of Ancient Britons from Lubbock's *Our Ancient Monuments and the Land around Them* (1880). This book was part of Lubbock's campaign to get his schedule of Ancient Monuments taken seriously.

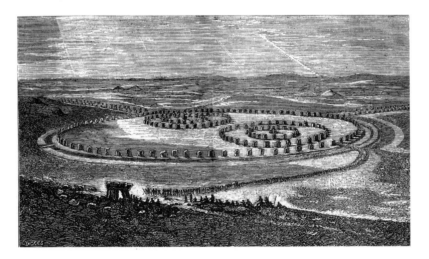

The fact is that in every session it ran out of time; it was never voted on, or directly opposed, just relentlessly sidelined. Some argued that the monuments were not important, others that the measures proposed were disproportionate, many that the element of compulsion exercised by a commission circumvented parliamentary responsibility. Gladstone's government saw it as an unjustifiable cost, Disraeli's as an attack on private property. And those who owned prehistoric monuments, or who had seen archaeologists at work, feared that the proposed system would do more harm than good. Archaeology had a bad name. Antiquaries were seen as glorified treasure hunters who, on the whole, did more damage to ancient monuments than the owners whose freedoms it was proposed to restrict. Barrows were randomly dug to find supposed buried treasures, as described by the owner of Stonehenge in 1874, who believed that 'it was the antiquarians who had done most mischief in England: and if ancient monuments were to be placed in their hands they would do still more'.[9]

Lubbock, however, stubbornly stuck to his guns; the bill through nine long years remained largely unmodified – no wonder it became known as the 'Monumentally Ancient Act'.[10] In 1880 Lubbock lost his seat, but returned the next year as Member for London University. By this stage even he realised that his bill would get nowhere and started to think not of legislation but of an ancient monuments inspectorate that could bring to owners' attention the value of the monuments in their care. At this point the Office of Works intervened.

THE ACT OF 1882

In November 1880 George Shaw Lefevre (1831–1928) was appointed First Commissioner of Works, a post he held for four years and then again from 1892 to 1894. Lefevre was on the radical wing of the Liberal party and his obituary recorded that 'for all subjects connected with art he had a natural taste, which was cultivated by assiduous study'. These aptitudes led to a particularly successful tenure at the Office of Works that included major metropolitan improvements, high-profile work at the Tower of London and Westminster Hall and the opening up of the Royal Parks to the public. He was also the leading figure in late Victorian environmental campaigning and founded, with a group of friends, the Commons Preservation Society in 1865. The establishment of the society marked a turning point in perceptions of common land, which had hitherto been seen as ground ripe for economic exploitation. Together with the society's lawyer, Robert Hunter (who was, from 1882, Solicitor to the General Post Office), Lefevre and his society had a series of successes in protecting public open spaces.[11] Thus Lefevre decided to break the decade-long deadlock on ancient monument legislation by drafting a bill, and gaining Government support for it.

Lefevre was himself an expert in property rights, and saw that Lubbock's bill implicitly recognised the right of an individual to destroy an ancient monument. During the debate for the 1874 bill he had referred to the case of Caesar's Camp on Wimbledon Common, one in which his society had been involved. The right of the owner to destroy a national monument needed, in his view, to be taken away.[12] His substitute act, however, unlike Lubbock's previous attempts, was a permissive measure that allowed an owner to place his monument under the protection of the State, which would then take care of it on their behalf. He had wanted to insert a clause that permitted the Office of Works to compulsorily purchase monuments that owners were reluctant to part with, but this was quashed in Cabinet. Yet the bill did contain a list of sixty-eight ancient monuments that the Office of Works could accept as a gift or purchase and, by the bill's provisions, it could accept additional monuments 'of a like character' by Order in Council (legislation approved by the monarch in Privy Council). Anyone convicted of damaging a monument was to be fined £5. Gladstone was happy to support Lefevre's bill as Government policy and it became law on 18 August 1882.[13]

Thus the mountain of ten years of debate produced the molehill of an act. As Lord Carnarvon pointed out in his Anniversary Address to the Society of Antiquaries on St George's Day 1883, 'in what a mutilated condition, shorn of many of its original provisions, crippled in its powers and limited in its scope that measure finally became the law of the land'. He placed the blame on the 'supineness of the public' and the 'prejudices of Parliament', as well as the all-absorbing political concerns of Ireland.

The act provided for the appointment of one or more Inspectors of Ancient Monuments to oversee and provide advice on their protection. The principal task was to persuade owners of monuments on the schedule to pass them over to the Office of Works in guardianship. Lefevre recognised that the character of the inspector would be crucial to the act's effectiveness and was successful in getting Gladstone to agree to the appointment of General Pitt-Rivers (1827–1900) as first Inspector of Ancient Monuments, thus creating a title that survives to this day.

Pitt-Rivers began as a collector of ancient and exotic arms and armour, and it was through this interest, rather than his embryonic archaeological activities, that he was elected to the Society of Antiquaries in 1864. In the early 1860s he was posted to Ireland, where he became much more intimately involved in archaeology, and by the end of the decade he had become one of the most active field archaeologists in England. He was also a substantial landowner, with some 25,000 acres to his name, and a close friend of (and relation by marriage to) Lubbock. All these attributes weighed heavily in his favour and his letter of commission explained: 'We believe there is no one in England who could fill the post so well as yourself, as besides a thorough knowledge of all the Ancient monuments ... your position as a land owner will enable you to bring more weight to bear on the present proprietors'.[14]

Immediately following the passing of the act, not a single owner came forward offering up his monument. Pitt-Rivers had naturally assumed that, at the very least, Lubbock would pass over the prehistoric mound of Silbury Hill in Wiltshire, which he had bought in 1873. But he declined to do so, presumably feeling that, because he owned it, it did not require any additional protection. In the end it was his first inspection – a Neolithic long barrow in Kent, Kit's Coty House, that led to his first acquisitions. Its owner was the Liberal MP Henry Brassey, son of Thomas Brassey, the greatest of all English railway contractors who had destroyed more than his fair share of national monuments. Brassey also offered Pitt-Rivers another barrow, the nearby Little Kit's Coty House, which, despite the fact that it was not in the schedule attached to the act, became the first monument to be offered into guardianship in April 1883 and eventually was accepted by Order in Council in August that same year. It was in a poor state: a former owner had dismantled the stones and tried to break them up to pave the garrison yard at Sheerness, and since he found this too difficult the stones were thrown down and scattered. Kit's Coty House was in better condition, but Pitt-Rivers suspected that it was being chipped away by visitors from a nearby cement works. In May 1883 he requested a strong iron fence to be erected round the monument as protection. The Treasury was horrified. The whole principle of the bill had been that such monuments would not require expenditure. A sum of £100 was eventually agreed, but only with reluctance and caveats.[15]

Few of the early monuments taken into State care were given fencing. Under normal circumstances a board was erected bearing a fierce notice warning against injury or defacement on pain of prosecution. Sometimes

Kit's Coty House in Kent surrounded by its original Victorian railing. In 1906 a
Cambridge undergraduate fell and was impaled on the fence after posing for a photograph
on the capstone. Reproduced by permission of English Heritage

there were also stubby boundary stones marked V. R. (Victoria Regina) to
indicate the extent of the monument. Pitt-Rivers thought these unnecessary for earthworks, but used them for standing stones. Not every owner
appreciated the paraphernalia of protection. Lord Brougham, the owner of
King Arthur's Round Table and Mayburgh, two important henges near Penrith, wrote in 1884: 'There is no kind of risk, or *decay-injury* or *depreciation*. I,
therefore will not permit, the surface to be broken: by the *insertion* of a *Notice
Post* or, *of a dozen stones*.' Pitt-Rivers, desperate not to antagonise landowners, informed the Office of Works: 'The letters are usually employed to mark
Government property and are liable to be misunderstood in country places',
and suggested that the letters V. R. be omitted and the owner's name added
to the noticeboard.

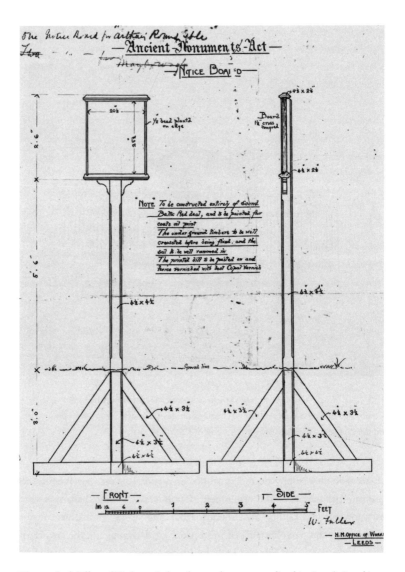

The standard Office of Works noticeboard erected at new guardianship sites, designed in the Office of Works architect's office. The National Archives

In May 1883 Pitt-Rivers was also successful with West Kennet Long Barrow, Wiltshire, and it seems that this was enough to persuade his friend Sir John Lubbock to sign over Silbury Hill. This was a spectacular acquisition, but a greater triumph was thought to be the long barrow at Uley in Gloucestershire. This belonged to Colonel Kingscote, MP for Gloucestershire West and later Commissioner of Woods and Forests. He had spoken out against Lubbock's bill and his agreement to guardianship was seen as a breakthrough. Commonly known as Hetty Pegler's Tump, after an earlier owner, Pitt-Rivers found the site to be in poor condition. Earth from the top of the mound had slumped, covering the entrance and the dry stone revetment; two of the chambers were ruinous and a modern doorway had been inserted. Pitt-Rivers recommended repair by a local archaeological society, which was duly carried out. But by 1888 it was again in poor condition: large stones had been dragged out, the new entrance forced and the official notice was lying 'obliterated' on the ground.[16]

Colonel Kingscote wrote to Pitt-Rivers that 'since it was put under the "Ancient Monuments Act" it has been very largely visited, consequently greatly pulled about, and I can well believe rendered dangerous'. This was, in fact, the effect that the act was having on a number of sites; for detractors of the bill, their warnings were coming true, and some owners were being put off handing sites over. The owner of the tumulus at Buckholt, Monmouthshire, for instance, had initially agreed to guardianship but then changed his mind, giving the state of Hetty Pegler's Tump as the reason.[17]

The general pressed on and, by the end of 1884, had been successful in bringing fourteen monuments from the schedule for England and Wales into guardianship. Though Pitt-Rivers was employed by the Office of Works, he could not exactly be described as an employee. He had no office at Storeys Gate, the headquarters of the Office of Works where all the bureaucratic mechanisms necessary to take monuments into guardianship were located. He was based at his country house, Rushmore near Salisbury, and at 4 Grosvenor Gardens, his London house from where he organised his itineraries. Though he claimed expenses, he normally paid for his drawing and surveying assistants himself. Though Lefevre had assured Parliament during the passing of the bill that the role of the Inspector would be limited, Pitt-Rivers's duties expanded to fit his interests. He certainly regarded excavation as part of his remit. At Pen Pits in Somerset, he conducted an excavation in 1883 in order to clarify the origins and purpose of the site in advance of a decision about guardianship. His report was emblazoned with his title 'Inspector of Ancient Monuments in Great Britain' and was printed by permission of 'Her Majesty's Commissioners of Works'.[18]

But from the start Pitt-Rivers saw the essential task as that of making a national record of prehistoric remains. He was well aware that the sites that he was protecting by guardianship held perhaps the least useful information by being best known.[19] In his final report to the Office of Works he recorded that, as well as inspecting sites that were eventually to be taken into guardianship, he had inspected 131 other monuments, mainly in the West Country and Scotland. In doing so a crucial tool had been the Ordnance Survey, part of the War Office since 1855 and the only other Government department with an understanding of archaeology.

The Ordnance Survey (os) was founded in 1791 under the sponsorship of the Board of Ordnance in order to provide detailed topographical information in the event of a French invasion. One of its earliest advocates had been the military surveyor Major-General William Roy (1726–1790), who recorded Roman antiquities such as the Antonine Wall. The first os map was produced in 1801, although it was not until the second half of the nineteenth century that a system for mapping antiquities was established. In 1865 an order by the Director, Sir Henry James (1803–1877), stated that surveyors should become acquainted with local history and objects of antiquarian interest in their districts, and in 1884 this was consolidated in instructions to the field officers of the os.[20]

In 1891 Pitt-Rivers wrote that he 'often thought it might work better if the Inspectorship was to be transferred to the Director General of the Ordnance Survey'.[21] In contrast to his own position, the os had a right of access to survey monuments on private lands. He considered it 'absurd' that he could not do the same. The os also had a large body of surveyors across the country that could potentially draw up plans and carry out works of protection. They could also record damaging changes and if necessary police them. In fact, in 1897 Pitt-Rivers instructed the War Office that they should inform his department of potential damage to earthworks within the army training area on Salisbury Plain. Arrangements were to be made for the protection of barrows wherever possible and the 25-inch os map was to be the main reference point.[22] The os depiction of antiquities was also used to determine the impact of the proposed Great Western Railway near Stonehenge.

This wider process of recording ancient monuments was having an impact in terms of owners' perception of their monuments. Pitt-Rivers himself argued that, although the act was limited, 'A good deal has been done by private communication with the owners and even in the case of monuments whose owners have refused to include them, it has generally been found that they are very anxious to protect them.'[23] At Whithorn Priory, Wigtownshire, which was refused guardianship by the Government, Lord Bute stepped in, laying out £1,000 to save it. This was more than the Government had spent on all the monuments in Britain since the act was introduced. But in fairness attitudes were changing anyway; in this, the activities of the Inspector played a part, but as will be seen much more was at work to change attitudes to protecting the past.

Despite these positive signs, by the late 1880s Pitt-Rivers had grown despondent both with the Government and the act. He thought funding for the protection of ancient monuments was 'totally inadequate'.[24] In 1884 he had requested at least £500, and £300 in 1887, but only £100 a year was allocated. In hope that more might be forthcoming, he decided to forego his travel expenses.[25] The amount was raised to £200, but this was still considered far too little. On the basis of expense the Government had refused to provide protective railings for the megalithic stones of Callanish on the Isle of Lewis. Worse still, they had declined to take three monuments offered by owners into guardianship. By 1890 he had been told that 'as the Act was permissive, the attitude of the Government towards it must be passive', and he was instructed not to take any further monuments except where owners actively offered them. Pitt-Rivers declared his post a 'sinecure' and resigned his salary, but continued as Inspector in an honorary capacity.

In 1891 he wrote to Sir John Lubbock: 'I feel that my time has been a good deal wasted in the attempt to carry out a measure, which, if it can be regarded as a success at all, has certainly not repaid me for the trouble it has caused.'[26] He questioned whether new legislation, by then being discussed, could be effective: 'I don't think much reliance can be placed on Government. I question whether it is right to tax the people for the maintenance of Antiquities, which none but the educated classes, and not all of them, are in a position to appreciate.' In the end he believed that 'Everything that is possible should be done to encourage owners to do the work themselves, and local archaeological bodies should be made to feel that the country looks to them to bring to notice any damage ... No Inspector of Ancient Monuments can stand sentry over all the Monuments in Great Britain.'[27]

4

THE OFFICE OF WORKS TAKES CONTROL
1882–1909

The Office of Works had responsibility for the Government's civil estates; its military and naval buildings, many of which were also important historic monuments, were cared for by other departments. The War Office had acquired the estates of the Board of Ordnance in 1855, giving it responsibility for castles, barracks and coastal fortifications; the Navy Office had responsibility for naval dockyards; and the Office of Woods cared for the hereditary estates of the Crown, today known as the Crown Estates. This too included many monuments, especially castles and some abbeys. In a series of steps from the 1870s, and much faster after 1900, the War Office and Office of Woods handed over to the Office of Works the bulk of their ancient monuments, to be opened to the public.

THE WAR OFFICE

The Boer War of 1899 traumatised the British establishment: it had taken 450,000 British troops to defeat 50,000 untrained and poorly armed farmers. The recriminations and self-examination that followed caused a major re-organisation of the British Army and a fundamental re-think of the responsibilities of the War Office. One of the features of this was a relatively rapid shedding of historic buildings no longer suitable for military use. The transfer of monuments was facilitated by the arrival at the Office of Works of two influential figures. The first was Aretas Akers-Douglas (1851–1926), a Conser-

Lord Esher was of fundamental importance in establishing the Office of Works as the official custodian of State-owned historic buildings opened to the public. © National Portrait Gallery, London

vative former Chief Whip, who was appointed First Commissioner by Lord Salisbury. He was a skilful politician, a manager of men and complex situations. His foil, and Secretary to the Board, was Reginald Brett (1852–1930; he became Lord Esher in 1898), courtier, historian and aesthete. Between them Akers-Douglas and Esher staged, with much acclaim, Queen Victoria's Diamond Jubilee in 1897, her funeral in 1901 and Edward VII's Coronation in 1902. They also were responsible for negotiating deals with the Office of Woods, the War Office and Queen Victoria, which hugely expanded the responsibilities of the Office of Works towards ancient monuments.

Crucial to their success was the position of Lord Esher vis-à-vis the War Office and the royal family. Esher had a life-long interest in military history and had been Lord Hartington's Private Secretary while he was Secretary of State for War in the early 1880s. Although he was to turn down the offer of being War Secretary himself, in 1903 he was asked to chair the War Office reconstitution committee (known as the Esher Committee) that brought in sweeping reforms to the army. Akers-Douglas was also involved in military reforms, chairing his own committee on military training in 1902.[1]

At the Office of Works, Esher's first engagement with the War Office came in 1897, when plans for a new barrack block at the Tower of London were put forward. The Office of Works, perhaps having learnt from their experiences in the 1870s, thought the proposals unacceptable. Esher wrote to Sir John Taylor, the Office of Works' Surveyor:

> I think the building that it is proposed now to erect has been brought too close to the White Tower. Further, although I do not agree that red brick is suitable for a building of this kind, or in place within the Tower, having in view the difference between the rest and other portions of the fortress, still I do not think the design a particularly happy one.[2]

Akers-Douglas visited the Tower with Lord Lansdowne, who had been Governor General of Canada and Viceroy of India before returning to England in 1894 and taking the job at the War Office the following year. He was a military reformer implementing the recommendations of Lord Hartington's Committee and knew Akers-Douglas and Esher well.

Lansdowne agreed that his department's plans for the Tower should be submitted to the Office of Works for comment and approval. The following year there was similar unease about a proposed hospital building to be erected at the north-west angle of Edinburgh Castle. In August 1898 Akers-Douglas wrote a private letter to Lord Lansdowne setting out the Office of Works' proposals:

> Considering the immense importance of places like the Tower and Edinburgh Castle from old associations of historic and national interest, and bearing in mind that the charge of nearly all ancient monuments and historic buildings under the control of the State has been entrusted to the Commissioners of Works, I should like to obtain your concurrence to a proposal that hereafter all designs for new buildings, or additions or alterations to existing buildings, within the precincts of historic places like the under mentioned, should *in so far as external elevations is concerned*, be approved by the First Commissioner of Works.

Lansdowne had already agreed the principle of the Office of Works' role at the Tower and he accepted the proposals, since the War Office, he said, wished to avoid 'erecting anything unsightly or in bad taste'. He also offered to hand over responsibility for the external appearance of historic War Office buildings in a list of specified locations. This was a coup, especially since the Treasury consented to the proposal in November 1898. The costs of works of repair, restoration or alteration to the external elevations of 'buildings of historical or national interest in the charge of the War Office' would now be paid by the Office of Works. A list attached to Akers-Douglas's letter included, amongst other fortifications, the Tower of London, Edinburgh Castle, Stirling Castle, Dover Castle, Walmer Castle, Deal Castle, Carlisle Castle, Chester Castle and Tynemouth Castle and Priory.[3] The War Office, however, retained operational control of these buildings, which, of course, included the three most important castles in their care: Dover, the Tower and Edinburgh.

The regulations of 1898 gave the Office of Works some leverage over these sites. Probably as a result of the regulations, the War Office erected roofs over a number of ruins at Dover, for the first time taking responsibility for the preservation of the non-operational estate and, by 1904, was in negotiation with the Office of Works for the full takeover of parts of the castle. James Fitzgerald, the Acting Inspector (below, pp. 53–4), piled on the pressure and in 1907 secured the transfer of all the most important historic parts of Dover to the Office of Works, though the army still retained some operational areas.[4] In 1902 the War Office suggested that it transfer all the military buildings at the Tower and Edinburgh to the Office of Works. After a summit held between the two departments that November, the Tower was transferred together with its warders, curator and workmen and collections plus the annual revenue of £2,500 that the War Office had been making from visitors. A similar deal was secured at Edinburgh Castle, and both national buildings fell to the control of the Office of Works in 1903.[5]

ROYAL PALACES

While the Office began to secure control over large numbers of castles from the War Office, Esher and Akers-Douglas brokered a stunning deal. Kensington Palace was, by the late nineteenth century, a large and unwanted problem, decaying, partly propped up and largely obscured by overgrown trees. Various uses had been proposed and demolition had even been mentioned. Its saviour was Esher, for, in a negotiation with Queen Victoria, he secured a deal that would see the Ranger's House in Greenwich, Kew Palace and Queen Charlotte's Cottage in Kew Gardens handed over to the Office of Works for public use in return for part of Kensington being restored as residences for her children. The state apartments would then be opened to the public by the Office of Works. The palace was in such a poor state that it must have seemed impossible that the Treasury would agree, but Akers-Douglas succeeded and the Chancellor of the Exchequer granted £20,000.

What followed was a pioneering event in the history of the display of historic buildings. Esher was determined that Kensington would not end up looking like a picture gallery, which had been the fate of the state rooms at Hampton Court (see also below, pp. 187–8). He wanted to restore the interiors 'as far as possible [to] exactly what it was in the reign of George II'. The historian and writer Ernest Law, who wrote the first historical guide to Kensington, noted that

> the most studied care has been taken never to renew any decoration where it was possible to preserve it ... it has been this minute – though no doubt sometimes costly – attention to details, this laborious piecing together of old fragments, this reverential saving of original material and work, this almost-sentimental imitation of the old style and taste ... which has produced a result and effect likely, we think, to arouse the admiration of all ...[6]

The completed rooms attempted to present the palace as a historic building in its Georgian glory. Later dividing walls were demolished; panelling was stripped of its later paintwork; walls were hung with flock wallpaper in imitation of the original damask; paintings were carefully selected; and furniture was arranged. Particularly pioneering was the restoration of the rooms in which Queen Victoria had been brought up, and the bedroom in which she had heard of her accession. These were not taken back to their eighteenth-century form but redecorated as the queen's nursery and furnished with some of her childhood toys. The work was under the supervision of Sir John Taylor and his clerk of works at the palace; but Esher was in charge of the detail and was the controlling mind. The palace reopened to the public in May 1899 and in its first year attracted 340,232 visitors.[7]

Kensington Palace was a major success for the Board and it was to be followed by another, almost more spectacular one: the acquisition of Osborne House, Queen Victoria's seaside home on the Isle of Wight. After her death in 1901 the Osborne Estate passed to Edward VII, who had no desire to live there. The following year he transferred the parts of the house that his

The lavish interiors of Kensington Palace in 1899, a pioneering venture by the Office of Works to display a suite of historic interiors. Reproduced by permission of English Heritage

mother had lived in to the Office of Works, for opening to the public and as a memorial to her. After some alterations, and new carpets in the state rooms, the historic rooms on the ground floor opened to the public in May 1904.[8]

FURTHER TRANSFERS

Esher was succeeded, as Secretary, in 1902 by Sir Schomberg McDonnell (1861–1915), the extremely well-connected fifth son of the Earl of Antrim, a former Private Secretary to Lord Salisbury and, through his membership of the late Victorian aristocratic clique the Souls, a close friend of the Prime Minister, Arthur Balfour, and of the Viceroy of India, George Curzon. His Assistant Secretary was James Fitzgerald, who also occupied the post of

Acting Inspector of Ancient Monuments, in the absence of a replacement for General Pitt-Rivers. Fitzgerald's position vis-à-vis ancient monuments was a difficult one. Lubbock could barely hide his contempt that a 'mere administrator' now occupied the post he had so long argued for. He told the Society of Antiquaries: 'The official at present acting for the Board of Works, with many qualifications and much good will, has not the status and cannot, however he might wish it, move in the matter.'[9] This was unfair, since Fitzgerald had continued the general's programme of inspections and had even secured the first successful prosecution for damage to an ancient monument in England (eased by the fact that the graffitist had scratched his name and address on the standing stones he had defaced).[10] As has been seen in the case of Dover Castle, Fitzgerald became the driving force behind the continued transfer of buildings from the War Office to the Office of Works.

In August 1903 the War Office decided to dispose of more buildings of 'historical and architectural interest' that were militarily redundant. Tynemouth Castle, parts of Dover Castle, Mont Orgueil Castle (Jersey) and Vale Castle (Guernsey), together with the castles of Deal and Walmer, were transferred.[11] This stimulated Fitzgerald, during his annual holiday in the summer of 1904, to undertake an inspection of historic buildings in the hands of the War Office. His conclusions were set out in a report to the First Commissioner:

> The condition of the buildings . . . leaves much to be desired. The funds at
> the disposal of the Military Works Department have been urgently needed
> for purely military purposes, and it is not unnatural that buildings should
> have been neglected whose claims rested merely on historical and ar-
> chaeological grounds. But damage has resulted, not merely from neglect:
> the modern buildings have been added in certain cases, to meet emergen-
> cies, as in the time of the Napoleonic and Crimean wars: and little beyond
> utility was considered in their construction.[12]

Fitzgerald argued that the time was ripe for all remaining Government historic buildings and monuments be transferred to the Office of Works, other than those retained in use by the War Office and maintained by the Office of Works under the agreement of 1898. The report was scathing about the activities of the Office of Woods in particular. Lindisfarne Castle, he said, had been adapted to form little more than a 'sea-side villa' and Yarmouth Castle on the Isle of Wight was 'practically part of the adjoining Hotel'. In contrast, he set out the beneficial treatment the Office of Works had given Linlithgow Palace and Carisbrooke Castle.

Not surprisingly, the Office of Woods claimed that it was the home of 'last resort' and those buildings in which they had 'pride and pleasure' should stay with them. The transfer of Yarmouth Castle, for instance, would cause 'unnecessary expense', that of Eltham Palace Old Hall would be 'inconvenient' and Tintern Abbey was a 'special case' that deserved to stay with the Woods. The Treasury, who mediated between the warring departments, accepted that transfers could be made on a case-by-case basis by mutual agreement. Meanwhile, the cost of protecting and maintaining ancient monuments and disused historic buildings was to become a separate item in future estimates in the Office of Works.

THE ANCIENT MONUMENTS PROTECTION ACT OF 1900

The ability of the Office of Works to transfer so many Government properties into its own care was smoothed by the passing of the 1900 Ancient Monuments Protection Act by the Marquess of Salisbury's Conservative and Unionist Government. The bill was introduced in 1899 by six MPs headed by David Lindsay (1871–1940). Lindsay, who enjoyed the courtesy title of Lord Balcarres, was at the time Conservative MP for Chorley, Lancashire, with a particular interest in cultural administration and a hand in the foundation of the Victoria and Albert Museum in 1899. He was later to serve as First Commissioner (below, p. 170), but the introduction of the bill was his first significant foray into conservation. He was supported by two veteran campaigners, Sir John Lubbock and James Bryce. Three others added their names, Sir John Maxwell-Stirling (1866–1956), a Scottish MP and landowner passionate about historic buildings and later Chairman of the Scottish Ancient Monuments Board; Sir John Brunner (1842–1919), Liberal MP for Northwich, an industrialist and philanthropist; and Edward Carson (1854–1935), the Ulster lawyer and leading politician who became Solicitor General for England in May 1900.

Their act was a belated response to agitation that had started almost immediately after the 1882 Act was passed. In 1888 the Society of Antiquaries had complained that it would not protect important medieval monuments such as Eleanor Crosses from defacement. Lubbock agreed to return to the fray and the Antiquaries set up a committee to consider the options.

The Eleanor Cross at Geddington, Northamptonshire, *circa* 1865, with a group of children on the steps. The Eleanor Crosses became a campaigning cause for preservationists. Reproduced by permission of English Heritage

What was galling to these campaigners was that in 1892 the Irish received an Ancient Monuments Act that extended protection beyond prehistoric monuments to 'any structure, erection of historic or architectural interest or any remains thereof', making it possible to add medieval monuments to the schedule. Soon after, the Irish Office of Works began to publish an annual report listing the places protected for the nation.[13] Pressure increased after this, with the Society of Antiquaries making a survey of protective legislation abroad and Lord Salisbury, as Foreign Secretary, seeking information on foreign protection systems from his ambassadors.

By the time that Lindsay's bill was introduced virtually every conservationist body had put forward their views on what ought to be in it and the National Trust's Secretary, the lawyer Sir Robert Hunter, was busy drafting clauses.[14] The Office of Works, however, had reservations. Although Esher was rapacious in his collection of castles and had taken huge pride in opening Kensington to the public, he regarded the preservation societies as 'the devil'.[15] In July 1899 he wrote to Akers-Douglas saying that he believed much pressure would be brought upon the Department to protect a 'great number of additional structures' such as churches, abbeys, castles and town walls. Meanwhile, 'awkward points' might 'arise as to the control, or transfer of control, over ecclesiastical fabrics'.[16] But Akers-Douglas was in favour and the bill went through in August 1900.

Essentially, the 1900 Act extended the provisions of that of 1882 to monuments of any date, thus opening the possibility of taking medieval monuments into guardianship and smoothing the way for the acceptance of the monuments transferred from the War Office and the Office of Woods. Another significant provision was that it extended guardianship powers from central government to county councils. Local government could now enter into agreements with owners and receive contributions towards the upkeep of ancient monuments and buildings. Akers-Douglas had argued the benefits of this to the Treasury in March 1900, but with the proviso that 'important monuments' should remain under the Board's control.[17] In some cases county councils had already taken action towards the preservation of monuments in their locality; Northamptonshire County Council had in fact taken steps to safeguard the Eleanor Cross at Geddington, Northamptonshire after the Office of Works refused to intervene in 1885. Other councils had moved in the same direction towards the end of the nineteenth century. In 1884 the City of Chester obtained powers for the protection of the medieval walls through the Chester Improvement Act. This specified that no new structures could be built within 6 feet of the city walls without the permission of the Corporation. Similar action was taken at Colchester and Newcastle. In Edinburgh the town council obtained powers to prevent unsightly advertisements damaging the amenity of their major historic buildings in 1899.

The revised act also required that the public should have access to all ancient monuments owned by the Government or a county council. For other guardianship sites public access was dependent upon the consent of the owner.[18] Although the royal palaces already took entrance fees, this was a significant development as applied to Office of Works sites, since guardianship sites, being almost exclusively prehistoric monuments, had not required a ticketed entrance or a full-time caretaker.[19]

Despite these new provisions, the 1900 Act also retained many of the limitations of its predecessor: specifically, there was still no power of compulsory protection when a monument was at threat of damage or destruction from its owner. Nor was there provision for a proper survey of national monuments as Pitt-Rivers had wanted. Yet, within a decade of 1900 the Government had agreed to this. To understand the reasons behind this we need to retrace our steps to the years around the passing of the first Ancient Monuments Act.

CAMPAIGNING FOR BETTER PROTECTION

Environmental campaigning, to use an anachronistic term, had been in its infancy in the 1860s and 1870s: there had been two bodies that had been active and successful, the Commons Preservation Society (founded 1865) and the Society for the Protection of Ancient Buildings (founded 1877). Between the passing of the 1882 Act and the end of the century a dozen more were added to their number. James Bryce, a very busy joiner of societies, told the annual meeting of the Selborne Society in 1900 that the 'existence of so many societies with cognate aims was a great source of encouragement . . . for with such a combination they could produce the impression that the attention of the whole country was directed to the question at issue'.[20]

The Commons Preservation Society had led the charge for the natural environment, followed by the Open Space Committee of the Kyrle Society (1875), the Metropolitan Public Gardens Association (1882), the Selborne Society (1886), the Society for Checking the Abuses for Public Advertising or SCAPA (1893), the National Footpaths Preservation Society, the National Trust (1895) and the Coal Smoke Abatement Society (1898), to name just the largest national bodies. These societies were very different from the mass movement membership organisations of today. No petitions were delivered to Downing Street; there were no rallies, no protests and few letter writing campaigns. They did not need them. These bodies were run by a small number of establishment figures with the wealth and connections that allowed them to press their case. Late Victorian environmental campaigns were posh pressure groups, not a mass movement.[21] They met in the Palace of Westminster, the Inns of Court, and in aristocratic town houses. Their membership, in terms of numbers, was small, generally bourgeois, and actually more-or-less irrelevant to their success. The SPAB had 443 members in 1910; in 1915 the National Trust had 700 and SCAPA fewer than 1,000.[22]

Although most of these societies championed the cause of historic buildings as a subset of landscape and natural history, there was also a group of campaigning bodies that focused on this single cause. The most prominent sprang up in London, where the rapid development of the City, in particular, alarmed those who loved its seventeenth-century charm. An early attempt at capturing some of old London's rapidly vanishing character was by the Society for Photographing the Relics of Old London established by Alfred Marks in 1875, which issued more than 100 large-format photographs over eleven years. In 1880 the London Topographical Society was founded to publish maps and views of the city and to record detrimental changes that were taking place, and in 1912 the London Society was founded to advance 'the practical improvement and artistic development of London'. The most important development was the foundation, by C. R. Ashbee (1863–1942), of the Survey of the Memorials of Greater London. Ashbee, best known as an architect, was a brilliant designer who was heavily engaged in social reform, teaching and writing. He had been appalled to see a sixteenth-century hunting lodge in Bow demolished for a modern school building and set up his committee to compile a register of important buildings and thereby halt their destruction. The survey started work in 1894 and its researchers were soon filling in standardised forms providing information about important buildings.

In 1896 it published its first monograph, a study of the seventeenth-century Trinity Almshouses on Mile End Road, a complex threatened with demolition. The book, and the fuss it stirred up, was successful in saving the building. The campaign came to the notice of Sir John Lubbock. Lubbock had been chairman of the recently constituted London County Council in the years 1890–2 and it was his continuing influence there that led to the convening of a conference of learned societies in December 1896 to discuss the council's policy towards historic buildings. Ashbee represented the

Survey Committee and won support for the idea of extending a register of buildings of historic or architectural interest across the whole LCC area.

The Statistical Officer at the LCC, a role that had significant influence on policy, was Sir Laurence Gomme (1853–1916), an enthusiastic recipient of this idea. Gomme was not only a polished administrator; he was also a leading expert in folklore and had been a co-founder of the Victoria County History (below, pp. 66–7). In 1900 he was to become Clerk to the Council – effectively its chief executive. He was instrumental first in shaping, then in executing, a system of listing and protection in the capital. In 1897 the LCC resolved to create a register of significant buildings based on that started by the Survey of Memorials, and to publish it. The following year it acquired the powers to buy historical places and works of art and to make contributions to maintaining them. In 1900 the LCC acquired its first historic building, 17 Fleet Street, followed by Marble Hill House (1902) and the Geffrye Almshouses (1908), and in 1908 it was instrumental in rescuing Crosby Hall on Bishopsgate by moving it, stone by stone to Chelsea.[23]

In 1901 the LCC took over, from the Royal Society of Arts, a scheme to put plaques on the houses of prominent citizens. This had been founded in 1866 in response to cries to identify publicly London houses that had, in the words of the MP William Ewart, been lived in by the 'ornaments of our history'. In the hands of the LCC the scheme became as much a means of identifying significant buildings for future preservation as a commemorative venture.[24] By 1904 the LCC declared, in its annual report, that the council would be 'the authority for preserving any structure, erection, or monument of historical or architectural interest' in London or any adjacent county.[25]

So the one part of Britain that had some sort of cogently organised State-sponsored survey of historic buildings in the early 1900s was London. This was a very different thing from the comprehensive survey of archaeological sites and monuments that General Pitt-Rivers had wanted. The pressure for this came most powerfully from Scotland. David Murray (1842–1928), a property lawyer, bibliophile and antiquary from Glasgow, argued for a proper national survey in a lecture delivered to the Archaeological Society of Glasgow and published as *An Archaeological Survey of the United Kingdom: The Preservation and Protection of our Ancient Monuments* in 1896. The basis of his argument was that the United Kingdom needed a comprehensive archaeological survey that would include buildings as well as archaeological remains. This, he thought, needed to be accompanied by a proper protec-

17 Fleet Street, London, sometimes known as Prince Henry's Room, purchased by the
LCC in 1900 for £20,000 and restored by its architect's department as a tourist attraction.
© Royal Academy of Arts

tion regime as had been established in Ireland. Murray was not the only
Scot to draw unfavourable comparisons with other protection regimes. In
1880 Gerard Baldwin Brown (1849–1932) was appointed to the new Watson
Gordon Chair of Fine Art at Edinburgh University, the first chair in fine

art to be established anywhere in the British Isles. In 1905 he published *The Care of Ancient Monuments*, which contained a comprehensive study of what he described as 'monument administration' existing elsewhere in Europe.[26] Baldwin Brown made an important distinction between 'classement' (a term he borrowed from France) and 'inventorisation'. Classement, or scheduling, was the process of identifying significant sites with a view to legal protection, while inventorisation was the process of making a comprehensive list of all the objects of artistic or historical interest in a certain district. He stated that 'it is recognised everywhere that this inventorisation is a necessary first step in any scheme for the care and protection of monuments'.[27]

Remarkably, Brown's book hit home. It came to the notice of Sir John Sinclair, Secretary of State for Scotland. He had taken up the post with a clear vision of leading Scottish policies by Scottish ideas. He was particularly interested in culture and education, and after a brief consultation put Brown's ideas into practice as the Royal Commission on the Ancient and Historical Monuments of Scotland, established on 14 February 1908. Brown was appointed one of seven Commissioners charged with making 'an Inventory of the Ancient and Historical Monuments and constructions connected with or illustrative of the contemporary culture, civilisation, and conditions of life of the people in Scotland from the earliest times to the year 1707'.[28]

Inevitably, this sent the English learned bodies into a frenzy. H. H. Asquith, the Prime Minister, received a barrage of requests to follow Scotland's lead from, amongst others, the Society of Antiquaries, the Royal Institute of British Architects and the Royal Society of Arts. As a result, on 27 October 1908 a Commission for England was appointed by royal warrant and Asquith invited the societies that had lobbied him to nominate Commissioners. They had two specific duties: the preparation of an inventory and the specification of monuments worthy of preservation. The method was to consult with national and local expert bodies to produce a draft list of sites, and, after fieldwork by the Commissioners, approved monuments would be added to the inventory. Pragmatically, they began in Hertfordshire, a well-researched county, and in 1910 it became the first volume to be published.

There was a major problem with the establishment of the Royal Commission in terms of advancing heritage protection. The link between what Baldwin Brown called inventorisation and classement was never clear. There was a recognition that this would be necessary, and to ensure a proper liaison with the Office of Works and in recognition James Fitzgerald and Sir

Schomberg McDonnell were appointed Commissioners. Later, Charles Peers, Inspector of Ancient Monuments from 1910 to 1933, was co-opted to help compile inventories. But there was never a formal link in which monuments identified by the Commission were given protection by the Office of Works. This was a shame, because the ambitions, and the energy, of the Commission were staggering. Between 1919 and 1923 it recorded 3,554 monuments, in 314 parishes, and the average rate of progress by 1930 was around 700 monuments a year. But they were, of course, recording all monuments built before 1714, not just those judged worthy of protection; and, as a result, in the first fifty years of their existence, had only covered 20 per cent of the country.[29]

The years 1907 and 1908 were important not only for the establishment of the Royal Commissions, but also for two other Acts of Parliament that, in their different ways, significantly advanced both the cause and the philosophy of heritage protection. The Advertisements Regulation Bill, championed by SCAPA, and passed virtually unopposed, gave local authorities power to make by-laws to prohibit advertising hoardings that 'disfigure the natural beauties of a landscape'. SCAPA was cock-a-hoop and announced in its journal that finally natural scenery had been recognised as 'a national asset'. This was an important development because it secured an explicit acknowledgement of the national value of countryside that had for long been applied to buildings and monuments.[30] The second noteworthy legislative change was a Private Member's Bill that gave special powers to the National Trust.

The National Trust was rather an unusual body in the context of its age, for it was primarily a property-holding company that focused on purchasing areas of beautiful and threatened countryside to protect them from development. In this way it provided the counterpart to the Office of Works, which was empowered only to protect monuments. The National Trust also had a related interest in historic buildings and could purchase or accept roofed structures capable of habitation, which the Office of Works could not. The Trust had a tiny income (only £2,063 in 1913) and so was limited in its scope, but nevertheless early on in its history had secured stretches of the Lake District, some Cornish coastline, two nature reserves and extensive common land in Surrey. It had also taken on a number of historic buildings such as Alfriston Clergy House, Sussex, and Long Crendon Court House, Buckinghamshire.[31]

Before the First World War, members of the National Trust's Council belonged to the hyperactive class of crusaders who were interested in the full

Alfriston Clergy House, Sussex, the first historic building purchased by the National Trust in 1896 after it had been earmarked for demolition by the Church of England. The Trust bought it for £10, and restored it according to SPAB principles. Reproduced by permission of English Heritage

spectrum of environmental protection, and so it was frequently represented, along with other bodies, in campaigning for all sorts of causes. Between the wars, after the death of the first generation of Council members, it fell back into being a safe haven for threatened natural and, to a lesser extent, built heritage. Yet in its first twelve years there was always a niggling problem. It was felt that despite ownership by a charity the necessary safeguards for long-term protection were not in place. Donors, it was thought, could be motivated more strongly if National Trust land could be held more securely for all time.

It was this ambition that was the most important provision of the 1907 National Trust Act that gave the National Trust power unprecedented before or since to hold land inalienably. It could therefore choose which parts of an estate were to be inalienable, and once declared, it could not be sold, mortgaged or compulsorily acquired except by Act of Parliament.[32] Though this power had little immediate influence it was, within fifty years, to be integral to the national system of heritage protection.

In the decade after 1900 the Office of Works established itself as the central government authority on ancient monuments and historic buildings with powers over other parts of Government. Meanwhile, it had acquired a sparkling, and growing, portfolio of historic sites. These included two furnished royal palaces, both of which were attracting huge numbers of visitors, and three of the nation's greatest castles complete, in the case of the Tower and Edinburgh, with major collections of arms and armour. But it was making little headway with the preservation of private monuments and in this it was lack of decisive expert leadership that was holding it back. In 1909 James Fitzgerald unexpectedly died and the Board decided to appoint a new, permanent Inspector. Charles Reed Peers (1868–1952), the man they chose, was to dominate the Office of Works for the next twenty-three years. Under his supervision its care of the nation's ancient monuments and historic buildings was to be transformed.

5

THE ANCIENT MONUMENTS ACT OF 1913

CHARLES PEERS

The appointment of Charles Reed Peers as Inspector in 1910 was a decisive moment in the history of heritage protection in Britain. Born in 1868, the son of a clergyman, he was brought up in Kent. As a teenager he had sketched buildings, and after he went up to King's College, Cambridge, he started a series of notebooks on the churches he had visited, arranged alphabetically with historical notes and plans. Every year he covered scores of sites. In June 1890, for instance, he bicycled with two friends across the fens visiting eleven towns and villages, recording churches in a sketchbook titled *The Journey of Three*. On leaving Cambridge, he studied in Dresden and Berlin where again he travelled and drew, not just buildings but also views of towns and hills. In 1893 Peers became a pupil of the architect and historian of medieval buildings T. G. Jackson. While in pupillage he travelled extensively, to France, Germany, Iceland and Italy, before, in 1896, spending a season in Egypt excavating at El Kab and elsewhere.

In 1898 Peers established his own architectural practice, but his interests were much less in contemporary design than history and archaeology. In 1900 he became the editor of the *Archaeological Journal*, the organ of the Royal Archaeological Institute. His duties included the organisation of their summer meetings, preparation for which further developed his knowledge of medieval England. The following year he was elected a Fellow of the Society of Antiquaries and then in 1903 gave up private practice to become architectural editor of the Victoria County History. The vcн had been

Sir Charles Reed Peers, Inspector of Ancient Monuments 1910–1933, photographed in 1922. © National Portrait Gallery, London

founded in 1899 as an act of private enterprise. It had big ambitions and hoped to be 'one of the greatest works ever attempted, in extent, interest and importance, and the largest enterprise of its kind ever undertaken by private effort'. Indeed, it set out to be 'a definite finality in English Local History'.[1]

Peers's methods at the VCH were enormously influential. He masterminded large-scale survey and mapping and the introduction of phase plans. This was particularly important for the development of medieval archaeology since it treated medieval buildings with scholarly weight in their historical context.[2] Work on the Hertfordshire Victoria Country History was fundamental to the Royal Commission's first volume that covered that county, which was published in 1910, using VCH plans rather than its own. In 1908 Peers became Secretary of the Society of Antiquaries, a position he retained until 1921 (he became Director in 1921, and was President from 1929 to 1934). With this background it is unsurprising that, when the Office of Works came to consider who might be appointed as Inspector of Ancient Monuments, Peers was the obvious choice.[3]

Peers immediately set about creating what was to become the Ancient Monuments Department of the Office of Works. He insisted that there should be a separate expert cadre of architects and surveyors who worked on the Board's historic structures. In charge was Frank Baines (1877–1933), a Board architect with a sizeable new works practice for the Office who had trained under C. R. Ashbee (above, p. 59) and who had won attention by his outstanding draughtsmanship and his swashbuckling approach to work (he first came to attention after climbing to the top of Nelson's Column to check on the quality of workmanship there). Peers then set out the approach of his new department to ancient monuments. There were six steps: prioritising structural repairs; second, enclosure by fencing; third, care of the site (signs, security and grass cutting); fourth, the preparation of plans, sections and an analytical phasing of the site; fifth, photographs; and finally the preparation of a guidebook. The first three were already largely established, but the other three steps were much more novel.

It was not only a methodical approach that was important, since Peers, for the first time, effectively and systematically exploited the powers of the 1900 Act. This involved taking into care, for the first time, privately owned monuments that were not prehistoric. In 1911 the first Roman site in England was acquired: the fort known as Richborough Castle in Kent.[4] The owner was the Archbishop of Canterbury, who met Charles Peers at Lambeth Palace to discuss guardianship proposals on 29 March 1911.[5] In a memorandum to Sir Schomberg McDonnell, Peers wrote: 'I think it is most satisfactory that this important Roman building should be placed in our charge, the first of its kind to be so placed.'[6] Upon taking over, Peers appointed a custodian, who

Richborough Castle, the Ministry's first Roman site, acquired in 1911. The handsome custodian's cottage and ticket office was later expanded to include a small museum. The Arts and Crafts design tendencies of Baines's office can be seen in the careful vernacular language of the building. Reproduced by permission of English Heritage

took a portion of the entrance fees and was given the right to graze his stock within the fort walls. It was not until 1913 that the position was formalised so that the Board took the gate receipts and the custodian received a weekly salary. He was paid ten shillings to open the fort from 10am to 7pm from April to October.

The careful arrangements for admitting and charging the public at Richborough were possible due to the 1900 Act. It was also thanks to powers under the act that Peers was able to take into guardianship his first medieval buildings. The Fish House near Meare in Somerset had been built in the years 1322–35 and had housed the Abbot of Glastonbury's water bailiff and provided facilities for fish salting and drying. Its owner was not willing to spend any money on its repair and in 1910 offered it to the Government. Peers travelled down to inspect the monument and found that despite the loss of the roof and floor the building was 'nearly complete, and of great interest, as small houses of this date are very rare'. The Deed of Appointment

Kirby Muxloe Castle, Leicestershire, the first privately owned castle to be taken into care, before and after restoration works. Reproduced by permission of English Heritage

was signed on 2 March 1911 and a neighbouring farmer appointed to act as caretaker for £1 a year.[7]

Kirby Muxloe Castle, a fortified house in Leicestershire, was acquired in similar circumstances. It had been built from 1480 by William, Lord Hastings, but was never completed because he was executed for treason by Richard III in 1483. Peers met the owner, Major Winstanley, in October 1911 and reported to Sir Schomberg McDonnell that the castle was of 'exceptional interest'; the details of the brickwork were 'extremely interesting' and the loopholes for cannon 'a remarkable feature'. It was, in fact, 'probably the latest example of a fortified house built in the Country' and therefore well worthy of protection. The structure, which was in terrible condition, was inspected by Frank Baines. He recommended urgent works, and the exclusion of a herd of goats that were 'proving most destructive to the wall heads'. Baines was particularly interested in the educational value of the buildings. 'These buildings', he concluded, 'have a decidedly educative value, illustrating as they do, the best work of the period within which they were erected, and it would be in the public interest to acquire control of them . . . many people visit this castle, in conjunction with an ancient camp and other historical remains within easy walk of it.'[8]

In May 1912 the Board brought the castle into guardianship and a major programme of repair began. This included excavating the moat, the garderobe shafts and the tower floor; re-pointing and repairing the walls using old bricks found in the moat; underpinning the gatehouse; waterproofing with Medusa cement and blue lias lime the vault of one of the turrets; and repairing the fifteenth-century oak doors, 'every bit of their old timber' of which was to be preserved. Through these measures the Department secured the preservation of the first privately owned castle to be taken into guardianship.[9]

In 1911 Charles Peers submitted his first annual report on ancient monuments and historic buildings to Parliament. It contained a detailed account of the number and classes of monuments and buildings in care, as well as their condition and repair works under way. There were already 104 monuments in care, including those transferred from the War Office.[10]

CONCERNS ABOUT WIDER PROTECTION

It should be emphasised that Peers's interests were not parochial. He was not only interested in making the Ministry's procedures smoother, but he also wanted to secure a more effective system for protecting and bringing into care important sites. To that end, immediately he was appointed, he invited his new employer, Sir Schomberg McDonnell, to address the Society of Antiquaries on how further legal progress could be made in protection. In the end McDonnell was unable to turn his mind to the issue until December 1911, since the Office of Works was absorbed by the funeral of Edward VII, the Coronation of George V and the Investiture of the Prince of Wales.

The appearance of the Secretary of the Board of Works was a remarkable moment for some of the Fellows of the Society of Antiquaries, who had often been hostile to the State's attitude towards protection. McDonnell was himself a Fellow, and was on the new Royal Commission on Historical Monuments, and his address was clear in setting out his approach to securing better protection. He spoke for at least half an hour on the problems of the current system, listing, in painful detail, the sites that had been lost or that were imperilled. Then he turned on his audience, warning that some of the agitation for new legislation had been, and would be, counter-productive. He made the point that Sir John Lubbock's original bill had failed to get through because it was too extreme: 'If you bring forward very drastic measures you will frighten people, and if you frighten people you will not get your Bill.' Instead, he felt it was best to remember that 'those who walk slowly probably walk furthest'.[11]

McDonnell favoured moderate reform: his Ancient Monuments Inspectors should have responsibility for identifying which buildings were endangered. They could report their findings to an independent advisory committee and, if this committee agreed, they would ask the First Commissioner of Works to declare the structure a National Monument and take it into his care. The proposal was extensively reported in *The Times*. As in the case of the first Ancient Monuments Bill, the opinions of the Office of Works were to prove decisive. But it was not Sir Schomberg who was eventually to put his ideas into action. After ill health forced him into early retirement, he was replaced by Lionel Earle (1866–1948). Like his predecessors in the post, Earle was socially adept and well connected: a long-time associate of a former Prime Minister, the Marquess of Salisbury, as his Principal Private Secretary, with artistic interests and an affable character, it was he who had to deal with an emerging national heritage crisis.

McDonnell had highlighted in his Antiquaries speech the issue of American collectors buying old houses and interiors and exporting them to the

Tattershall Castle, Lincolnshire, in September 1911 showing the gaping scars left by the removal of its famous fireplaces. © The British Library

United States. He was even worried by the idea that the Royal Commission volumes could become a sort of shopping list for American speculators. His concerns were well founded. Panelled rooms, staircases, fireplaces and even ceilings had been removed from important houses and exported across the Atlantic. In 1910–11 one such case came to national attention.[12]

Tattershall Castle, Lincolnshire, was a large fifteenth-century brick tower, the surviving part of a residence that the Office of Works had been concerned about for some years: McDonnell mentioned it in his speech and Peers, who considered it 'probably the finest piece of medieval brickwork ... in England', had shown lantern slides of it afterwards. It had been sold to a speculator in 1910 and it was realised that its large stone fireplaces (used as models for fireplaces in the Palace of Westminster by A.W.N. Pugin) were valuable antiques in their own right. As the castle passed through various hands, each attempting to turn a profit, it was offered to the National Trust, who turned it down. A scheme whereby Baroness Eckhardstein would buy the castle and put in the charge of the Office of Works also fell through. As the fireplaces were removed for sale a storm of protest broke out and the case came to the notice of George, Lord Curzon (1859–1925).

In the late 1880s and 1890s Curzon had travelled the world, visiting the ancient sites of Persia and Afghanistan and riding through the countryside alone on horseback.[13] This had a profound effect on his attitude to the past, and as Viceroy of India (1899–1905) he revived the Archaeological Survey of India (ASI), which had been established in 1861 to survey and list India's archaeological monuments, but which had been dormant since 1889. In 1900 he announced that he could not 'conceive any obligation more strictly pertaining to a supreme government than the conservation of the most beautiful and perfect collection of monuments in the world'. Curzon reorganised the ASI, strengthened its central powers, recruited a brilliant new Director General, John Marshall, and for the first time allowed Indians to be considered for officer-level posts. In 1904 this work was crowned by a comprehensive Ancient Monuments Act that afforded blanket protection to all sites, including those in private ownership, and made their conservation mandatory. It also tightened the regulations against the traffic in antiquities. By the time Curzon left India in April 1906 the future of the great monuments was secure.[14] This, however, was not what he found in his homeland, where the protection system was, as has been seen, virtually non-existent. Back in Britain Curzon threw himself into a series of conservation causes. He became President of the Royal Geographical Society, a trustee of the National Gallery, a leading figure in the Royal Society for the Protection of Birds and an enthusiast for the National Trust. The case of Tattershall Castle drew him in, and, informed that he had twenty-four hours to save the building, he hurried to Lincolnshire and made an offer to buy the castle, which its owners accepted. Then, showing characteristic single-mindedness, he tracked down the fireplaces, raised the money to buy them and returned them to the castle in 1912.

THE 1913 ACT

With the Tattershall case as a background, the Royal Commission on the Historical Monuments of England submitted a report to Parliament. It admitted that the work of identifying monuments of national importance would take many years to complete and that, in the meantime, many valuable sites were being damaged or destroyed.[15] This news was the trigger for no fewer than three bills being introduced into Parliament. The first was introduced into the Lords by Lord Southwark on 14 March 1912, and then taken

The return of the Tattershall Castle fireplaces in 1912, an event that was part carnival, part Roman triumphal procession. © National Trust Photo Library

to the Commons on 26 April by Russell Rea MP at the instigation of the National Trust, which had felt badly bruised by the Tattershall case. Also on 26 March the Government's bill – the Ancient Monuments Consolidation and Amendment Bill – was introduced into the Lords by the First Commissioner, Lord Beauchamp, who had taken office under Asquith in November 1910. In its essentials it was the measure proposed by McDonnell in his speech at the Society of Antiquaries. A bill drafted by the SPAB was taken into the Commons on 2 April by the radical and reforming MP Noel Buxton, owner of the spectacular timber-framed house Paycockes in Coggeshall, Essex, which he was to leave to the National Trust in 1920. This bill was taken into the Lords on 25 April by George Shaw Lefevre, now Lord Eversley, who had himself drafted the 1882 Bill.

Before the bills were even introduced their opponents began to take positions. The Duke of Rutland led the charge in *The Times*:

The system with meddling with and spying into every one's private affairs which is just now in vogue is as mean and petty a one as was ever legislatively created; and I trust that no other measures of the kind may be brought forward under the cloak of the preservation of ancient monuments; and that if they are, they will be strenuously opposed by those who loathe the system of interference with personal liberty as much as I do.[16]

Rutland spoke against the bill in a similar vein at its Second Reading in the Lords. In the same debate Curzon spoke at length, arguing that buildings such as Tattershall

are part of the heritage of the nation, because every citizen feels an interest in them although he may not own them; and they are part of the history of the nation, because they are documents just as valuable in reading the records of the past as is any manuscript or parchment deed to which you can refer.[17]

This view of monuments as documents of national history was one shared by Charles Peers and raised on a number of occasions during the Select Committee hearings that followed the introduction of the bills. Perhaps the most important contribution in Committee was made by Charles Trevelyan (1870–1958), Parliamentary Secretary to the Board of Education. Trevelyan came from a family of historians: his brother, George Macaulay Trevelyan, was the outstanding historian of his generation and a strong believer in public education. Charles was a radical Liberal like his younger brother, and after the First World War left the Liberals and stood as a Labour MP, becoming President of the Board of Education in Ramsay MacDonald's government of 1924. His evidence to the joint Committee on Ancient Monuments put forward the view that ancient monuments were increasingly an integral part of the education system, a way of making history come alive. He explained that his Board was very anxious that the bill

should not be regarded as merely an antiquarian question, but that it should be realised that part of the character of the nation which depends on the appreciation of its past may really be affected by the preservation of these monuments now that the idea has really got into our system of education that the nation ought to learn about its past through what is left of its monuments.[18]

It has been seen that there was widespread and enthusiastic popular engagement in history, but, before the last decade of Victoria's reign, there was little or no official recognition of this. Before 1890 history was barely taught in English schools, but as education expanded beyond reading, writing and arithmetic the subject became increasingly popular, and by 1903 almost all England's elementary schools taught it. Central government responsibility lay with the newly formed Board of Education, which had published its first *Code of Regulations for Day Schools* in 1900. This suggested that children between nine and fourteen should learn English history chronologically and focus on great figures and events. Later, they could progress to themes such as the development of parliament and the acquisition of colonies.

A band of inspectors was responsible for informing the Board on educational progress in the localities. They had a book of *Instructions* that set out what should be encouraged and discouraged. Importantly, the *Instructions* confirmed that time spent out of the classroom in museums, galleries and 'other places of educational value, or of national or historical interest' counted as school time provided that there were not more than twenty such outings a year. These were not just recreation, for the *Instructions* also hoped that on such trips a person should be present who was 'competent to give information of a kind interesting to young children', and that children who were old enough should write an account of what they had seen.

In 1908 guidance was published on history teaching in secondary schools by the Permanent Staff Inspector of Secondary Schools, James Wycliffe Headlam (1863–1929), a former professor of Greek and ancient history at Queen Mary College, London. He reiterated the desire for children to grasp chronology through great individuals, events and inventions, but was also concerned that other civilisations should be understood, especially where their history touched on our own. Strongly alive to the dangers of rote learning, he was an advocate of using pictures of people, objects and buildings to bring history alive. He also saw local history as a way into the national story. He wrote: 'it is far more important that pupils should leave school with their eyes trained to observe historical remains which are to be found in almost every part of England, than that they should attempt to remember the whole of the political history which they cannot understand'.[19]

On 15 August 1913 the Ancient Monuments Consolidation and Amendment Act was passed. It expanded the definition of an ancient monument to 'any monument or part or remains of a monument, the preservation of which is a matter of public interest by reason of the historic, architectural, traditional, artistic, or archaeological interest'. Ecclesiastical buildings in use were totally excluded from the provisions of the act and inhabited houses largely so (although curiously they could be purchased by the Commissioners, or accepted as gifts). An expert advisory committee was set up known as the Ancient Monuments Board. It was formed of representatives of the Royal Commissions on Historical Monuments, the Society of Antiquaries, the Royal Institute of British Architects, the Royal Academy of Arts, the British Museum and the Board of Education. On the advice of the inspectors, the Ancient Monuments Board was to alert the Commissioners if an ancient monument of national importance was in danger of damage or destruction so that a Preservation Order could be made. This would place the monument under protection giving powers of entry and inspection, and, if necessary, an order preventing damage or destruction for a period of eighteen months. In order to protect the monument permanently, the Preservation Order had to be confirmed through an Act of Parliament, at which point compensation equivalent to the market value of the site would be payable.[20]

It will be seen that this cumbersome system proved almost impossible to use (below, pp. 165–70), but the act also introduced another form of protection, which was sometimes known as 'scheduling'. The term schedule was borrowed from the 1882 Act, but, confusingly, had nothing to do with it. 'Scheduling' hugely widened the scope of protection to thousands of monuments on private land rather than just those in Government or local authority care. Inspectors recommended lists of monuments to the Ancient Monuments Board, which would decide which were of national importance. Those agreed were 'scheduled' through a notification letter to the owner. By scheduling the owner was required to give the Board of Works a month's notice before carrying out any proposals to alter, demolish, remove or add to a monument.[21] Any person found convicted of contravening this rule was liable to a fine of up to £100 or imprisonment for up to three months.

The third important provision of the act was to extend the guardianship powers granted to county councils in 1900 to borough and district councils. It also allowed a borough or district council to relax by-laws where these impeded 'the erection of buildings of a style of architecture in harmony with other buildings of artistic merit existing in the locality'. In this way local authorities were empowered to provide new buildings that enhanced the setting of the existing historic buildings. In addition, by-laws could be made to prohibit or restrict advertisements that were detrimental to the amenities of an ancient monument.[22]

The 1913 Act is often referred to as a weak and toothless measure. In terms of preservation orders this is perhaps a fair criticism, but, as will be seen, scheduling did much to protect monuments in private ownership. The act also crystallised a division of the Office's activities into three parts: operating the protection system of preservation orders and scheduling; acquiring sites for guardianship and opening them to the public for education and enjoyment; and giving more general advice about how best to protect monuments of national importance.

The hub of the Office's ancient monument activities now became the Ancient Monuments Board that held its first meeting on 1 April 1914. It was chaired by the Secretary to the Board of Works, Lionel Earle, and comprised a heavyweight list of architects, historians, archaeologists and educationalists, many of whom have already featured in this story.[23] The powers and duties of the Board set out in detail the criteria for determining which monuments were to be considered of national importance: 'Generally speaking, monuments must be considered from two aspects: – Their actual and relative importance and their topographical value. The point to be kept constantly in view being that the preservation of the evidences of the history of the country is the end to be secured.'[24]

The Board was asked to consider the distribution of monuments across the country, as well as selecting examples that were representative of 'the Stone, Bronze and Iron Ages, the Roman Occupation, the Early Christian Settlements, the Saxon, Danish and Norse Invasions, the Norman Settlement, the social and economic developments of the Middle Ages, the Renaissance, the Great Rebellion, the Restoration and the development of industries'. In addition, they were to consider local or regional specific sites, including such monuments to 'explain and illustrate the special features' of particular districts. Guardianship sites were expected to be identified as of national importance by the Ancient Monuments Board before they were taken into care. Foremost in the mind of the Board was thus the task of choosing the most representative monuments across time and across the country that illustrated the story of Britain.

HISTORY AND THE BRITISH STATE

The 1913 Act thus instituted a project to create a great outdoor museum of national history. This extraordinary ambition should be seen as part of a late nineteenth-century concept of collecting, categorising and popularising the national story. The Public Record Act of 1838, followed by the completion of a magnificent new Public Record Office in Chancery Lane in 1861, marked, in many senses, the start of the State's appropriation of national history. The *Calendars of State Papers* and a series of *Chronicles and Memorials* began to be published in 1856–7 to provide a guide to what was in the Record Office. It was believed that these books

> would show to the people of the country, that as their history yields to no other, in ancient or modern times, in the vast importance of the acts which it records, in their variety, their fullness, and their paramount interest, so the chronicles, records and state papers, in which these acts are registered, bear the like impress of the national character.

The *Calendars* and *Chronicles* were published in short print runs but gave nationwide access to the raw materials of national history. A reviewer of the *Calendar of Colonial State Papers, 1574–1660* in *The Reader* wrote proudly of English subjects who had fought their way through 'ice and mist to the other side of the world ... to plant the standard of Protestant Christianity and English Civilization in regions yet unknown'.[25]

In 1869 the Government turned to historic manuscripts in the muniment rooms of private castles and country houses. The Historical Manuscripts Commission founded that year met, at first, with opposition – its inspectors characterised as Government-employed snoopers. But it quickly won over aristocratic owners who had never properly sorted their own papers. Between 1870 and 1884 it reported on 424 private collections in seventeen volumes. In 1883 it started to produce calendars of the most important collections, such as the manuscripts at Hatfield House.[26]

The hunger for history was also expressed in the search for authentic images of Britain's past. From the mid-1840s until after 1870 painters were preoccupied with creating accurate depictions of the past. The most spectacular enterprise was at the new Palace of Westminster, which was being decorated with giant murals illustrating the national story. The programme was under the control of the historian Thomas Babington Macaulay, MP for Edinburgh, who was then writing his hugely successful and popular *History of England*. The murals were designed to show 'the long and uninterruptedly increasing prosperity of England as the most beautiful phenomenon in the history of mankind'.[27] The parliamentary murals were costume drama. A more serious State-sponsored effort to capture the images of national history was the foundation, in 1856, of the National Portrait Gallery. It was given a board of trustees and a grant of £2,000 a year. Its first acquisition was a portrait of Shakespeare. The gallery's focus was collecting images of men of political power and influence, amassing, by 1877, 500 portraits and 50 pieces of sculpture visited by more than 70,000 people.[28]

The British Museum was also undergoing changes that would bring national history to more people. Its Keeper of Printed Books was Anthony Panizzi (1797–1879), who came to post in 1837 and set out to make the British Museum the world's greatest library. He was particularly interested in British works and of 'works relating to the British Empire; its religious, political and literary, as well as its scientific history'. He wanted to bring these to the 'poor student' as well as to the richest man in the kingdom. He secured an incredible £10,000 a year from the Treasury to achieve this; as a result, the British Museum was buying 30,000 volumes a year in the late 1840s. Its extremely cramped reading rooms were replaced with a stupendous new circular reading room in 1854. William Makepeace Thackeray wrote of it in 1862: 'What peace, what love, what truth, what beauty, what happiness for all, what generous kindness for you and me are here spread out . . . I own to have said my grace at the table, and to have thanked heaven for this my English Birthright, freely to partake of these beautiful books, and speak the truth I find there.'[29]

These currents of collecting and national history were also strong in the Office of Works. Lewis Harcourt (1863–1922), First Commissioner 1905–10, together with Lord Esher put together a daring scheme to create a museum that told the history of London in 1910. Through their contacts, skill and energy, in three short years they had assembled a collection, found it a home, and secured an ongoing Government grant for its operation. A major spur for them and their supporters was the sale of a number of important collections of London material and the fear that they would end up in America. The museum opened its doors at Kensington Palace in April 1912 and on the first day there were at least 13,000 visitors. Its first Director, Guy Laking, wrote to Harcourt: 'Its popularity is nothing short of astonishing, indeed the queues waiting to get in, suggest the attractions of a musical comedy or a football match, rather than visitors calmly viewing a museum that purports to be educational? And instructive?'[30]

This, then, was the context within which the new Ancient Monuments Board operated. Lord Beauchamp and Lionel Earle, immediately after the passing of the 1913 Act, had a clear ambition to construct, with their new powers, a National Heritage Collection, both in the activities of the schedule and in guardianship. The first lists for scheduling were intended to include the most outstanding national monuments.[31] The initial lists were prepared by Harry Sirr, Assistant Inspector of Ancient Monuments and Secretary to the Ancient Monuments Board. At the second Board meeting in May 1914 a list of monastic buildings and a list of city and town walls were considered and discussed. At the third meeting the Board considered a list of castles, but a provisional list of 'prehistoric forts and Roman military works' drawn up at the following meeting was deferred for consideration until after the war. By this time notification letters had been sent out to owners of monastic buildings and castles. A total of 129 had been scheduled, some of which were Crown property and already under the act. Of the seventy-three owners who had received letters, twenty-eight had already replied, most with 'encouraging' responses.[32]

Meanwhile, the Board was very active in collecting new sites for itself. Between August and December 1913 the Office of Works took over Mattersey Priory, Nottinghamshire, Framlingham Castle, Suffolk, and Penrith Castle, Cumbria. Mattersey was a particularly rare example of its type, one of the few surviving buildings of the Gilbertines, the only purely English monastic order. The initiative was taken by Nottinghamshire County Council, which persuaded the owner, Captain Laycock, to transfer it into Government care. He did this willingly, but admitted: 'My only fear is that so little is left of the old Abbey, and what there is is so overgrown with ivy and filled with blown sand, that I fear it is not of very great interest.'[33] This was certainly not the case. The priory was on a list of sites targeted for acquisition held by Lord Beauchamp since at least 1912. The list does not survive, but it illustrates that the Board had clear ideas about how it would like its own collection to grow.[34]

In the first half of the nineteenth century history had captured the popular imagination through the efforts of novelists and antiquaries; in the second half it was appropriated by professionals; and after 1900 it was owned by the State. In 1913 the Government acknowledged, for the first time, that the

An early photograph of Framlingham Castle, Suffolk. Framlingham was taken into care
in 1925, adding to the magnificent royal castles transferred from the War Office and the
Office of Woods. © Francis Frith Photographic Collection

State had a cultural responsibility for the physical remains of its own history and set out to collect them. The first list of scheduled monuments and
the increasingly large portfolio of sites in guardianship open to the public
now represented an established view of the nation's history. The custodians
of this were the staff of the Ancient Monuments Department of the Office
of Works, and it heavily influenced the way in which they repaired and displayed the sites in their care.

6

THE ANCIENT MONUMENTS DEPARTMENT IN INTER-WAR BRITAIN

THE INTER-WAR OFFICE OF WORKS

After the First World War there was an increasing demand for the services of cultured aristocrats on the boards of national cultural institutions, and a small number of grandees circulated as their chairmen and presidents. The First Commissioners of Works were, with few exceptions, drawn from this class of men tightly networked into the world of museums, galleries and cultural campaigning. The Earl of Crawford and Balcarres, who was briefly First Commissioner in 1921–2, was, for instance, President of the National Art Collections Fund and was on the boards of the National and National Portrait Galleries. He was also variously President of the London Society, the Society of Antiquaries, and the Survey of London Committee, and Chairman of the Royal Commission on Historical Monuments, the Royal Fine Art Commission and the Council for the Preservation of Rural England.[1]

The contributions of various inter-war First Commissioners will be charted in the following chapters, but it should be emphasised that, for most, despite the increasingly broad range of responsibilities in the Office of Works, the Ancient Monuments Department was a particularly attractive and interesting part of their brief and most made direct, personal and lasting contributions to its work. Under them served only two Permanent Secretaries.

Sir Lionel Earle was the dominant figure in the inter-war Office of Works. Appointed by Asquith as Permanent Secretary in 1912, he remained at the

Lionel Earle photographed in 1909 by Sir John Benjamin Stone. Earle was the dominating figure in the Office of Works in the inter-war years. © National Portrait Gallery, London

helm until his retirement in 1933. Suave, well connected and deeply cultured, his interests were artistic rather than financial or managerial. As well as being Chairman of the Ancient Monuments Board for England, he was a member of the Royal Commission on National Museums and Galleries (1927–30), and had a significant influence in founding the Royal Fine Art Commission in 1924. His private passion was gardening, and his interest in trees and shrubs found an outlet in his responsibilities both in the royal parks and in his work with ancient monuments.[2] His successor as Permanent Secretary was Sir Patrick Duff, who had been Private Secretary to Stanley Baldwin and continued to serve until 1941. He was an important figure in nature conservation, serving as Chairman of the National Parks Commission (1949–54) after the Second World War.[3]

Under the Permanent Secretary were several Assistant Secretaries who were important in the day-to-day running of the Ancient Monuments Department. In the inter-war period they included James Eggar, M. Connolly and Frederick J. E. Raby. Raby came into the office in 1927 and, through his combination of academic ability and administrative efficiency, made a big contribution to the Department's success. Like many senior figures in the Office of Works, Raby was a member of the St. James's club the Athenaeum.[4]

The Ancient Monuments Department was headed by Charles Peers as Inspector of Ancient Monuments,[5] with the support of his Principal Architect, Sir Frank Baines. These two men, with Earle's support, effectively invented the Ancient Monuments Department, its policies and procedures. What they set out remained almost unaltered until the formation of the Directorate of Ancient Monuments and Historic Buildings of the Department of the Environment in 1970 (below, p. 235). It was, perhaps, an unlikely partnership.

Baines had trained under the Arts and Crafts architect, designer and social reformer C. R. Ashbee. His articles began in 1892, while Ashbee was preoccupied with his Guild and School of Handicraft on Mile End Road. Here Ashbee, his employees and pupils designed and made furniture, metalwork and painted decorations. Baines was in the office while Ashbee designed his own house on Cheyne Walk, and during the foundation of the Committee for the Survey of Memorials of Greater London (above, p. 59). In February 1895 Baines joined the Office of Works as an assistant draughtsman in the royal palaces section.[6] Energetic and talented, he quickly amassed a deep knowledge of the buildings in his care. Yet it was the First World War that made his career (below, pp. 99–100). He was knighted in 1918 for his work with the Ministry of Munitions, Ministry of War and Ministry of Air. On his retirement in 1927 he received a KCVO for his work for the royal family and became known to his colleagues as 'twice a knight Baines'.

After the First World War he moved to Loughton in Essex, where he shared a house with his sister and brother (the latter was Chief Engineer at

James Eggar, Frank Baines, W. J. Downer, Schomberg McDonnell, A. Durrant, Sir Charles Peers and E. Bright in civil uniform levée dress at the Investiture of the Prince of Wales at Caernarfon Castle in 1911. Reproduced by permission of English Heritage

the Office of Works and had been in charge of Civil Defence of London). Baines was part of an artistic and politically active inter-war set in Loughton mixing with academics, writers and artists, but he was a complex man who had lied about his age to join the Office of Works and kept his marriage secret, living with his siblings in Loughton rather than with his wife and children in south London.[7]

Charles Peers, who has already been met (above, p. 66), was altogether more conventional, an establishment figure, but made so only by birth; his brilliance and abilities were recognised by everyone. In 1914 it was realised that a single inspector could not manage the workload, and so Peers became Chief Inspector and acquired three deputies: Wilfred Hemp as Inspector for Wales, James Richardson as Inspector for Scotland and, in 1920, Jocelyn Bushe-Fox as Inspector for England. Bushe-Fox became Chief Inspector on the retirement of Charles Peers and Paul Baille Reynolds took over as

Inspector for England. In 1929 George Chettle, the first of three assistant inspectors, was appointed; in the following year he was joined by R. S. Simms in England and Margaret Simpson in Scotland. Simpson is notable as the first woman to serve in an inspector role, albeit as an assistant; she was the co-author of the Office of Works guide to Stirling Castle published in 1936.[8]

A separate team led by Baines, as Principal Architect and then Director of Works, carried out preservation works to ancient monuments and historic buildings. After 1920 he was assisted by the Architect, Arthur Heasman; under him were between fifteen and twenty draughtsmen. A much larger body of foremen and labourers was directly employed on the sites themselves. The architects saw to it that the Department immediately had a recognisable identity, casting the letters 'AMD' for Ancient Monuments Department on lead hopper heads at Eltham Palace, where they had been working in 1914.

These, then, were the men from the Ministry in charge of Britain's ancient monuments in the twenty-five years between the two World Wars. Their attitudes and opinions will be examined in some detail in chapter Nine. Philosophy, however, is not enough to understand them, because a number of streams of thought in the inter-war years moulded departmental attitudes and actions.

THE BIRTH OF TOWN PLANNING

This book is not a history of heritage protection or a book about the history of town and country planning: there is already an extensive literature on both these topics.[9] Yet, from 1900 the notion that local government should exercise greater control over development grew, and while in the inter-war years this had only a minor impact on the Office of Works, in due course it was to become the backbone of the national heritage protection system.[10]

Statutory planning grew out of the imperative to improve the living conditions of the inner-city working classes. During the nineteenth century a measure of progress had been made through local by-laws, and the growth of suburbs had relieved some of the pressure on city centres. But there was still a feeling that cities had somehow failed and in 1909 a Housing and Town Planning Act gave powers to local authorities to draw up planning schemes that would regulate things such as construction and open space. An amendment to the bill, put forward by the Liberal MP Philip Morrell, gave authorities powers to preserve 'objects of historical interest or natural beauty', and so, through the enthusiasm of an individual, the protection of historic places and town planning were linked.

These powers were entirely different and separate to those that the Office of Works gained in 1913, but in 1919, in response to a proposal to develop the Royal Label Factory in Stratford-upon-Avon (below, p. 157), it was suggested that the two should be combined. The 1913 Act could be amended, it was thought, to include 'a clause enacting that in approving of Town Planning Schemes the Ministry of Health should have regard to the preservation of artistic and historical features of national sentiment'. At the time Charles Peers rebuffed the suggestion, remarking to Sir Lionel Earle:

I think we have enough on our hands at present without such things as this. If certain towns or villages (or streets) could be scheduled as of national importance on aesthetic or historic grounds – as is done in other countries, we should be in a position to deal with such matters as the industrialisation of Stratford. We must await legislation on the subject.[11]

Legislation took a very long time and when it came it did not give powers to the Office of Works to schedule large urban areas. Despite amendments to the 1909 Planning Act in 1919 and 1923, and a major reorganisation of local government in 1929, it was only in 1932 that the Town and Country Planning Act significantly changed the scope of statutory planning. This bill, for the first time, conjoined town planning with country planning. It was introduced by the Minister of Health, Sir Edward Hilton Young, who carried the brief for housing and planning, and it was primarily concerned with raising housing standards, addressing poor sanitation, controlling urban sprawl and attempting to regulate the housing market, but it also introduced protection for inhabited buildings by preservation orders. This, at first sight, was a huge step forward for preservation campaigners, but the power was, in fact, no easier for a local authority to use than the Office of Works' existing powers. A local authority had to get an order signed off by the Minister of Health (responsible for planning) on the advice of the Office of Works. Once agreed, permission to demolish or alter the building had to be signed off by both the ministers at Health and Works, and, crucially, the local authority had to pay compensation for any loss to the owner.

The Labour Party endorsed the bill and its approach. The Tories were appalled. Sir Derek Walker-Smith stood up in the House to say: 'this is just the sort of measure a socialist government would introduce. An enormous amount of power and control over the rights of property are invested in local authority and government departments.' The Marquess of Hartington said: 'these buildings have been preserved to us not by Acts of Parliament but by the loving care of generations of free Englishmen who did not know who the Minister of Health was'. These were not the only concerns. Although both the Office of Works and the Royal Commission on Historical Monuments were making lists of buildings worthy of protection, it was felt that local authorities would have no guidance as to which buildings should be protected. Viscount Cranborne complained that 'one of the chief failings of local authorities is a complete lack of artistic sensibility' and proposed that ministers have an expert committee that draw up a list of what should be preserved. 'There is no lack of experts in this country – innumerable people who have not very much to do, and plenty of taste, who would be able to do this work very well'; in fact, he argued, 'all they would have to do, would be to take a large scale ordnance survey map and mark the buildings which ought to be preserved, there would not be a day's work in it'.[12]

The bill went through, without listing provisions, in its original form. Several preservation orders were served through the inter-war period, the first being on the medieval watergate to Bridgwater Castle in Somerset. This was followed by an early eighteenth-century town hall in New Romney, Kent, and a seventeenth-century market hall called Grange Court in Leominster, Herefordshire. Sixteen orders were issued between 1936 and 1939, covering thirty-eight buildings.[13]

THE COUNTRYSIDE

Historians disagree about attitudes to the countryside, Englishness and preservation in the inter-war years. One school of thought sees the establishment reacting to modernity and progress using notions of rural England and preservation as a way to protect the traditional social order. This reaction was so successful, the argument goes, that England's entry into the modern world was stifled, condemning the nation to economic decline and stagnation. An alternative view rejects the picture of economic decline and sees inter-war Britain as perhaps less obsessed with the past than many European countries. Though an increasingly post-urban society, the argument goes, the countryside and its Englishness was part of Britain successfully re-defining itself in the modern world.[14]

What is certain is that after the First World War the countryside was flooded by visitors. Increasingly long holidays meant that by 1937 fifteen million people (a third of the population) took an annual holiday, and many of those who did not head for the seaside spent it in the countryside. They came in trains, buses, cars, bicycles and on foot. During the First World War there had been 331 stage bus operators; by 1930 there were 3,962 and by 1932 buses carried more passengers than the rail network. At the same time there was an explosion in car ownership. In 1918 there had been no more than 100,000 private motor cars, but by 1939 there were two million. The internal combustion engine took people to places that railways and even motor buses could not.

In writing this history, which tells the story of the Office of Works' activities in protection and conservation, it would be easy to focus, at this point, on the vast literature, both contemporary and subsequent, that bemoaned this influx of people to the countryside: the effects of suburbanisation, of ribbon development, of roads and cars, of cafés, tea shops, picnickers, hikers and advertising hoardings.[15] These were certainly the concerns of a very vocal group of intellectuals and campaigners, but the books and pamphlets they produced (and there were quite a number of them) were drowned out by material celebrating the countryside and what it had to offer. It will be seen (below, p. 149) that guidebooks and travelogues were produced in their hundreds of thousands, and were used by urban holidaymakers and tourists to explore the countryside.

So the countryside was full of people wanting to visit places and see things, clutching the guidebooks and maps that took them there. The countryside and its monuments were, for the first time, permeable to almost everyone. Was this rush to the green fields of England more than a leisure pursuit and a boost to hoteliers, petrol companies and tea-shop owners? Was it something more fundamental that helps us to understand the enthusiasm and success with which the Ancient Monuments Department took hundreds of rural historic sites into its collection? Since the seventeenth century, and perhaps before, the countryside has been a huge creative force inspiring British writers, musicians, painters and sculptors. This was no less the case in the interwar period; indeed, it could be argued that the countryside as a source of creativity was at a particular peak. All the major creative figures of the period lived in villages, not in cities: Virginia and Leonard Woolf, John Piper, E. M. Forster, Stanley Spencer, Cecil Beaton and Evelyn Waugh are just a few examples. Their work was fundamentally inspired by landscape and especially the monuments within it. So, for example, the work of Paul Nash, Barbara Hepworth and John Piper all acknowledged their fascination with megalithic art, and in the late 1930s Piper made a series of studies of the remains of Knowlton Church in Dorset, a lovely ruin set amidst a Neolithic henge.[16]

Medieval ruins were also important. The First World War had made ruins part of many people's world picture, either by direct contact in Flanders or by images of them transmitted by photograph and paint. The two principal British fronts, the Ypres Salient and the Somme, were both dominated by iconic ruins: the Cloth Hall at Ypres and the ruins of the Basilica at Albert on the Somme. Looking at war artists' records of bombed Flemish cities, it is hard to distinguish them from a monument in the care of the Office of Works. The work of the brilliant war artist Paul Nash was dominated by haunting ruins of this sort. After the First World War ruins struck a

Rural tourism in the motor car. The photographer, W. J. Brunell, specialised in taking images of new model cars in all manner of settings. Here a Singer stops to admire Ludlow Castle. © National Motor Museum/MPL

The Cloth Hall at Ypres after the ravages of the First World War. Images such as this were impressed on the minds of combatants and those at home in equal measure.

chord in people's imaginations, and those of the Reformation and Civil War were rendered more poignant by association. Reginald Smith of the British Museum compared the Neolithic flint mines at Grime's Graves with the cratered landscape of no man's land, describing them, in 1917, as like 'a mass of shell-holes, but the trees are standing'.[17]

It would take more than these two examples to argue convincingly that the rural neo-romanticism of contemporary artists and the haunting images of the Great War lay behind the Ancient Monuments Department's success in collecting megaliths and ruins in the post-war period. Yet it would be foolish to ignore this important background to their activities.[18]

THE PRIME MINISTERS

As background to the inter-war activities of the Office of Works, Prime Ministers need to be added to town planning and the countryside. Stanley Baldwin (1867–1947), the dominating political figure of the inter-war years,

Grime's Graves, Norfolk, from the air in 1997. Was this Neolithic England or the Somme?
© Crown copyright

clearly saw the importance of England's rural heritage.[19] The First World War had a transforming effect on his outlook and opinions and on his political career. He was too old to fight and in 1916, with a healthy inheritance, turned to politics with a determination to serve his country in a different capacity.[20] In a speech in 1931 he laid out his motivations for entering politics. He said that 'after four years of slaughter and destruction many times four years would be needed to repair even part of what had been lost ... and after such a storm should there not be calm, and would not the sun come out and the world be more beautiful than before?'[21]

Baldwin was Prime Minister in the years 1924–9 and 1935–7, and was effectively deputy Prime Minister from 1931 to 1937. Like Margaret Thatcher, he successfully conveyed his personal vision with considerable influence. He saw the inter-war world as a fragile place, inherently instable and in need of careful handling. He strove and succeeded to be a figure that almost rose above politics, evoking images that he believed would unify the nation. They were traditional Christian ones of charity and patience, respect and generosity of spirit, but they were underpinned by a sustaining idea of the rural heritage. The carefully manufactured image of Baldwin as a countryman was a central part of his appeal, especially in the early years of his first premiership.

Speaking at the handing over of Haresfield Beacon in Gloucestershire to the National Trust in January 1931, he asked why it was necessary to preserve spots such as this. 'I think', he said, 'it answers to a very deep and profound instinct of the English people. The country represents the eternal values and the eternal traditions from which we must never allow ourselves to be separated'.[22] In June 1931 he unveiled a memorial stone at Old Sarum, Wiltshire, a site that had been taken into guardianship in 1892. 'What', he asked, 'is the site value of Old Sarum? The site value arrived at by any value ... can be but small. But the value to us and all England is infinite. The spiritual value is beyond all computation.'[23] Baldwin was not afraid to campaign for this heritage 'of infinite value'. He spearheaded a campaign launched by the Royal Society of Arts to save old rural cottages, buildings he thought captured the essence of England, and supported efforts to save the landscape round Stonehenge.

Ramsay MacDonald (1866–1937), who was Prime Minister in 1924 and then in the years 1929–31 and 1931–5, also signed up to the campaign to save Stonehenge. Unlike Baldwin, who, in fact, was essentially an industrialist, MacDonald was a countryman who yearned to be in Lossiemouth and the Highlands where he was born; he was a keen ornithologist and perhaps did more, in actuality, than Baldwin to support the cause of preservation. He had been decisive in instigating the 1932 Planning Act, having written to George Lansbury, First Commissioner of Works, and to the Health Minister, Arthur Greenwood, in 1931 saying that the Government needed to consider 'the whole question of how to deal with our national amenities'. With the question of Stonehenge in his mind he stated that 'we cannot go on dealing with this part and with that separately, raising funds for purchase and so on, otherwise the vandalism that is going on in our country will soon destroy some of our most precious historical monuments and our finest bits of natural scenery'. The solution, he thought, was for 'some national policy regarding them'.[24]

Stanley Baldwin, 1st Earl Baldwin, photographed by Vandyk in 1927. © National Portrait Gallery, London

It is important not to see this interest in, and concern for, rural heritage as a backward-looking force: it was regarded by both Baldwin and MacDonald as an integral part of a modern society comfortable with itself. Baldwin's Conservative Government set up the Empire Marketing Board to promote imperial products worldwide. Its secretary was Sir Stephen Tallents, who invented the concept of national projection – the projection of images about Britain that were to marry dynamic forward-looking characteristics such as industry, tourism, universities and scientific research with a more established group of icons: the monarchy, London buses, the Oxford and Cambridge Boat Race and the countryside. In 1937 Britain sported a pavilion at the Paris International Exhibition intended to convey exactly this. The building was partly modern and partly traditional, a white box with curvaceous lines but with Georgian-shaped windows; inside it contained a traditional vision of England with tennis, weekend cottages, shepherds in white smocks and a cardboard cut-out of Neville Chamberlain fishing.[25]

The proper funding of the Ancient Monuments Department, even in harsh economic times, should be seen against this cultural background, one where art, memory and politics gave weight and value to the rural ruins of the past as part of a modern and progressive society. For though almost every year the Treasury resisted the Office of Works' pleading for more money for ancient monuments, when the votes were allocated officials were overruled and more resources were made available. So from a position when the first Inspector, Augustus Pitt-Rivers, had resigned in despair, the Office of Works believed that they now had 'considerable' scope to take on the best of the nation's heritage. Charles Peers was able to establish a corps of deputy inspectors and a whole works office for conservation and repair. The general trajectory of funding was upwards and reflected the growth of interest in the work of the Office.

A VIEW FROM THE SECRETARY'S DESK

In 1934 Sir Patrick Duff wrote to the Treasury summarising the position of the Ancient Monuments Department. He began:

> It is now just over 20 years since the Act was passed on which the main body of our work is still based, but, owing to the War and its after effects, only the last ten years or so can be counted as years of real activity and progress. During those years remarkable changes have taken place which have not failed to affect profoundly the extent and nature of our work.

The first of those changes, he thought, was a huge upsurge in popular interest: 'there has been an unprecedented growth of interest in archaeology. Not only has the study of prehistoric archaeology been entirely revolutionised as a result of excavations carried out on innumerable sites, but an equal interest has been focused on medieval civilisation and its material remains.'

This, he thought, was the cause of popular campaigning for preservation.

An immediate response has been forthcoming to propaganda in recent years on behalf of the preservation of the amenities of the countryside, and of buildings – from Cathedrals to humble cottages – which might be in danger from various causes. All these movements have received support, not only from persons more immediately interested, such as archaeologists, architects and men of letters, but also from a growing pressure on the part of the general public whose conscience is becoming more and more stirred in respect of those matters, and Parliament, in passing the Town Planning Acts and the Ancient Monuments Act of 1931, has given full recognition to this remarkable growth of opinion.

The implications of this for his Ancient Monuments Department had been quite remarkable:

Our correspondence has grown to vast dimensions; our advice is sought on innumerable occasions; our work, and the way we conduct it, are jealously watched, and, though on the whole we have earned a great deal of praise, we are being made to feel more and more that we are falling short of what people, in the light of the obligations laid upon us by the Ancient Monuments Acts, expect us to perform.[26]

Well he might feel this. For though the Office of Works was widely recognised as being the official guardian of the nation's monuments, it still had very limited powers to do anything other than acquire them. And, after the First World War, this is what it did with gusto.

7

CREATING A NATIONAL HERITAGE COLLECTION
1913–1939

In 1914 the Office of Works became one of the front-line departments prosecuting the war. It was responsible for constructing arms factories and building housing estates for naval and munitions workers. Ten thousand civilians in internment camps fell into its remit, as did the preparation of a venue for signing the armistice; by 1918 the Department had spent more than £25 million on war-related activities. The aftermath was no less arduous: the housing estates it had erected were now let out commercially and the Department found itself landlord to thousands of working-class tenants. To it fell responsibility for the Commonwealth War Graves Commission and for British war memorials across Europe. This rag-bag of duties was gradually expanded during the 1920s: responsibility for Government hospitality came its way together with the arduous task of sampling wine and cigars before purchasing them in bulk.[1]

At the outbreak of war the staff either signed up or were assigned duties at home. Frank Baines wanted to go to the Front, but failed the medical more than once. He was instead crucial to the Office of Works' ability to implement the huge building programme assigned to it. Attached to the Ministry of Munitions in 1917, amongst other tasks, he was given the job of building a large estate in Eltham to house munitions workers. Conceived, planned and built in less than a year, the estate was intended to be a model solution for the wartime housing crisis. The 1,000 houses and 200 flats were designed as an old English village along principles established before the war in places such as Hampstead Garden Suburb.[2] Baines went on to design two more estates amongst other large-scale commissions. Sir Lionel Earle, Permanent Secretary, wrote that he knew 'no one who did more to win the war in a civilian capacity than this man: his energy and determination was remarkable and his power of work Napoleonic'.[3]

During the war the activities of the Ancient Monuments Department were wound down. Many guardianship offers were either deferred or rejected. In November 1917 Charles Peers replied to a request to take over Wayland's Smithy, a magnificent long barrow in Oxfordshire. 'In normal times', he said, 'the State would no doubt be prepared to assume charge of, and maintain, so valuable a monument, but for the moment it is useless to consider that question.' A similar request for Witcombe Roman Villa in Gloucestershire was filed and marked 'End of War'.[4] Despite this, some offers were accepted, especially those that were already in train. These included Farleigh Hungerford Castle in Somerset and Clifford's Tower in York, both transferred in 1915. The owner of Farleigh Hungerford, Lord Cairn, was commanding a regiment on the front line and the deed had to be signed by his wife under power of attorney, while Clifford's Tower was in use as a prisoner-of-war camp.[5]

Without a doubt, the most spectacular wartime acquisition was Rievaulx Abbey in Yorkshire. The first great Cistercian church to be built in England, it was modelled on the church at Clairvaux, France. In the early thirteenth century the presbytery was rebuilt and the transepts remodelled, creating one of the most important churches in the Early English style in Britain. In addition, the abbey was surrounded by a massive agricultural and industrial estate, staffed by lay brothers and intended as the progenitor of a family of daughter houses throughout northern Britain. Rievaulx was owned by Lord Feversham, who had created a rifle regiment from the labour force on his estate. In September 1916 it saw action on the Somme, where, tragically, nearly the entire regiment was wiped out, including Lord Feversham himself.[6] His death left the estate in the hands of a minor and the decision was taken to transfer the abbey into guardianship in May 1917.

Despite the tragic circumstances of the transfer, the Office of Works was delighted. Charles Peers wrote:

This offer needs no recommendation from me. Rievaulx is perhaps the most beautiful of all our ruined abbeys, and its permanent preservation is

Rievaulx Abbey, Yorkshire: a view eastwards along the chancel showing the classic Office of Works aesthetic. Nobody would guess that the standing ruins were filled with iron railway rails and concrete. © English Heritage

a work which would meet with everyone's approval. It has long stood in a neglected state, and though we cannot at present undertake repairs on the scale which its condition demands, there is much temporary shoring and supporting which can be done at small cost, and will prevent further falls of masonry until we can give the Abbey the care it deserves.

The Assistant Secretary remarked: 'this is emphatically the class of building which we ought to take over', and Sir Lionel Earle added that it was the 'greatest offer' of guardianship that the Department had ever received.[7] The deed was signed on 20 July 1917. Although work was urgently required, it did not start until later that year when an explosion at a nearby munitions factory provided second-hand timber for use as scaffolding.[8]

After the war, Whitby Abbey and Scarborough Castle in Yorkshire were transferred to the Ancient Monuments Department, to repair damage suffered during German bombardment from the sea in 1914. The owner of Whitby, Mrs Tatton Willoughby, reluctantly handed over her damaged family heirloom in 1920: 'We must admit that we had rather manage the place ourselves as had been done by our family for centuries and, we think, greatly more in the public interest than our own. But times have changed and we are changing with them – hence our conclusion now.' The Office of Works literally pieced the west front together from the broken fragments piled up around walls, transforming its appearance.

FINANCIAL WOES

The mini economic boom that followed the end of the war turned into a slump in 1920 and, though the Office of Works was again able to bring some focus to bear on ancient monuments, it was against the background of Britain's dire economic state. Economic crisis was both the Department's greatest problem and its greatest opportunity. At the root of its success as a collector of monuments were the financial difficulties of landowners. Between 1928 and 1931 the value of all agricultural produce fell by a third. As a result, agricultural rents collapsed; in 1936 they were at the same level as in 1800. The value of land collapsed too: by the mid-1930s land was selling for barely a third of what it had fetched in the 1860s. On top of these woes, the top level of death duties doubled to 50 per cent in 1918 and rose again in 1925. These events triggered a huge sell-off by the great estate owners to their tenants and to newcomers. It was a transfer of land on a scale not seen since the dissolution of the monasteries: owner-occupied land in England and Wales grew from 11 per cent in 1914 to 37 per cent by 1927.[9]

By no means all estate owners faced ruin between the wars, but without doubt the changes in land ownership, and in the economic structures of the countryside, made the maintenance of non-productive parts of any estate

Buildwas Abbey, Shropshire, before conservation work was undertaken by the Ancient Monuments Branch of the Office of Works. © The Francis Frith Photographic Collection

a luxury and, amongst these, ruins were near the top of the list. Captain Herbert Moseley was the owner of the twelfth-century Cistercian abbey at Buildwas, Shropshire, and, when pressed by the Office of Works to take action to arrest the decay of the abbey ruins, he gave a response that summed up the problems faced by hundreds of owners of medieval ruins:

> I think it very hard lines to expect the unfortunate owner of such a property as this to make good the dilapidations and ravages of time which have been going on for 400 years – especially in such a period as this of costly living, high taxation, and, for a landowner at any rate, greatly reduced income – a time too when we are all being told not to spend our money on unproductive objects. I have not raised my rents during the past six years, my spendable income is just half what it was six years ago, being almost entirely from rentals of land, etc. and I am very hard put to maintain my very much reduced establishment and make both ends meet.[10]

Understandably, he was reluctant to pass the abbey, a treasured family possession, into Government hands. Negotiations went on for several years until the collapse of part of the vault in the chapter house in November 1923

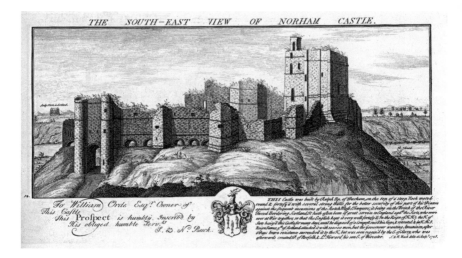

encouraged the captain to open guardianship discussions, but it was only after a Preservation Order had been drawn up, and after Moseley had been sent a final warning, that the abbey passed into Government care in November 1925.

Yet despite the difficult position in which many landowners found themselves, the Office of Works' position was little better. Until 1923 it was under tight financial controls, and so most landowners who offered their monuments were simply turned down. Others, who presented the most tempting sites, were told to wait three years until things improved. A small number were accepted through the agency of private philanthropy. Spofforth Castle in Yorkshire is reputed to have been the spot where the rebel barons drew up the Magna Carta in 1215. The castle was plundered by the Earl of Warwick during the Wars of the Roses, but it was restored by Lord Percy in 1559. In 1920 Charles Peers received an alarming letter informing him that it was to be sold and possibly dismantled for its materials. It was clear, however, that the financial situation made it unlikely that the Government could accept a transfer. Remarkably, a private individual, Major Nichols, stepped forward, promising to provide repair funds for the next twenty years. The cost was considerable, estimated at £300 or £350 for urgent works, and then £5,000 for repairs over the next four years. The offer was one the Government dared not refuse and the Deed of Guardianship was signed in February 1924.[11]

Norham Castle was another happy story. A border castle, besieged at least thirteen times by the Scots and commanding a vital ford over the River Tweed, it was purchased by Charles Romanes in 1920 when it was fast falling into decay. Stone was falling each winter and the tenant was taking it away to use elsewhere. Immediately after buying the castle Romanes opened guardianship negotiations. Considerable repair work was required: the architects estimated £3,900 for immediate repairs and then £17,400 for further work and excavation. The offer was put on hold. But Romanes was determined and wrote to Sir Frank Baines in November 1921 with a generous offer: 'I purchased the property with the sole aim of offering its guardianship to the Nation under the provision of the Ancient Monuments Act ... I am ... so anxious that this magnificent Monument should be preserved that I am prepared to contribute a sum of £500 per annum for three years towards the immediate works of preservation.'[12] Romanes's gesture is among the most notable acts of public benefaction in the formation of the National Heritage Collection.

COLLECTING IN THE 1920S

One of the fiercest battles fought by the Office of Works in the 1920s (apart from with Treasury) was not with a private owner, but with another Government department. Grime's Graves in Norfolk is a vast Neolithic flint mine with more than 300 shafts covering an area of 16 acres (6.5 ha). In 1917 Reginald Smith of the British Museum had requested the monument be scheduled, given that it was 'incontestably the finest Stone Age site in England and probably anywhere else', a request to which the Ancient Monuments Department was happy to agree.[13] The Forestry Commission purchased the mines and the surrounding estate in 1926 and, as it now came under a Government department, the scheduling effectively became void. The Office of Works reminded the Commission that they were expected to 'take every care' of the mines and should consult them over any changes in management.[14] Within a year, however, a large part was planted with young trees. An urgent meeting was called in August 1927 at which the Forestry Commission emphasised that they needed to maximise the profits from the site. Charles Peers was determined to 'point out that this is not a question of mere finance, and that the treatment of such a monument by a Government department cannot be dictated by £-s-d. The state must set an example, or it is hopeless to expect private owners to abstain from profiting by the destruction of any monuments they may own.'[15]

It was too late. A damning letter in *The Times* on 8 October 1927 was headed 'Grimes Graves. Forestry on a Scheduled Area' and emphasised flagrant contravention of the Ancient Monuments Act, not by a private individual, but by a Government department.

In January 1928 Lord Peel (1867–1937), the First Commissioner, met a representative of the Forestry Commission at Grime's Graves. Peel had been appointed by Baldwin in 1924. It was perhaps a demotion for a man who had previously been Secretary of State for India, but he stayed the course and remained in the post for four years. Peel was a man of common sense and promised to speed up excavations currently under way by the Prehistoric Society of East Anglia, and do everything in his power to meet the wishes of the Commission. Peers felt betrayed:

> we must, as a Department, remember the exceptional importance of this site to science, and should not acquiesce in a treatment of it to which we should strongly object in the case of tumuli and earthworks scheduled under the Act. Our policy must, I fear, conflict with that of the Forestry Commission and indeed it is our duty to see that it does.[16]

Negative press continued and in 1928 a report by the excavators suggested that if the monument were to be permanently preserved it should be purchased by the Office of Works. At the same time it was revealed that a Neolithic mine shaft, which had been left uncovered since excavation in 1914, had been vandalised by the Ipswich Motor Cycle Club.[17] The Office had no option but to start negotiations to buy the site. In this the Forestry Commission was difficult, but not the problem. It was the Treasury that said no. 'We are not sure', they wrote,

> that any useful purpose will be served by this transfer; am I not right in thinking that the main object of transferring Ancient Monuments to the Office of Works is that your expert staff may see that the structure is not allowed to deteriorate? Since here there is no structure or, alternatively, the structure is underground; there is nothing calling for the work of your expert to be done.

The Office persisted and the Treasury eventually gave consent in July 1929; the site was handed over in the latter part of 1931.[18]

The attitude of the Treasury to the purchase of Grime's Graves (for a knock-down price of £400) was typical. At junior levels there was unconcealed hostility towards expenditure on ancient monuments. In 1924 their vote was considered 'entirely a luxury' and the officials refused to 'waste its resources on schemes which, however desirable from the aesthetic point of view, do not enrich the country or add to its commercial equipment'.[19] The problem, as one official noted in 1935, was that 'the service is in fact perpetually vulnerable to our attack as being one which however desirable, is not imperatively necessary'.[20] These were the arguments of junior officials; but whatever their views may have been, the monument vote increased until 1925 and then, after a couple of lean years, grew even faster to 1931. Though acquisition averaged around five a year from 1922, in 1929 the Department took on no fewer than fourteen sites, a further nine in 1930, and another eleven in 1931.

INVESTIGATIVE ARCHAEOLOGY

Archaeology had always been at the heart of the Ancient Monuments Department. The first Inspector, Augustus Pitt-Rivers, is often called the 'father of British field-archaeology', and he introduced the concept that archaeological evidence should be able to stand up in a court of law. The proof of evidence rested on the vertical stratigraphic section, a practice he borrowed from geology. Pitt-Rivers was meticulous at recording his archaeological work and appreciated the worth of every find no matter how insipid: 'the value of relics, viewed as evidence,' he wrote, 'may ... be said to be in inverse ratio to their intrinsic value'. By the 1920s this was no longer the crusade of one man but the accepted principle of the archaeological discipline as a whole.[21]

Many sites subsequently taken over by the Office of Works had been subjected to archaeological investigation, some for many years. A famous Roman site like Corbridge in Northumberland had been excavated in the nineteenth century by William Coulson. It was again excavated, more professionally, between 1906 and 1914 by Francis Haverfield and Leonard Woolley in preparation for the Northumberland volume of the Victoria County History. So when the site came to the Office of Works it was excavated and well known.

From 1920 investigative archaeology developed in the Office of Works under the leadership of Jocelyn Bushe-Fox. He had learnt his trade under Sir Mortimer Wheeler at Wroxeter and from 1922 conducted excavations at

Richborough Roman Fort. Funding and manning such digs at guardianship sites was just about possible, but conducting excavations on private land was virtually impossible. In April 1928 the Ancient Monuments Board reported that it had been very difficult to find supervision and funding for excavations at the Iron Age hill fort of Chilworth Ring in Hampshire, where redevelopment for housing was imminent. The Board proposed that the Ancient Monuments Act should be amended to enable the Office of Works to spend money on research in urgent cases such as this. These were the first mutterings of both a research policy for archaeology and the importance of rescue excavation.[22]

In 1929 Charles Peers published 'A Research Policy for Field Work' in the *Antiquaries Journal*. It was drawn up with the assistance of a sub-committee of the Society of Antiquaries formed of his Inspector for England, Bushe-Fox, Robin Collingwood (1889–1943), Harold Peake (1867–1946) and Mortimer Wheeler (1890–1976). The paper stated that the time was opportune for the establishment of a research policy:

> a general agreement on the direction of archaeological enquiry in Britain would be of the greatest possible value. By such means the energies of all the archaeological societies and institutions of the country might be concentrated on a definite programme of research, in which all might take part, avoiding side-issues and useless repetitions.

The policy was to be based on the presumption that every excavation should now have a specific aim and definite line of enquiry, which would benefit the archaeological world in general. What was important to Peers was the knowledge and record gained from the excavation, not the quantity or quality of the finds:

> The examination of ancient sites can no longer be regarded as was unhappily the case in former days, as a mere search for antiquities. The thing found is of value, whether to history, art, or science, but the circumstances of its finding are of even more evidential worth. The ideal excavation is one in which all the evidence is recognised and recorded, a task which demands no ordinary degree of knowledge and experience ... The choice of a site should not be at haphazard, but made with a particular problem in view ... Provision must be made for complete and accurate record by measurements, drawings, and photographs of all evidence disclosed ...[23]

The specific policies set out by Peers were organised under three headings: Prehistoric, Roman and Post-Roman. The first two categories were long-standing interests, but in the Post-Roman section the emphasis was on identifying Anglo-Saxon occupation sites, dating medieval pottery and understanding the architectural development of later medieval buildings. Field archaeology was not considered as a useful tool for the interpretation of later medieval sites. This is reflected in the sweeping clearances that were undertaken by Peers at sites taken into care (below, pp. 140–1).

The terms of the Ancient Monuments Act of 1931 (below, pp. 175–6) gave the Office of Works new powers; they could, for the first time, excavate any site they had reason to believe contained an ancient monument.[24] They could now also spend money on a site not in their charge, and Peers soon authorised excavation of Viking remains on the Orkney and Shetland islands. Some digs would be undertaken by the Department's inspectors; others were by approved archaeologists under the condition that they published their results and sent a copy to the department.[25] Its activities eventually widened to encompass a large number of rescue excavations during the Second World War (below, p. 199).

THE DEPRESSION

The recession of 1920–1 was but a foretaste of the crash of 1929–31. Three million people were unemployed in 1933 and the figure remained at more than two million until 1935. A major priority for the Government was reducing unemployment and this brought an unexpected opportunity for the Office of Works. Their new First Commissioner, George Lansbury (1859–1940), was a committed socialist who had visited, and admired, Bolshevik Russia and later became leader of the Labour Party. His appointment in 1929 had been met with dismay by the Permanent Secretary, Lionel Earle, who saw only his reputation as a 'visionary revolutionary'. Earle had probably not known about his strong interest in London's heritage, campaigning with a fellow socialist, William Morris, to save the Trinity Almshouses on Mile End Road (above, p. 59).

Lansbury was a completely different breed of First Commissioner from the suave, aristocratic royalists who had previously held the post. Indeed, he had been kept out of Ramsay MacDonald's first Cabinet because George V thought him a Bolshevik sympathiser. Working-class, radical, representing

George Lansbury, First Commissioner of Works, inspects the Neolithic houses at Skara Brae on the Orkney Islands in 1929. © Library of the London School of Economics and Political Science, ref: Postgate/13/9

an impoverished constituency in the East End of London, he had been appointed to appease the left wing of the Labour Party. The Office of Works was a small department where it was felt that 'he would not have much opportunity for squandering money, but he would be able to do a good many small things which would improve the amenities of Government buildings and the public parks'.[26] He did indeed do good in the royal parks, where he embarked on a radical programme of recreational improvements, including 'Lansbury's Lido' in the Serpentine, Hyde Park. Though this work demonstrated his sure popular touch, winning him more news coverage than the Prime Minister, it is often said that he felt frustrated locked in a small department when what mattered was unemployment.[27] The evidence of the Office of Works files tells a different story.

MacDonald's publicly stated priority was unemployment and, with a relatively light load at the Office of Works, Lansbury was put on an unemployment committee with a small group of ministers and officials. This was where he wanted to be and he proposed a series of schemes for employing out-of-work miners at the Board of Agriculture. These, and others, were stifled by the Treasury, and so he turned to his own department where he devised, with Earle, Baines and Peers, a way of using unemployed men to restore recently acquired ancient monuments. Predictably, this led to barbed comments from his parliamentary colleagues, who were surprised at his sudden passion for medieval castles.

Lord Crawford, who had been a First Commissioner in 1921–2, teased him in committee in February 1931:

> We remember the revolutionary, the iconoclast, of former days, but now ... the right honourable Gentleman is spending his time and the money of the public in propping up relics of feudalism and in building medieval castles. By such means the ancient traditions of the Old World redress the balance of the New. By such means is Socialism in our time being made possible? If it were in order, one might invoke the shades of Lenin to try and find out what he now thinks of the decadence and fall from the path of virtue of his one-time disciple and ardent admirer. While we congratulate the right honourable Gentleman on his change of heart, probably his one-time master is turning in his grave.

Lansbury, in reply, reassured the House 'that the mausoleum where Lenin lies is all right'.[28]

It was at Helmsley in Yorkshire where labour from the Increased Employment Programme was first directed to recreate the castle moat. The monument had been taken into guardianship in December 1923 and was in poor condition. Its surrounding moats and ditches had been filled in during the eighteenth century when the castle became an ornamental ruin in the grounds of Duncombe Park. As a result it did not look very castle-like and proposals were drawn up to remove 10,000 cubic yards of soil and dump it next to a meander in the River Rye.[29] Work utterly transformed the castle,

Portchester Castle, Hampshire: the west curtain wall from the gatehouse in the early 1920s, before the Office of Works started restoration. © English Heritage Photo Library

giving it deep, clean cut, ditches on all sides. Similar schemes were implemented at the Saxon Shore forts of Pevensey and Portchester, taken into care in 1925 and 1926, respectively.[30] These had been built by the Romans but were later colonised by the Normans, who added new masonry structures. The substantial earthworks associated with them provided perfect employment for unskilled labour. At Portchester, Hampshire, unemployed Welsh miners were used to dig out the moats, using the spoil as backfill behind a new protective sea wall. A railway was built inside the castle on which mine trucks ran. Supervision was provided by an 'antiquarian'.[31]

Work started without fully appreciating the consequences. By 1931 the re-creation of moats at the castles of Helmsley and Pickering in England and of Ogmore, Kidwelly and Beaumaris in Wales had been pursued so enthusiastically that work had cut off public access entirely.[32] The Department had been forced to create makeshift gangways of scaffold boards, which were dangerous for public use. Plans were hurriedly drawn up for the construction of permanent bridges. At Helmsley four were built using the original drawbridge entrances. All this was starting to cost a lot of money; nearly £3,200 had been spent at Goodrich Castle alone and the Department had to go back to Parliament and ask for an increase of £60,000. This was uncomfortable for Lansbury at a time of economic crisis.[33]

When the request came into the House of Commons in February 1931 Captain Cruikshank MP led the charge:

> He [Lansbury] talks about improving an ancient monument, but, after all, an ancient monument is not a thing to be improved like a small boy by being sent to school. What does the right honourable Gentleman mean by improving an ancient monument? ...What is the standard of improvement? Is it laid down by the architects of the Department, by the First Commissioner's professional advisers, or has he consulted the Royal Commission, which has had a great deal to do with ancient monuments, or the Fine Art Commission? Or perhaps he sees that there are a great many unemployed in some parts of the country and says, 'There are some funny looking mines in some fields there, let us dig them up.'

Brendan Bracken went further, making a personal attack on Lansbury:

> Through a process of severe cross-examination, we have learned that the object is not the upkeep of cathedrals. What is it? Perhaps it is on Roman walls. We know the right honourable Gentleman's passion for Roman walls. We know that he travelled at the expense of the Office of Works all over the North of England searching for those interesting curios. But to come here at a time when the finances of the State are in such dreadful peril, and to ask us to find this sum of money for the upkeep of monuments, is disgraceful.

In summing up, Lansbury was able to answer the question as to the purpose of the work directly:

> I was asked whether the object of spending this money is to give work to the unemployed, or to preserve ancient monuments. The expenditure has both objects in view ...The bulk of the work is unskilled work, and, when I speak of restoring, preserving or improving, I mean the removal of vast quantities of rubbish from works that it will reveal buildings as they were originally.

He went on to say that 1,300 men had been employed in total.[34]

The moat-digging unemployment schemes transformed the appearance of a number of castles in a way that could never normally have been afforded. It is hard today not to be pleased that these works took place, but it is clear that at Helmsley, at least, they distorted the castle's history. In 1923 Peers and his fellows considered Helmsley as a major military site, with massive defensive earth outworks. When he began the clearance of these he found to his intense confusion that there was a gap in the banks at the south corner of the defences. This certainly did not conform to his model: the ditches could not possibly have been filled with water with a hole in them, and the circuit of banks would have not provided an adequate defence. So strong was this paradigm that the hole at the south corner was filled in to complete, or 'restore', the site – in fact, completely changing its nature.

The castle is now understood in a rather different way and the earthworks are not seen as a mechanism for retaining water (there was never a wet moat), but about showing off the castle to visitors. It is now thought that the earth banks defined a ceremonial approach, not the sides of a ditch.

While the Office of Works thrived in the early 1930s, thanks to the huge resources made available by unemployment schemes, the same could not be said for private owners of monuments. The impact of the Depression on landowners continued to be severe and, as before, many of the monuments that came into State care in the 1930s were from owners who were desperate to give away large medieval sites.

Bowes Castle, a twelfth-century tower keep that guards the approach to the Stainmore Pass over the Pennines, was in a particularly bad state. An article in the *Yorkshire Evening Post* commented on the attitude of the local villagers to its ruinous state: 'Nobody cares. "We've enough troubles of our own" said a parish councillor . . . "It is a derelict castle," adds the Vicar. "Nobody cares about it." The villagers do not seem to bother. There is none to take pride in its preservation, and, shame for it to be said, it is going to destruction.'[35] An Office of Works architect visited the site and sent a technical report to the owner, prompting a reply from her land agent:

> Lady Curzon-Howe regrets that owing to the present high taxation and Death Duties to which the Estate is subject, she regrets that she does not see her way to carry the very large out-lay which would be necessary to preserve this ruin. If as you say the preservation of the ruin is of national importance, I shall be glad to know whether your Department would be willing to consider taking it over.[36]

The Augustinian abbey of Haughmond, Shropshire, was in an equally bad state, despite the fact that the owner, Hugh Corbet, had been spending money on it. By 1930, though, he felt that his estate could now barely support

Helmsley Castle, Yorkshire. This remarkable photograph taken in 1929 shows the Ancient Monuments Department's work under Sir Charles Peers under way. The keep is scaffolded and the ditches are being re-profiled. © English Heritage Aerofilms Collection

itself. He wrote to the Office of Works saying that he was 'much surprised and disturbed to notice the difference in its condition since my last visit in November – also, I fear that further falls may take place, unless the structure is properly attended to ...Therefore, I have decided, (reluctantly, as I must admit) to ask HM Office of Works to help maintain the Abbey.'[37] It was taken over by the Government in May 1931.

Other monuments taken in were structural emergencies. Muchelney Abbey in Somerset is a spectacular example. A Benedictine abbey on the Somerset Levels, part of it had been transferred into guardianship in 1927. In 1931 the neighbouring farmer proposed to demolish his 'old Cider House with apple loft' in order to construct a new house on the spot.[38] The building was, in fact, a unique and extremely well-preserved thatched reredorter (communal WC). It was in a very fragile state with a huge crack in one

The reredorter at Muchelney Abbey, Somerset, before and after its restoration in 1931. *Before image:* Reproduced by permission of English Heritage. *After image:* © Francis Frith Photographic Collection

wall and a thatch roof that was about to cave in. The Department came to an agreement with the farmer; they would restore the reredorter as a cart shed if his house could be sited elsewhere. It was taken into guardianship in February 1932.

Not everything that the Office took on in the 1920s and 1930s was on the verge of collapse. In 1930 the freehold of the spectacular Norman castle at Middleham in Yorkshire was given to the nation, although it had passed into guardianship four years earlier.[39] There was some structural work, but it was mostly a question of tidying up the site: a cattle loose box and pigsty stood against the castle walls and a colossal manure heap lay next to the tower. The Ministry was particularly pleased with the acquisition because the donor was a Government minister, Sir Philip Cunliffe-Lister. He greatly complimented the work of the Ancient Monuments Department, to the satisfaction of Sir Lionel Earle.[40]

The most spectacular acquisition of the whole of the 1930s was, however, Kenilworth Castle, one of the greatest fortresses in the land and already a famous and popular attraction. The castle belonged to Lord Clarendon, who had inherited his earldom, and the castle, in 1914. He had spent some £10,000 on it in the decade after 1926 but found that it was impossible to keep up with the costs. A local industrialist, Sir John Siddeley, stepped in with an offer of purchase. In 1935 Sir John received £1 million for merging his huge automobile company, Armstrong Siddeley, with Hawker Aircraft. Hawker Siddeley went on to produce the Hurricane fighter planes that, along with the Spitfire, served as Britain's front-line defence in the Battle of Britain. On merger he was already aged seventy and the following year he gave up his business to retire to the Channel Islands. In April 1937 he called into the Office of Works to see the Chief Inspector, Jocelyn Bushe-Fox. What took place is best described by Bushe-Fox himself:

Sir John Siddeley (of Armstrong-Siddeleys) called this morning and saw Mr Simms and myself. He has it in mind to purchase *Kenilworth Castle* and make it over to the nation. He thought first of the National Trust but was not sure that they would be able to preserve and maintain it properly. I explained the conditions of guardianship to him and assured him that the Department would have no hesitation in accepting guardianship of what we considered one of the most important monuments of the country. He would have to pay about £30,000 for it to Lord Clarendon and he would

Kenilworth Castle, Warwickshire, one of the jewels of the Office of Works in the early days of guardianship. © English Heritage Aerofilms Collection

be willing to make a grant of £5,000 towards the cost of preservation so that we could go on with the work without delay.[41]

The purchase went ahead and the castle was handed over the Office of Works, though his family retained the Elizabethan gatehouse until 1958.[42] The extraordinary gift was widely applauded and Sir John was raised to the peerage of Baron Kenilworth by the king, an honour that compared well with the titles given to Cecil Chubb, who donated Stonehenge, and Sir John Lubbock, who gave Avebury.

COLLECTING POLICY

This cavalcade of acquisitions opens the important question of how systematic the Office of Works was being in building the collection. It is clear that throughout the period they were tightly constrained by money, but it is also the case that the Office refused to be bound only by this. A file minute from

1929 claimed: 'It would hardly be in accordance with fact to say that the Department has ever refused to take over a monument of first class importance solely because of lack of funds.'[43] A list of monuments refused guardianship dating from around 1932 records reasons for not proceeding: fifteen monuments were not considered of national importance; five were in the ownership of Government departments or local authorities (and therefore safe); in four cases guardianship negotiations collapsed and in four cases the decision was postponed. In only nine out of twenty-eight cases was money the problem.[44]

It is clear that the decision to acquire turned on the definition of national (or 'first rate') importance and this, on most occasions, came down to the opinion of the Chief Inspector. As each case was considered the Chief Inspector was consulted first, then the Assistant Secretary, the Permanent Secretary and finally the First Commissioner: only on very rare occasions was the Chief Inspector's opinion overruled. The most common reason for rejection was that monuments were not important enough. St Michael's Tower is a medieval church tower on the summit of Glastonbury Tor overlooking the Somerset levels. The church was rebuilt in the fourteenth century but with the exception of the tower was torn down at the Dissolution. The site was offered for guardianship in April 1933 by Neville Grenville after another one of his properties, Glastonbury Tribunal, was taken into care.[45] From the outset Peers did not consider it of sufficient importance. The Assistant Secretary, Frederick Raby, contacted the National Trust asking whether they might wish to take it on, stating: 'This Tower is not included in our list of Ancient Monuments and we are inclined to think that it is not suitable to be placed under our guardianship as its value is primarily on account of its position and the fine views of the surrounding country which it affords rather than on account of its archaeological or historical interest.'[46]

In August 1937 the Department was invited to take over the medieval remains of St Benet's Abbey, Norfolk, by the Ecclesiastical Commissioners. These were refused on several grounds according to the Assistant Secretary: 'partly because they are in reasonable repair and partly because they are so scanty. There are many buildings a good deal more important than this site that we should wish to take over as funds permit.'[47] A more controversial case was that of the Elizabethan country house of Moreton Corbet in Shropshire. It was marked on the guardianship refusal list simply as 'ruined house unsuitable for guardianship'. It is clear, however, that other such houses such as

The lovely Elizabethan Moreton Corbet House, Shropshire, at first rejected, but then embraced. © English Heritage

Kirby Hall were taken on. The fact was that Peers himself did not consider the monument of sufficient architectural or historical interest. In 1937, however, Jocelyn Bushe-Fox, by then Chief Inspector, thought that 'there should be no question that these ruins are worthy of preservation'.[48] The Permanent Secretary, Sir Patrick Duff, agreed: 'The cost of preservation will be high but I feel pretty strongly that this period of English Domestic Architecture is of the greatest interest and that the expenditure will be more than justified.'[49]

Not only ruined houses, but also complete mansions with their contents were offered to the Office of Works in the 1930s. In late 1932 or early 1933 a young man, A. F. Maitland, offered his house, Friston Place in Sussex, and all its contents to the nation, along with an endowment. His intention was that it should pass to the Government after his death. After visiting the house, which dated from the early fifteenth century with sixteenth- and seventeenth-century additions and alterations, Peers wrote: 'The attractions of the house are undeniable and it would be appropriate for the state to maintain it.' Despite a provisional acceptance by the First Commissioner, for some unknown reason the proposal never came to fruition.

When The Grange at Northington, Hampshire, was offered to the nation, it provoked a very different response. This seventeenth-century country house had been transformed into a remarkable Greek Revival building in the early nineteenth century. The solicitors of the owner, Lewis Charles Wallach, contacted the Government in February 1936 with a view of gifting it to the nation given its 'intrinsic interest' and 'historical associations'.[50] The building was, after all, one of the foremost examples of Greek Revival architecture in England. When it was brought before the Office of Works, however, it was not classed as a proper monument,

> since The Grange belongs to a type of building which is hardly within the intentions expressed by Parliament in the Ancient Monuments Acts, the Commissioners regret that they have no alternative but to decline your client's generous offer. They have, however, sent your letter to the National Trust, in case the Trust may possibly be in a position to consider accepting the care of The Grange on behalf of the nation.[51]

A letter from the Department to the Treasury the following year reveals the case more fully:

> [Our view is still] that a building of this kind is not an appropriate one for us to take over, with or without endowment fund. We could not make any use of it and I'm sure it would be a white elephant. I cannot think of any close precedent; the nearest seems to be Lancaster House which the late Lord Leverhulme gave to the Government, but that is on Crown Land and a definite use was in view.[52]

By 1975 the Department of the Environment, as successors to the Ministry of Works, saw the case differently and took over the building, at that time under threat of total demolition (below, p. 237).

Under the 1913 Act national importance was the primary consideration for adding a monument to the collection, but it was also acknowledged that a good geographical spread of sites was desirable. Brough Castle, Cumbria, was considered by the Department as less impressive than other sites in guardianship, because, while the keep stood to a good height, the medieval residential quarters had burnt down following a 'great Christmas party' in 1521. The castle ruins were expensive to repair, but Sir Lionel thought it important to acquire because it would be 'the only monument in that part of the country' in guardianship.[53] During the acquisition of Castle Acre Priory several years later Sir Lionel Earle remarked: 'This is a most important monument and very fine . . . We should certainly I think take it over particularly as we are not rich in monuments in the Eastern Counties.'[54]

TWENTY-SIX YEARS OF COLLECTING

Of course, ultimately, the Government was limited to taking on monuments that were offered to it but, as has been seen, there were a few cases of compulsion and many more of heavy persuasion. These, combined with the legally established notions of national importance and geographical spread, led to the construction of an extraordinary collection. In 1913 there were 44 British monuments in the Department's care; by 1933 this had risen to 273 and by the outbreak of war there were many more. Of these, 147 sites were in England.[55] This was a formidable list in both number and quality: forty-six medieval castles, thirty medieval ecclesiastical buildings (mostly monasteries), thirty-two prehistoric monuments, twenty-one Roman sites, eight post-medieval domestic sites, six medieval domestic sites, three medieval monuments and a single Victorian one. Most were acquired in a frenzy during the twenty-six years after 1913: fourteen English sites came in 1929, eleven in 1931 and eight in 1938. It was a glittering bag that included Stonehenge, Maiden Castle, Carisbrooke Castle, Rievaulx Abbey and Richborough Roman Fort. Scotland had seventy monuments in the 1930s, of which more than twenty were acquired between 1911 and 1920.

Never before had such a collection been assembled. The rapidity with which the sites came in, their poor condition and the determination to open them to the public immediately brought big challenges. But before turning to these we must pause and consider the greatest and most important acquisition of all – Stonehenge.

8

STONEHENGE

The story of the Office of Works' acquisition of Stonehenge in Wiltshire is long and complex and too important to be included in a more general account of the Office's work. While in 1918 the Office eventually acquired the stones, this, in some ways, only started the problems that have dogged the site since then. By the 1950s it was already thought that there were too many visitors, and too many cars, and by 2000 the situation was agreed by everyone to be desperate. Yet as this book is written the aspirations of the inter-war inspectors to close the A344 are being met and the disfiguring car park is being removed. So a new chapter in the monument's history will begin.

Tourism was nothing new to Stonehenge in 1918. It had been a popular attraction since the Middle Ages. In the early nineteenth century tourists would stay in Salisbury visiting the cathedral, then venture out onto Salisbury Plain via the abandoned town and hill fort at Old Sarum and visit the stones. There was only a thrice-weekly coach service to the stones at 3pm on Tuesdays, Thursdays and Saturdays,[1] and so anyone who could afford it would hire a carriage; one horse at 15 shillings and two for a guinea. This allowed for a morning stroll at Old Sarum and an afternoon picnic at Stonehenge. Many were welcomed to the stones by Henry Browne, who became the first, albeit self-appointed and unpaid, custodian of the monument in 1822. He claimed to be a resident 'Lecturer on Ancient and Modern History' and told visitors that Stonehenge was the last surviving building from the age before Noah's flood; the fact that it was battered on the south-western side proved the great flood had engulfed the world from that direction.[2] He made a living through tips or by selling handmade cork models of the monument. His son, Joseph, took over nearly twenty years later and became 'attending illustrator'. The process was modernised when his successor introduced a horse-drawn 'Photographic Van'.[3]

The railway reached Salisbury in 1847 and ten years later this joined the London main line and it became possible to visit the monument on a day trip from the capital. By the later nineteenth century the principal annual event was the summer solstice sunrise; in 1872 there were only about thirty-five spectators, but by 1878 there were perhaps as many as three hundred.[4] Nearby pubs stayed open all night; the rich came from afar; and the Devizes cycling club made it an annual event. By the end of the century a small band of Neo-Druids began to celebrate their rites at the solstice.[5]

Victorian Stonehenge was unsupervised and people regularly chipped the stones for souvenirs and scratched their names on the monoliths; one visitor, in 1871, complained that 'a constant chipping of stone broke the solitude of the place'.[6] Stopping this was one of the principal factors behind Sir John Lubbock's campaign for protective legislation. Stonehenge had long been considered a national monument of which preservation should be a 'national interest'.[7] What was especially alarming was that even after the passing of the 1882 Act the most famous monument in Britain remained entirely at the whim of its owner, Sir Edmund Antrobus (1818–1899), the MP for Wilton, who jealously guarded his family heirloom. He had fallen out with Lubbock at an early stage. In 1870 a senior committee of five archaeologists of the British Association for the Advancement of Science, including Lubbock and Pitt-Rivers, approached him to excavate Stonehenge. They were flatly refused. Theirs was only one request from what Sir Edmund considered were 'mischievous antiquarians',[8] who had scarred much of the surrounding landscape by their diggings. Earlier in the century William Cunnington (1754–1810), prescribed archaeology by his doctor as a healthy outdoor activity, opened up hundreds of barrows in search of treasures.[9] Antrobus spoke openly against Lubbock's bill in Parliament and subsequently resisted the overtures of the new Inspector, General Pitt-Rivers, to place the monument in guardianship in 1883.[10]

This was very frustrating for Pitt-Rivers since many people believed that as an official Government inspector he had the powers to protect the monument. One letter told him that:

Barrow diggers from the *Gentleman's Magazine*, XXXVII (1852). It was exploits like these that aroused such hostility against archaeologists in the minds of landowners.

In company with two friends I have just visited Stonehenge and I never yet saw it in so filthy dilapidated and wretched a state, full of Rabbit bones and Chalk inscriptions on most of the stones, low pic-nickers at horse play ... It should be deemed a *national* monument, suitably enclosed regulated and guarded ... I declare it made us sick to see it. My friends were Scotch and abused the English for it freely.[11]

Pitt-Rivers shared their concerns, especially regarding the state of several of the monoliths that were leaning badly. Sir Edmund was willing to take advice but only from those he appointed himself. When a stone began to fall in 1880 his architect hastily installed timber props, but they were both a temporary and an unsightly measure.[12] Pitt-Rivers wanted to straighten up the leaning monoliths to prevent any more from falling down, digging out their bases and setting them in cement. But because the monument was not in guardianship there was little he could do. In 1887 he drafted a passionate letter to *The Times* appealing for the restoration of the fallen trilithons for Queen Victoria's Jubilee: 'no more suitable way could be devised for com-

Visitors at Stonehenge in the nineteenth century. Reproduced by permission of English Heritage

memorating the 50th year of the Queens reign than by securing to posterity the most remarkable monument in the world, viz Stonehenge. This stupendous memorial of an unknown age and people is slowly but surely perishing through natural causes.' The letter was never sent and nothing was done.[13]

By the end of the nineteenth century, when it was clear that most of Wiltshire's other great prehistoric monuments were safely in the hands of the Office of Works, agitation to protect Stonehenge goaded the Ministry to call Pitt-Rivers from retirement to inspect it. When he visited in September

1893 he found little had changed: freshly scratched names defaced the stones and rats feeding on picnic scraps were burrowing under the monoliths. Pitt-Rivers recommended that a resident policeman be appointed and a cottage be built within sight of the stones.[14] He later wrote, in a personal letter to a friend, that given the chance an excavation would within two months definitely determine the age of Stonehenge.[15] Sir Edmund Antrobus stood firm, refusing all suggestions; and this is how it remained until he died in April 1899. His successor, the fourth baronet, announced that he was willing to sell Stonehenge and the surrounding downland to the nation for £125,000, retaining the shooting and grazing rights himself.[16] The Chancellor of the Exchequer thought the price astronomical and the conditions impossible. The press speculated that Stonehenge would be bought by an advertising contractor, a showman or an American millionaire to ship across the Atlantic. In the event, at that price, nobody came forward.

The impasse was, quite literally, broken in December 1900 when an upright of the outer sarsen circle fell and its lintel snapped in half. There was a predictable outcry, and almost immediately several of Pitt-Rivers's earlier recommendations were implemented. A police constable was appointed, a caretaker's cottage built and one of the leaning stones restored. The ground around it was dug out by William Gowland (1842–1922), who carried out the first scientific excavation of the monument, dating it to the Late Neolithic or Early Bronze Age.[17] Stonehenge was also enclosed by a fence for the first time. This provoked outrage from the National Trust and the Commons and Footpaths Preservation Society. A High Court case opened in March 1905, but the judge ruled in favour of the owner, who now began charging a shilling admission.[18]

The 1913 Act finally gave the Government power to protect Stonehenge. They could now prosecute anyone (except the owner) who damaged it, but, with control remaining in the Antrobus family, little could be practically achieved. In any case the outbreak of the First World War brought a new peril. Military camps sprung up in the surrounding landscape and an airfield to the west flattened the caretaker's cottage. Worse still, mine explosions on Salisbury Plain shook the ancient stones; the surrounding bank and ditch was mutilated by horse-drawn artillery; and half the nearby Cursus was ploughed up to grow corn and potatoes.[19] The conflict also led to a change in ownership, since the baronet died in 1915 and his heir was killed in action. Stonehenge was put up for sale and purchased by Cecil Chubb (1876–1934),

Repairs to Stonehenge by the Office of Works in November 1919. A lintel is being temporarily removed so that the position of the leaning uprights can be jacked back to the vertical. © Crown copyright

a local barrister, for £6,600.[20] Three years later he wrote to the Government, offering it to the nation:

> Stonehenge is perhaps the best known and the most interesting of our national monuments and has always appealed strongly to the British imagination. To me, who was born close to it and during my boyhood and youth visited it at all hours of the day and night, under every conceivable condition of weather – in driving tempests of hail, rain and snow, fierce thunderstorms, glorious moonlight and beautiful sunshine, it always has

had an inexpressible charm. I became the owner of it with a deep sense of pleasure ... [but] it has ... been pressed upon me that the nation would like to have it for its own ...[21]

The offer was greeted with rapture at the Office of Works. The king said that he was 'interested and gratified' and the Prime Minister expressed his 'deep appreciation'. A special handing-over ceremony took place in October 1918 and Chubb received a knighthood, gaining the local nickname 'Viscount Stonehenge'.

Taking charge of the stones, the Government honoured a request to hand over remaining wartime revenue to the Red Cross. The custodian's salary was now set at 25 shillings a week but with free rent, grazing for his horses and fuel.[22] The resident policeman was replaced by an assistant caretaker so that the custodian could take his first day's holiday in seven years. After the war the Office of Works with characteristic exactitude undertook a painstaking structural survey. The engineer's report ran to 101 pages, providing an account of the weight, tensile stresses and angle of every stone.[23] Nothing was left to chance. A modest programme of restoration was planned, although Charles Peers warned that anything 'considered as "smartening up" of this venerable monument' should be wholly avoided.[24] Several of the leaning monoliths were jacked back to the vertical and set within reinforced concrete. In March 1920 the animated-picture cameras of the Gaumont Cinematographic Company filmed a lintel being ceremonially placed back into position by a wooden crane. Alongside the restoration went a seven-year programme of excavation, declared the most important ever undertaken in Britain.[25] It was directed by Lieutenant-Colonel William Hawley (1851–1941), who made several significant discoveries. Among them were the so-called Aubrey holes' and the prosaically named 'y and z holes'.

In 1926 the requisitioned land of the nearby airstrip was finally handed back to its owners and the dilapidated aircraft sheds, stores and barracks became a pig farm.[26] On the other side of the monument a café was built and there was talk of colonies of holiday bungalows. A national appeal was made to restore and preserve the surroundings of Stonehenge to its former wilderness. The Prime Minister, Stanley Baldwin, lent support, George v contributed 20 guineas, and even the Druids provided 10.[27] In 1929, 1,500 acres of the surrounding downland were purchased by the Government and vested in the National Trust. The unsightly aerodrome buildings were demolished,

An Ancient Monuments custodian at Stonehenge with members of the public in the 1950s. © English Heritage

together with the nearby café and custodian's cottages. An effort to move the A344 (the road running across the avenue) failed. None the less, it could, at last, be declared that Stonehenge and its setting had been safeguarded for the future. The stones became the jewel in the crown of the Ancient Monuments Department. In 1920, 20,000 people visited, but in 1951 there were 124,000 and by 2009 nearly a million.[28]

9

AESTHETICS AND PHILOSOPHY

From 1913 Lionel Earle's Office of Works, with Peers and Baines at the helm, and a series of educated and discerning First Commissioners, devised a distinctive aesthetic for the presentation of its sites. This was poetically described by Edmund Vale in his book of 1939 about the Office of Works monuments:

> The decayed monastery which before treatment is generally the most meaningless jumble regains that orderliness that was, in fact, the keynote and background of the Rule. You can now see the outline of the cloisters and how the church had transepts with apsidal chapels; the cream line running in the green sward gives you back the exact boundary between ground hallowed and profane.[1]

This is the look that still dominates the sites in the care of English Heritage, Historic Scotland and Cadw. It was deliberately created after 1913 as the best way of rescuing and showing the new national collection to the public.

THE OFFICE OF WORKS' APPROACH

Long before the SPAB set out coherent principles of building conservation and repair, the Office of Works had established an approach to work on its historic buildings. This philosophy was, in essence, that set out for the Office in 1846 by Edward Blore and William Twopenny (above, p. 30), which drew a clear distinction between restoration and preservation. The same was stated by Philip Hardwick in a report for the Office of Works on the condition of

Carisbrooke Castle in 1856: 'In any repair of an old structure the first object to be gained is to arrest the progress of decay without altering in any way the character or features of the building. The restoration of an ancient fabric ... usually ends in its destruction as a work of interest and study.'[2]

The debate over techniques and ethics of restoration that raged in Victorian England had been centred on the appropriate treatment of medieval churches, which were being rebuilt on a massive scale from the 1840s. The Ecclesiological movement promoted the reconstruction of churches to their original or early form, with the resulting loss of post-medieval alterations and the effective rewriting of the buildings' history. The reaction to this movement led to a consensus against restoration, placing the Office of Works in the mainstream of architectural opinion.

It was recognised, however, that different approaches were needed depending on the condition and future use of any structure. In 1850 George Gilbert Scott, the most active of all nineteenth-century church restorers, published a statement of his principles in which he distinguished between the treatment of ancient churches, which still had a function to fulfil, and ruins or other structures that had lost their original function. Ruins were valuable principally as historical documents and as such should be preserved as found, however damaged or fragmentary their present state. Churches, by contrast, were living buildings and opportunities should be taken to reverse past alterations and replace failing fabric for the sake of the building's historic design and its future usefulness. This was, as has been seen, his approach at the chapter house of Westminster Abbey while working for the Office of Works (above, p. 29).

In 1862 Scott returned to the subject, in a paper presented at a meeting of the RIBA. In it he endorsed John Ruskin's recommendations for the treatment of ruins, anticipating the work of the twentieth-century Ancient Monuments Branch. He prescribed the protection of wall tops, the grouting and bonding of masonry, and underpinning or buttressing where necessary, but all in ways that would not alter the original appearance or character of the ruin. New work, he thought, should be undertaken only to sustain the original structure. In 1865 the RIBA published advice on the conservation of ancient monuments and remains, based mainly on Scott's paper. This stressed the value of preserving authenticity at the same time as condoning the clearance of modern additions that obscured the historic structure. While the later nineteenth century saw the development of William Morris and the

SPAB's distinctive conservation ethos, the Office of Works remained rooted in this earlier interpretation of an anti-restoration approach.[3]

In his introduction to the Inspector of Ancient Monuments Report of 1912, the First Commissioner, Lord Beauchamp, set out the aim of the Ancient Monuments Branch as

> to avoid, as far as possible, anything which can be considered in the nature of restoration, to do nothing which could impair the archaeological interest of the Monuments and to confine themselves rigorously to such works as may be necessary to ensure their stability, to accentuate their interest and to perpetuate their existence in the form in which they have come down to us.[4]

Both Charles Peers and Frank Baines were of the same mind. Baines wrote that preservation was 'the retention of the building or monument in a sound static condition, without any material addition thereto or subtraction therefrom, so that it can be handed down to futurity with all the evidence of its character unimpaired'.[5] In similar mode Peers wrote: 'treatment must suggest itself within the limits of the maxim that nothing should be added or taken away without absolute cause. An understanding of what has been is necessary, but imagination must be kept in bounds and not translated into material: repair and not restoration is the essence of the matter.'[6]

Repair quite simply had to be the overriding concern of the Department. The ivy-clad state of decay so admired by the Victorians was now realised to be unsustainable. By the early twentieth century most major medieval ruins were in an incredibly poor state. Almost all were privately owned and there was no incentive for owners to invest in them. Some owners shored up their remains; others were happy to let them gently collapse. Large numbers were literally held up by the ivy that enveloped them. At Goodrich, one of the most magnificent ruins on the Welsh borders, the face of the south-west tower suddenly began to fall in 1925. The wall section, weighing 300 tons, was restrained by steel cables erected by men working all night. The tower was eventually saved, but only because the Office's men were already on the site. Cases like Goodrich (and there were many others) demonstrated that reconstruction was the only solution for many monuments. It also was a solution that was seen as having significant side benefits. While major structural intervention would transform progressively decaying romantic ruins into static ones, at the same time they would be transformed into instructive ruins. The tangled mass

Goodrich Castle, Herefordshire: emergency repairs under way. A very serious movement occurred in the south-west tower at midday on Thursday, 19 March 1925. The existing fractures suddenly widened, and mortar and crush core began to fall out whilst part of the tower moved outwards towards the moat. The whole of this section of wall, weighing more than 300 tons, was in imminent danger of collapse. The foreman, Mr Roberts, and the whole of the staff worked throughout the night of 19 March and steel wire ropes were fixed by Friday. Foremen in the neighbourhood from Tintern Abbey, Grosmont Castle and White Castle assisted in the work. They continued to work in shoring up the tower over the weekends of 21st and 28th March. Reproduced by permission of English Heritage of ivy, undergrowth and saplings, piles of fallen stone and mounds of earth obscured both architecture and archaeology. Clearing ruined medieval sites made them easier to understand. So the loss to the imagination would be more than repaid by the gain to the intellect. By repair and reconstruction the Ministry's great collection was better able to be a national educational tool.

The Office of Works' attitude towards ivy neatly illustrates the transition from romantic to instructive monument. In the surveyor's report for Richmond Castle, written in November 1907, it is clear that the ivy was regarded as an integral part of the site's attraction:

> The luxuriance of the ivy and other growths is such that it was only with difficulty that a way could be forced through portions of it when examining the tops of the walls, and this needs unsparing pruning (not total destruction) . . . some of the [Yorkshire Archaeological] Society's suggestions make for restoration, which is not the intention of the Board . . . to round the tops of the old walls, would be to reduce one of the most picturesque ruins in Yorkshire to a bald, uninteresting antiquarian record of doubtful value.[7]

It was unquestionably the 1913 Act, and the advent of the Ancient Monuments Department, that changed this point of view. Two reports exist in the file for Finchale Priory near Durham, one from 1906 and the other for 1915.[8] In the earlier report the architect admitted that, though it was necessary to remove ivy damaging the stonework, it added to 'the charm of the ruins' and such actions would cause 'outcry among lovers of the picturesque'. He himself thought that one of the chief values of the site was its 'picturesqueness'. The 1915 report stated, without equivocation, that all ivy was to be removed. In 1923 Sir Lionel Earle described ivy as 'a rank and odious plant', which not even the royal family tolerated at their properties. As a result, a dramatic description of the damage it might cause was included in *Notes on Repair and Preservation* handed out to staff.[9]

Tintern Abbey, Monmouthshire, Wales, was one of the first major repair programmes undertaken by the Board and, to some extent, set the pattern for later work. Tintern was transferred from the Office of Woods, Forests and Land Revenues in spring 1914. It had been purchased by the Crown in 1901 and the Commissioners of Woods had already undertaken a remarkably severe clearance and consolidation programme. This involved the demolition of two cottages, which obscured medieval architectural details; tearing down

Tintern Abbey, Monmouthshire, during repair work undertaken by the Office of Works in 1925. © Crown copyright: Royal Commission on the Ancient and Historical Monuments of Wales

the Ship Inn, which blocked a view of the abbey church from the nearest road; and chopping down trees so that a vista of the west front could be provided for visitors approaching from the railway station.[10]

The Office of Works carried out a thorough survey of the abbey and were critical of the approach adopted by the Woods, which had involved smearing

Portland cement across joints: a 'wretched apology for repair'. The survey showed that the south nave arcade of the roofless abbey was leaning to the north, causing an eccentric load on columns supporting it and that these were now cracking under the stress. The Office of Works' architect in charge, Arthur Heasman, suggested supporting the overhanging nave wall with four new buttresses of local stone that would harmonise in colour and texture with the surrounding ancient stonework. They would also, he thought, be compatible with the Gothic tradition as well as provide the most efficient and permanent structural support. Baines was in agreement. Peers, however, argued that new buttresses would be wrong since they were not part of the original scheme and would obscure the evidence of the moulds and shafts, spoiling the simple appearance of the nave wall. Baines was asked to draw up an alternative.[11]

His was an ingenious but complex solution involving the erection of a braced steel frame on the south side of the nave on the plane of the medieval roof, reflecting the form of the original roofline. Both schemes were put before the Ancient Monuments Board on 26 January 1921. The Architect, Sir Reginald Blomfield, made a strong case against the steel girder scheme and the Board did not come to a unanimous agreement. The final decision was taken by the First Commissioner, who admitted that he 'disliked each necessity with equal cordiality', but adopted Baines's proposal as the most effective. So work went ahead: the nave crossing was strengthened by a system of steel reinforced concrete beams set within stonework. Concrete grout was pumped into the wall cavities to strengthen and solidify them. In 1925 the arcade piers were dismantled, hollowed out, and old rail tracks were inserted. This was a form of 'invisible repair', which proved very attractive to the Works Department and was later used at a number of other abbeys, such as Furness.[12]

CRITICS OF THE OFFICE OF WORKS

As the first major excursion for the Office of Works there was much interest in their work at Tintern Abbey. Perhaps predictably, the Society for the Protection of Ancient Buildings had its doubts. At a dinner held at the RIBA in December 1913 Charles Peers had spent the evening in debate with Thackeray Turner, Secretary of the SPAB. They had begun holding separate views and finished it 'by holding them more strongly still'. Turner argued that the Office of Works approach was not always honest. He suggested that decayed medieval stonework should be repaired in a way that visually revealed modern intervention in the historic fabric. So, for instance, tiles might be used instead of stone. Peers, on the contrary, thought it important to retain a harmonious outward appearance and that historic structures should be free from obvious signs of modern intervention. He argued that the SPAB methodology would 'find London a city of stone and leave it a city of tiles and cement'.[13]

By 1920 the SPAB had a new Secretary, Bertie Powys, a thirty-three-year-old architect on a mission: his family nicknamed him 'brother positive', so strong were his convictions.[14] He started a concerted campaign against the work of the Ancient Monuments Department, presenting his criticisms in person at the Ancient Monuments Board in 1920. The work at Tintern particularly enraged him and he gained an audience with the First Commissioner, Lord Crawford, to complain about it. Crawford passed him onto Lionel Earle, who told him: 'we have nothing to hide and I hope and believe nothing to be ashamed of'; and to prove it, Sir Frank Baines agreed to address the Society of Antiquaries on the Department's work in 1922, followed by a debate chaired by Sir Aston Webb.

Powys got to work, writing first to the newspapers, urging them to attend. He told the editor of the *Manchester Guardian* that 'the Department is doing very useful work there is no doubt, but there is weighty opinion that some of its methods should be modified, and it is this opinion which my committee fears might be ignored'. The next batch of letters and cards were sent to his friends and supporters asking them to speak up at the debate. His note to William Rothenstein, Principal of the Royal College of Art, was explicit: 'The Committee would be very grateful if after Baines has spoken you would rise and criticise his methods – uniformity of treatment in all parts of the country – disregard of the picturesque in favour of mechanical perfection – failing desirability to refrain.' Other letters ranged from the circumspect to the *crie de cœur*, but all were intended to create a public showdown with the Ancient Monuments Department.[15]

On the day Baines gave a careful and technical account of the work of the Department before handing over to Peers to speak. He referred to a leader that had been in the *Morning Post* that day stating that the Department's work ought to be restricted to minor repairs, and important repairs left to professional architects. Did this imply, Peers asked, that Sir Frank Baines was not an architect? He went on to say that the Department had decided to risk criticism – they might be called 'wicked vandals' now, but he hoped that looking ahead ten or twenty years, it would be seen that their work was justified. A member of the audience, one J. Leighton, thought that repair took away the romance of building 'as it appealed to a painter, a poet, or average person'. He went on to suggest 'the genius of Sir Frank Baines is misapplied. He should be expressing the spirit of his day in new buildings.' Sir Aston Webb retorted: 'I would rather have Jedburgh repaired than no Jedburgh at all.'

Baines, for all the criticism of him as the arch-technician, fervently believed in architecture as one of the Arts. In his final reply of the evening he spoke not as an official, but as an enthusiast, and said that if one were to let great buildings of the past go one might as well burn famous libraries or collections of paintings.[16]

The matter did not end there, for a few months later the SPAB arrived at Tintern for a site inspection. After some minor design criticisms the SPAB noted, in their report, the transformation of the abbey from a romantic ruin to an instructive one:

> There remains one consideration which it would not be right entirely to overlook and that is the physical change – it might almost be called a spiritual change ... the walls [are] ... monolithic ... the building is no longer alive with the poise and counter-poise of medieval work and the thrust of the arch 'which never sleeps'. Everything is now fixed, solid and secure, a medieval ruin frozen, as if by cold storage, into perpetuity. This however is not a criticism, but a distinction to be remembered – it is the price we pay to enable us to hand on such relics to posterity.[17]

Peers must have thought the conclusion of the affair the most gentle of rebukes.

The nub of the matter was that the SPAB and others thought that the Department was doing too much to the monuments, but for Peers and Baines this was exactly the point: they favoured thoroughgoing repairs because they were inexpensive and long-lasting. They were, after all, men from the Ministry. They were custodians of public money, under an obligation to spend it in the most efficient manner possible. According to Baines, the rule should be to 'spend as little as possible' and 'aim at some finality'. Peers stated that no one should need to touch the Department's work at Tintern for another fifty or a hundred years.[18]

For them the notion of doing a little here and there over a long period was the romantic musing of people who had no real responsibly. Indeed, it was only recently with the advent of greater technical expertise at the SPAB under Thackeray Turner that conservation campaigners were dealing with anything other than the abstract.[19] The fact was that for the first time in history Peers and Baines were coping with hundreds of monuments in dire condition with limited resources. Their priority was to save them.

THE OFFICE OF WORKS' AESTHETIC

Yet it was not only the repair of the great abbeys that transformed their appearance, it was also the thoroughgoing clearance of their sites. This was a major operation sometimes employing systems of light railway and turntables. Site clearance went ahead over several years at Rievaulx, where Baines called the nave little more than 'a dimpled mound of ruins'. Beginning in 1919, clearance was organised on a grid system so that the location of significant objects could be plotted in three dimensions. The work may have been methodical but it was not archaeological. The clearance was carried out by a team of unskilled workers, under a foreman, not an archaeologist, and by present standards this entailed a loss of evidence for the post-dissolution history of the site. This is, of course, a modern judgement, for at the time nobody was really interested in the later history of the buildings. The excavations at Rievaulx revealed a huge number of architectural fragments, many of which were reburied on site. However, when the nave piers were revealed lying next to their bases and the possibility of reconstruction was discussed, it was not to go ahead since it would require the insertion of new material, breaking up the authenticity of the original work.[20] Similar clearance schemes were undertaken at a number of sites, including Middleham Castle, Yorkshire, and Portchester Castle, Hampshire.

Site clearance at Byland Abbey in Yorkshire took place in 1921–2 when finances were particularly restricted. For this reason Heasman had suggested that the ground simply be levelled and turfed. Peers, however, insisted that such an approach was a waste of time and the full 2.5 metres of soil needed to be cleared and removed. The results were reported with enthusiasm in a gushing article in the *Yorkshire Herald*:

> ...while the Earl of Carnarvon and his co-workers have been startling the world by unearthing the magnificent relics buried in the tombs of the Pharaohs ... relics and architecture of wonderful beauty, if of lesser impor-

Light railways were used to clear debris from the moats and ditches at Portchester Castle, Hampshire. Reproduced by permission of English Heritage

tance, have been laid bare in one of the ruined Yorkshire abbeys – that of Byland ... under all the debris was buried a tessellated floor, in a wonderful state of preservation, unique so far as the ruined abbeys of England are concerned, in extent, in exquisiteness of design, as well as the almost miraculous manner in which it has escaped destruction ... [21]

The Office of Works saw that clearing sites allowed the possibility of revealing their layouts clearly for the first time. This, in fact, had first been suggested in an architect's report on Finchale Priory of 1906 that proposed that the entire plan of the site should be revealed: 'it is a question whether the Board as guardians of the ruins, and I suppose, as an example to private owners should not have the foundations of these buildings, searched for, exposed if found, and enclosed ... as an example of the arrangement of a Benedictine Priory'.[22] This is what was to take place at nearly every medieval Office of Works site up to the 1970s. Peers, it must be remembered, had pioneered the use of phased plans during his time at the Victoria County History; for him

Rievaulx Abbey, Yorkshire, above as seen in 1917, the year the monument came into Guardianship, and opposite in a modern photograph, transformed by the Office of Works. *This page:* Reproduced by permission of English Heritage. *Facing page:* © English Heritage

it was vitally important to be able to read the building, like a manuscript or a map. In his own words, 'The recovery and demonstration of its plan adds enormous significance to an abandoned building, and though it can never recall it to life it can show to all and sundry what that life has been.'[23] To do this it was necessary to display ruins in a carefully designed setting.

Both Baines and Peers were keen gardeners, but Baines's house in Loughton offered only limited scope to develop his interests. The same could not be said for Peers, who, during the First World War, inherited Chiselhampton House in south Oxfordshire that had been in his family since the mid-eighteenth century. Its gardens and their wildlife were a passion.[24] In true Victorian style he kept a cabinet of butterflies and moths. They were all sketched in his notebooks; later the sketches give way to photographs,

arranged alphabetically. In his obituary in the *Antiquaries Journal* it was noted that 'His love of gardens rejuvenated the neglected piles of castles and abbeys with mown lawns and bright flowers.'[25] This was indeed the case and, from 1913, Office of Works monuments were set in carefully designed lawns with gravel paths and well-thought-out tree planting and areas of longer grass.

Peers thought brick and stone against mown grass was a visually pleasing combination. This view may well have been influenced by the college courts of Cambridge with their neatly clipped lawns that Peers had inhabited in the 1890s, but equally cathedral closes, churchyards and private houses were all combinations of grass and stone. The Office of Works was also responsible for the Commonwealth War Graves Commission, where stone monuments were laid out in mown grass for a different sort of quiet contemplation. But in the 1890s it would have been impossible to set hundreds of ruined monuments in manicured lawns. The ability of Peers to do so was entirely thanks to the invention of the motor mower.[26]

The view up to the house of Sir Charles Reed Peers, the Chief Inspector of Ancient Monuments. His eighteenth-century house at Chiselhampton, Oxfordshire, was set in smooth lawns, like the monuments he saved. © Country Life Picture Library

Managing vegetation on ruined sites is very expensive. Keeping sites trim and clear of undergrowth was one of the challenges for Victorian monument owners. Although the hand mower was invented in 1830, the machines simply did not work on the humps and bumps of unrestored sites, and the scythe and sickle were the only options. Once clearance had taken place, however, and sites were levelled and smooth, it was possible to use mowers. Small hand mowers were already a status symbol in suburban homes in 1900 but they were not robust enough for large-scale work. The first petrol mower, a ride-on contraption bought by the Cadbury Chocolate Sports Club in 1904, was too big to weave its way through the maze of walls in an ancient monument. It was only with the development (mainly) for cricket clubs of a series of compact petrol mowers that it became possible to contemplate their use in ruins. In 1913 these mowers were still new technology; they were also newly cheap technology, for before the First World War mowers were not only big, they were also expensive. It was now possible for the Office of Works to buy hundreds of small motor mowers to be kept at remote sites.[27]

One of the consequences of this approach to the neat and beautiful exposure of historic plan forms was the merciless removal of later additions, usually anything post-medieval in date. This occurred at the abbeys of Tintern, Rievaulx, Haughmond and Whitby, among others. At the Roman fort of Portchester, the Department even felt the need to remove the Victorian bandstand that had long provided a useful local amenity.

Moreover, this attitude affected the extent of the monuments taken over. The Board was only really interested in the core of medieval sites, which for monastic buildings meant the abbey church and claustral buildings. The abbot's lodging was rarely taken in. So at Buildwas and Much Wenlock, two fine Shropshire abbeys, the even finer abbots' lodgings were outside the guardianship area. This was, of course, in part because these were still in occupation and so fell outside the Office's powers. Yet even core remains that were uninhabited were of little interest. The opportunity to take the important abbey fishponds at Netley into guardianship was declined. It was felt that their inclusion, even as a gift, would 'not improve the site to a very great expense', although Baillie Reynolds admitted that it would be 'a pity' if modern villas were built on the land.[28]

The exception to the rule was medieval castles. Here the surrounding landscape was taken more seriously: castles were perceived as defensive sites and outworks as necessary to understand them. As has been seen in the 1930s, moats and dry ditches were recreated with gusto. The clearing and re-flooding of the moat at Beaumaris, Wales, was described as returning a magic that had long been absent.[29] Charles Peers's successor, Bushe-Fox, went so far as to propose re-flooding the great mere surrounding Kenilworth Castle:

> . . . we should certainly endeavour to re-establish the lake so as to give the Castle its proper medieval setting. The dam is, I believe, still in existence, as is, I presume, the stream that fed the lake . . . It would be a most wonderful addition to the castle making it one of the most attractive monuments in the country. Revenue might also be obtained from it by letting out boats![30]

Following the retirement of Sir Charles Peers in 1933 there was a reaction to some aspects of the earlier approach. Almost immediately the First Commissioner, William Ormsby-Gore, requested that some reconstruction take place at the abbeys of Rievaulx and Byland:

At Rievaulx particularly, I think the 'purism' of the Department in not re-erecting any stones that have been found detached has been carried to excess. Personally I would like to see at any rate one small bit of the great cloister arcade re-erected. There are dozens of columns, capitals, and arch mouldings lying outside the hut museum, and the re-erection of one bay, as has been done in the infirmary cloister, would enable the visitor to see how the typical Cistercian cloister was constructed. At Byland it might be possible to replace in the transept or choir at any rate a bit of the fine thirteenth century arcading, so much of which lies in the overcrowded museum.[31]

This would have been anathema to Peers. It is all the more significant that it was sanctioned at Rievaulx, far and away the most important monastic ruin then in guardianship.[32] Following the reconstruction of a bay of the cloister in December 1933, Ormsby-Gore visited. He was so delighted with the results that he sanctioned the construction of another bay on the west side. In the same visit he observed the 'neat and unobtrusive' white metal tablet stating simply 'reconstruction' on the cloister arcade, and requested that similar labelling be placed elsewhere.[33] This was the beginnings of the distinctive, and sometimes esoteric, labels that appeared across guardianship sites (below, p. 157).

THE ACHIEVEMENT

Criticism of the work of the Office looms large in the files, but that is because criticism generates paperwork. In fact, outside a very rarefied circle led by the SPAB, there was staunch admiration for the Office's approach. The sites that were repaired and presented to the public were recognised by visitors and commentators to be in terrible condition. What the Department did was to save them, to make them accessible and understandable. *The Times*, for instance, was a strong supporter of the work at Rievaulx Abbey. An article in the *Yorkshire Post* in February 1926 called out for Government intervention at Easby Abbey. It stated that the 'neat and ordered lawns' of other abbeys in Yorkshire in Office of Works hands contrasted 'painfully' with the neglected state of Easby, which was little more than a cattle shelter.

Where Peers and Baines were culpable, from a modern standpoint, was in the removal of so many later phases of the buildings they restored. In almost every case they were most interested in the earliest phases of occupation. This led, in the Office's abbeys in particular, to the destruction of evidence for late monastic life and certainly of all post-dissolution uses. Similar interpretive decisions were problematic at a number of castles. At Conwy, for instance, the walls were cleared of later medieval domestic buildings, exposing the original fortifications but destroying evidence for the later occupation of the site.

But for people at the time these would have been seen as niceties. During the second reading of the 1930 Ancient Monuments Bill, Lord Ponsonby gave his verdict on the Department's achievements:

> Those of your Lordships who have visited these monuments, which are under the guardianship of the Office of Works, may have noticed how admirably they are preserved, how well the amenities are looked after, and how they form a focus of interest in the districts where they are situated ... it is undoubtedly the case that this preservation of ancient monuments is a movement which is popular and increasing.[34]

Charles Peers characteristically felt assured of his own legacy. In 1933, the year of his retirement, he spoke proudly of the work carried out under his watch:

> ... the cumulative effect of a great ruined church and cloister, still retaining a goodly measure of its architectural beauty, and set reverently in a simple setting of grass lawns, can hardly fail of its appeal ... [these monuments] may now become objects of pilgrimage to the traveller in Britain ... and as years go on, their number will increase and still further justify those who just fifty years ago first set legislation for the protection of ancient monuments in the Statute Book.[35]

IO

INVENTING THE HERITAGE INDUSTRY

RURAL TOURISM

By the outbreak of the Second World War the Office of Works was running by far the largest visitor attraction business in the country. No official tallies were kept but in 1925 the combined visitors to the royal palaces, ancient monuments and historic buildings in their care was probably already 1.43 million and the total revenue £31,400. By 1935 total receipts at the 122 sites open to the public had risen to £56,036, suggesting visitor numbers in the region of 2.5 million. The Tower of London and Hampton Court had been the backbone of the Office of Works attractions before 1913, but by the mid-1920s Carisbrooke Castle, Stonehenge, Tintern Abbey and Caernarfon Castle were all receiving more than 50,000 visitors a year. More significantly, there were large numbers of remote rural sites that were for the first time attracting substantial numbers.

Access to ancient monuments had been hugely boosted by the motor bus and then the private car. Sir Patrick Duff, Permanent Secretary at the Office of Works, wrote to the Treasury in December 1934:

> There was a time when, even if these monuments were preserved, few people could get the benefit of them. But today the great improvement in means of transport, the growth and increase in comfort of char-a-banc excursions, the spread of motoring to classes which formerly could not afford it, and the recent revival of bicycling and walking, have combined to create an interest in ancient monuments, both as objects for excursion, and as places interesting in themselves.[1]

Cars were, at first, not a means of business conveyance; they were a leisure accessory. Early motor magazines focused not on cars, but where to drive them.[2] As a result the market was flooded with guidebooks aimed at the motor tourist. In 1907 James Edmund Vincent, the distinguished *Times* journalist and former editor of *Country Life*, wrote *Through East Anglia in a Motor Car*, one of the first books written specially for motor touring. Vincent announced in his introduction: 'A new method of travel, in fact, brings in its train the need for a new species of guidebook.' He recognised that for the first time the principal enjoyment of a day out was not reaching the destination, but getting there. The tour was the thing and his guidebook gave advice on routes and roads, even on the best place to buy driving gloves. His tourist could easily reach Castle Acre Priory, 4½ miles from Swaffham, which the Office of Works would take on in 1929. In 1907, though, his readers were taken through the lumps and bumps of the site by the two resident custodians.

Ordnance Survey maps were stuffed into the glove pockets of thousands of touring cars. In 1924 the OS archaeological officer O.G.S. Crawford, under his own steam, published a map of Roman Britain. The *Daily Mail* described it as one of the most wonderful maps ever made and claimed that it would open up a whole new era in motor touring. It sold out and soon the OS produced more period maps opening up archaeological monuments everywhere.[3] More specialised books helped visitors to interpret remote Neolithic barrows and stone circles precisely located by the OS. The Homeland Association, founded to encourage knowledge and love of Britain, published a range of guidebooks in which monuments featured large. In 1930 came a guide to prehistoric Sussex with an introduction by O.G.S. Crawford. Maps, diagrams and air photographs directed people to obscure Iron Age forts and Neolithic barrows. Some may have had in their pocket *Our Homeland Prehistoric Antiquities and How to Study Them* (1922), one of a series of Homeland Pocket Books only 4 inches deep that helped a public hungry for reliable information to appreciate ancient monuments, churches and cathedrals.

The most successful of all the motoring guides were those published by the Shell Oil Company under the editorship of John Betjeman. Cornwall was the first in the series published in 1934; twelve more were published before the Second World War, selling at two shillings and sixpence. They were personal, quirky and took readers to unexpected places to see buildings then thought unfashionable. Often little effort was wasted on the Office's sites. Of Launceston Castle, Cornwall, Betjeman wrote: 'for those interested in ruins, it is a ruin'.[4] But if Betjeman thought his readers uninterested in ruins he was wrong. In fact, the Office's monuments were enjoying a heyday, attracting visitors who once would have visited country houses.

Country house visiting had been at a peak in the 1870s; dozens of houses received more than 10,000 visitors a year and many more had even larger numbers in their parks and gardens. Eaton Hall in Cheshire was one of the most popular with 24,000 visitors in 1901. Few originally charged an entry fee and those that did imposed one to restrict numbers rather than to make a profit; from the 1880s, however, more sites began to charge, partially to control numbers, but also to offset costs in a time of agricultural depression. By 1883 Blenheim, Alton Towers and Burghley were all charging visitors a shilling a head.

Charging was one trend, closing was another. Of the hundred or so country houses that were advertised as open in the 1860s and 1870s, half were closed to the public by 1914, including Blenheim, Woburn, Knebworth, Alton Towers and Kedleston. This was certainly often a cost-cutting measure but it was also a generational change; new owners wanted a quieter, more private life without their drawing rooms invaded by the working classes. Many also felt no obligation to offer old-style hospitality as had their predecessors. It is also perhaps true to say that, on the other hand, many working people were now less inclined to be herded through echoing aristocratic halls.[5]

While country houses closed their doors, Office of Works sites, donated by their owners, scrubbed up and laid out for visitors, were a magnet for tourists – map and guidebook in hand. The consequences for the sites were unforeseen. Many, without proper car parks, were overrun by cars. At Kirkham Priory, Yorkshire, visitors without a ticket to the abbey were charged a deterrent five shillings to park their vehicle.[6] One writer, Henry Williamson, on a visit to Stonehenge lamented the proliferation of advertisements for motor tyres that had sprung up over Salisbury Plain; ironically, it was increasing tourism on Hadrian's Wall that required improved roads, built with stone from quarries that threatened the monument itself (below, p. 171).[7]

THE HERITAGE INDUSTRY BEGINS

Although the Office of Works had long charged admission at the Tower and Hampton Court, it was the 1900 Act that gave them power to charge at Ancient Monuments. At first, there was no reason to use the powers but then came the case of Walmer Castle, Kent. In 1904, the year of its transfer to the Office of Works, the castle had been partly renovated to accommodate Lord Curzon, the new Lord Warden of the Cinque Ports, whose official residence it was. Curzon was eager to take up residence and moved in before work was complete. At this point his wife died, a tragedy blamed on the 'insanitary condition of the castle'. Curzon resigned his office, and after some debate the Office of Works was permitted, in 1905, to use Walmer as what they called a 'show-place'. The practical implications of this were significant, because, other than Hampton Court and Osborne House, none of their monuments had furnished rooms. Acting Inspector James Fitzgerald had the job of devising a way of showing the castle.[8]

Three custodians were to be employed, to open Walmer for the same hours as Hampton Court. A turnstile, barriers, lavatories and exit gates were provided at a cost of £700. A visitor route was devised and, to help tourists on their way, the rooms were labelled 'like the Courts at Hampton Court'. Turning to the interiors, the Office of Works spent £1,000 on purchasing furniture from Lord Curzon, which included several items considered to be of 'national historic importance' relating to himself and former Lord Wardens, including the Duke of Wellington, who had died there. In April 1905 Edward VII instructed that a marble bust of the duke and a metal cast of his death mask should be sent to Walmer. The mask was found to be a fake and the Office of Works returned it to Windsor.[9] The admission fee was set at threepence per person and receipts amounted to £200 in the first year.

Walmer was the first attraction that the Office of Works made itself – the first of several hundred assembled over the following eighty years. But it was then a novelty and in 1912 they debated whether to drop the charge, since it was 'not very usual to charge fees for similar buildings under the Works'. But a precedent had been set, and it was decided to maintain the fees, which kept out 'the worst of the undesirables' as well as providing a modest income. Over the seven years between 1905 and 1912 average admission receipts at Walmer were £172 per annum – equivalent to nearly 14,000 paying visitors a year. The Office of Works believed that numbers were increasing due to 'improved means of transit'.[10]

The 1913 Act, with its presumption of an active acquisition programme, entrenched the idea of admission tickets. In fact, it was agreed that 'as a question of general principle there would seem to be no reason why admission fees should not be charged in respect of ancient monuments'. The usual

An Ancient Monuments custodian welcomes visitors to Rievaulx Abbey between the World Wars. Reproduced by permission of English Heritage

entry charges were set at sixpence and threepence, with smaller charges at a handful of monuments, and no charge at all for small or remote sites.[11] The introduction of season tickets was also discussed in 1913 on the basis that the Office of Works had such a scheme at Tintern Abbey, but it was determined that Treasury approval would be needed for such 'special arrangements'. It is not recorded when a season ticket was first introduced and the documents are almost certainly lost, but one was certainly in operation soon after the Second World War.

In 1918, in response to frequent questions about charging, Sir Alfred Mond issued a strong defence:

> We now have a very large number of important Monuments in England, Scotland and Wales under our care, and the expenses for custodians, cutting the grass and keeping the grounds neat and tidy amount to a considerable annual sum. If we were to get no appropriation in aid from the tourist element, it would, I am convinced, hamper us with the good work.

But the real concern, as it had been previously to country house owners and at the Tower of London, was deterrence. 'Persons without interest or understanding of Ancient Monuments', he wrote, 'will not pay anything to see it, and as they are precisely the people who may be expected to scratch their names on it and otherwise damage and disfigure it, their exclusion is all to the good.'[12]

PROMOTING AND EXPLAINING MONUMENTS

Despite their negative attitude to charging, after 1920 the Office of Works became increasingly commercial in its outlook and began to take advertising space in guidebooks and on station platforms. In 1922 Sir Lionel Earle wrote to the Treasury regarding his plans for Furness Abbey:

> Next year, under the new railway grouping system the North Western railway take over the Furness railway, and through my long-standing friendship with the Honourable Charles Lawrence, the Chairman of the North Western railway, I believe I could persuade the company to advertise the Abbey pretty freely in their railway carriages, and stations, by photographs.[13]

First the railways, then the petrol companies, became the biggest promoters of the Office's sites. The Shell Oil Company started to advertise petrol in 1920. At first they advertised to attract chauffeurs and technicians, but as car ownership widened they moved away from technical promotion to woo people with the pleasures of touring. The most innovative poster designs were produced from 1932, when Jack Beddington became responsible for the company's advertising. Under his direction a list of artists, not instinctively associated with commercial art, were commissioned to convey simple messages, including Paul Nash, John Piper, Vanessa Bell and Graham Sutherland. A major thrust of these compelling designs was to get people to visit historic places and ancient monuments. John Betjeman was asked to compile a list of historic places for the campaign, and artists were invited to choose a landmark from the list. Many were monuments run by the Office of Works. An advertisement for Stonehenge with a linocut by Edward Bawden bore the memorable pun: 'Stonehenge Wilts. But SHELL goes on forever.'[14]

William Ormsby-Gore (1885–1964), later Lord Harlech, became First Commissioner in the National Government of 1931, a post he retained until May 1936. His appointment marked a turning point in the promotion and presentation of the national collection of monuments. It also coincided with

STONEHENGE *WILTS.*

BUT SHELL

GOES ON FOR EVER

Office of Works sites were frequently depicted on posters designed
by petrol companies. Here Edward Bawden puns on the county
name of Stonehenge while three Druids watch in horror.
© Wiltshire Natural History Museum

the end of the long and hugely successful reign of Sir Lionel Earle as Permanent Secretary and the appointment of Sir Patrick Duff (1889–1972) in 1933.
The new men at the top brought a new focus to the Ancient Monuments
Department. Duff had spent most of his career at the Board of Trade, but
then had become Private Secretary to both Ramsay MacDonald and Stanley
Baldwin as Prime Minister. He was worldly, wise, well connected and aware
of the potential business opportunities of the Ancient Monuments Department. Ormsby-Gore, as a successful banker, was also commercially minded,

but more significantly was an art and architectural historian and trustee of the National Gallery, Tate Gallery and British Museum. He was interested in both the art-historical and the business issues of showing art and architecture to the public. In 1933 he asked that the Office negotiate with the London and North Eastern Railway to establish a series of posters of Office of Works monuments based on the beautiful and successful railway cathedral posters promoted by the Great Western Railway and the London, Midland and Scottish Railway. Later, he asked the Office to design and produce its own promotional coloured linocuts that could be used by the railways and motoring bodies in their advertising. These stylish posters contained a special logo designed for the Office of Works: *HMOW Ancient Monuments*, the Department's first attempt at branding. Ormsby-Gore was also instrumental in advising the National Trust on the design of its first logo, the omega sign, adopted in the same period.[15]

A 1930s Office of Works poster, advertising Goodrich Castle and travel by railway to get there. The Ancient Monuments Department's logo appears on the bottom right corner. Reproduced by permission of English Heritage

Ormsby-Gore also recognised that the growing portfolio of monuments needed some coherent historical and topographical explanation and, in 1934, commissioned six *Illustrated Regional Guides*. These were the forerunners of the handbooks made available to season-ticket holders from the 1960s, containing lists of monuments, a map, opening hours and admission fees. More importantly, they set out to give some general historical context, for, as the preface to the first volume explained, 'The story of our past is written not only in history books but in stone.' Four of the six volumes, including the first in 1935, which covered the northern counties, were written by Ormsby-Gore himself. Further volumes were then produced covering individual building types such as castles and abbeys.[16]

The *Illustrated Guides* were supplementary to the Office or Works Official Guidebooks that had been introduced by Charles Peers in 1911. The first guidebook to be produced was for Kirby Muxloe, Leicestershire, and was published in 1917. Normal practice was for a small temporary pamphlet, costing twopence, to be produced immediately on the acquisition of the site. A fuller guidebook would then be produced after research, and clearance priced at sixpence. The guides contained a description and history of the monument and a pull-out phased plan. They were either prepared by the Department's inspectors or an approved archaeologist of established repute. By 1937 a total of seventy-six guides had either been produced or were in production.

The importance of the Office of Works Blue Guides cannot easily be over-emphasised. The measured surveys undertaken of monuments newly in care were, in almost every case, the first accurate record to be made of them. In due course hundreds of plans of British medieval and prehistoric monuments were made available to scholars through the Blue Guides. These were, of course, guidebooks, but they were also, crucially, primary documents essential to the understanding of British history and archaeology. They revolutionised the study of Britain's past, providing for the first time accurate, dimensioned and phased plans of crucial monuments. Both the plans and Office of Works photographs were widely reproduced. This had a profound long-term effect on the direction of scholarship. The Office of Works collection of monuments, as the only one properly recorded, became virtually the sole source of cited examples; the same plans and photographs were reproduced over and over again in hundreds of books and articles. In this way the selection of sites in the care of the Government became the ac-

A Royal Label Factory green sign points the way at Goodrich Castle. © English Heritage

cepted foundation on which scholars based chronology and development. It has only been since the 1980s, with the increasing availability of surveys of monuments in private ownership, that some of this bias has been redressed.

Of course, not all visitors bought a guidebook; indeed, those who did must have often been perplexed by their technical nature and complete lack of any social context. Most people who wanted to understand the monuments turned to the signs fixed to the various parts of the buildings explaining what they were. These green signs with raised white lettering were manufactured by the Royal Label Factory, which started life in Stratford-upon-Avon making signs for Queen Victoria's rose garden. By the 1960s it made all the road and street signs in Britain and also exported thousands to the colonies. Cast in aluminium, the signs were indestructible and thousands were ordered by the Office of Works to instruct and warn visitors. The strategy was to be terse. Signs read, 'east end', 'dorter', 'kitchen', 'well', and though they used technical language they enabled all but the most ignorant visitors to understand the layout of the monuments. After many changes the factory still exists; ironically, its main client today is the National Trust.

Ormsby-Gore was clear in his *Illustrated Guides* that, as well as guidebooks, the site custodians had an important role in 'assisting visitors with such information as they are able to give'. These custodians were not under the Chief Inspector but under the Chief Architect, Sir Frank Baines, who, during the 1920s, brought them into a formal employee relationship with the Office. Previously, many had received perks such as grazing rights as part of their remuneration, distracting them from the joint purposes of protection and education.

In August 1922 Warkworth Castle, famously described by Shakespeare as a 'worm-eaten hold of ragged stone', was taken over by the Office from the

Portrait of a custodian at Old Soar Manor, Plaxtol, Kent, in uniform cap and coat, 1956. © English Heritage

Duke of Northumberland.[17] In August 1922 three candidates were interviewed for the job of custodian, including the duke's existing employee. His occupation of the site had left it in a poor state: 'Cattle, pigs and poultry', we learn, were 'housed in some of the ruined portions of the building or in wooden erections built against or near the Castle Walls ... There is, at present, no attempt made to keep visitors from doing damage to the low walls and foundations, and children freely clamber over the masonry.' Mr Scott, the incumbent, also had 'in spite of his long connection with the Castle, a very poor knowledge of the building and its associations'.[18]

In contrast, the Office's favoured candidate was a thirty-seven-year-old joiner who lived nearby and who was of 'good appearance and education and of pleasing disposition, having at the same time a commendable interest in the Castle buildings'. Warkworth was, and still is, a demanding site, since, amongst the custodial duties, was the task of rowing visitors up the River Coquet to the nearby medieval hermitage. The best custodians everywhere were outstanding. A letter written to the Office by the Secretary of the Archaeological Section of the Bournemouth Natural Science Society in 1936 raved about their visit to Muchelney Abbey, Somerset:

> I wish to say on behalf of myself and the party that we greatly appreciate the way in which the Office of Works has laid out this very interesting building ... The carefulness in both the Archaeological and Architectural detail and the entire absence of commercialism greatly commend it to the sympathy of the public ... the Custodian, Mr H. Hall, makes the history of the Abbey so understandable to the layman. Seldom does one find a custodian so accurate with Archaeological data. His wife looked after the wants of the ladies in a most satisfactory manner.[19]

The care taken in the selection of custodians in the inter-war years was typical of Peers's and Baines's regime: nothing was left to chance; visitors needed to be helped to understand the buildings by all means available; and while security was an important role for the custodian, educating the public was just as important.

Security was most effectively achieved by the custodian living on site. The earliest surviving custodian's house is at Richborough Castle, Kent, a charming timbered Arts and Crafts structure commanding access to the monument. Few of the many early custodians' buildings remain today, but at Furness Abbey there is the sole survivor of a pre-war ticket office. Just

The 1920s ticket office at Furness Abbey, Cumbria, just large enough for one custodian and his dog. © Mr C. J. Wright. Source English Heritage

large enough for one man and a small till, some postcards and guidebooks, the hut has its own fireplace and chimney, a generous amenity for its occupant. Both of these were designed in the office of Frank Baines and were part of the strong aesthetic developed by the Office of Works before the Second World War. Interventions were almost always of elm; walkways, staircases, handrails and barriers were all oak allowed to silver naturally and harmonise with the walls of the monuments. Understated and traditional, they contrasted strongly with the Ministry of Works' buildings of the 1960s to 1970s (below, p. 244).

Another of Ormsby-Gore's concerns for the public was the provision of proper site museums. In 1933 he wrote to Sir Patrick Duff: 'Both at Rievaulx and Byland the great need is the same, viz: a properly constructed and arranged museum where the more important detached finds, carved stones, tiles, etc., can be better housed and shown. The present huts are unsuitable, unsightly and a definite disfigurement to the amenities of the ruins.'[20] Duff had to go to the Treasury, which referred the idea to the Royal

Commission on Museums (a body that Ormsby-Gore was to chair after the war). By April 1936 the Department had been given the green light. It was decided that two museums would be erected: one at Byland Abbey and another as an extension to the existing building at Richborough.[21] No other museums were built before the war, but these two set the tone for dozens of others after 1950.

By the outbreak of the Second World War the Office of Works had invented the entire apparatus of the heritage world that we know today: a large portfolio of centrally managed historic sites, carefully presented and interpreted to the public who arrived by car, paid to get in and bought guidebooks and postcards. There were site museums, interpretative panels, helpful, well-informed custodians and illustrated handbooks laying out the history and location of sites in the portfolio and how to visit them.

It was big business for a small Government department. In 1935 the entrance fees amounted to £42,089 and the total revenue, including sales of guidebooks, postcards, etc., amounted to £53,036. The annual expenditure on ancient monuments was £77,750 and thus before the Second World War the Office very nearly covered its own costs. In a persuasive letter to the Treasury in 1934 Sir Patrick Duff explained:

> Except for the years of depression, 1930, 1931 and 1932, when there was a slight falling off, these [visitor] figures have shown a steady annual increase over the last ten years, and in that period have reached a total of not far short of £100,000. The population is growing more alive to the interest of these places, and at the same time gets, and will get, more and more mobile, and I look forward to a time when every well cared for and attractive monument will be a source of a respectable revenue.[22]

Before the war the Office of Works as an operator of historic attractions had no real competition. Private owners were scaling down and the National Trust had not yet started scaling up. It was the men from the Ministry's golden age.

II

PROTECTION IN ACTION
1913–1939

THE LIST OF MONUMENTS

While part of the energy of the Ancient Monuments Department was focused on the acquisition of sites for its own portfolio, equal efforts were made to develop the new schedule of monuments. Scheduling was in abeyance between 1915 and 1918, and by the time it resumed properly in 1919 the need was urgent. The Ministry of Transport Act had set aside £10 million for bridge improvements and Professor Lethaby, an Ancient Monuments Board member, was instructed to form a sub-committee for the rapid scheduling of historic bridges before they were damaged by widening or demolished and replaced.[1] It was decided that all bridges of national importance pre-dating 1800 were to be scheduled. This was far too ambitious, as the first list of monuments scheduled, published in 1921, shows. Most of the monuments on it had been scheduled many years before and they were a traditional selection of the most important and prominent prehistoric and medieval sites. In Shropshire, for instance, there were five abbeys, three castles, a seventeenth-century chapel and a stone circle. On Anglesey, other than Beaumaris Castle there were eighteen prehistoric monuments.[2] A second list was published in 1923, a third and a fourth in 1924, and a fifth, sixth and seventh each year from 1925 to 1927. By 1930 there were 1,735 Scheduled Ancient Monuments in England and Wales.[3] Unquestionably, the advent of scheduling was a very significant development in the protection of historic sites in Britain, since it widened the scope of preservation to non-guardianship sites and provided a rapid mechanism for State protection merely by including the name of a monument on a list.

A Treasury report on the workings of the Ancient Monuments Department in 1935 observed that:

> The one field of activity where purely archaeological considerations prevail is in the scheduling of Ancient Monuments i.e. protecting them from active abuse by their owners. Apart from overheads the procedure costs nothing and the figures show that the Office of Works staff etc. costs do not grow to any extent with the increase in the numbers of scheduled monuments. Most of the additions to the lists are I gather thrown up (a) by the Royal Commission's surveys as they proceed. Others are brought to notice (b) by archaeological societies etc. or by the general public.[4]

One of the notable features of the scheduling system was its democratic and participatory nature. From the start the Ancient Monuments Board recognised that considerable organisation would be required to identify monuments for scheduling and then establish effective supervision over them. A system for overseeing the sites was discussed in March 1915, but was not fully in place until the summer of 1922. The task was carried out by unpaid 'Honorary Visitors' and 'Honorary Correspondents', which were either Fellows of the Society of Antiquaries or members of local archaeological societies. They were organised on a county basis with a Chief Correspondent in each and below him a network of Local Correspondents. Their duties were to oversee the monuments in their district, and to report any damage or any scheme that might have a detrimental impact on the monument, or any change in ownership.

During the 1930s the system of scheduling began to mature and people both within the Ancient Monuments Department and members of external organisations began to suggest sites that pushed the traditional boundaries. In July 1931 a seventeenth-century post mill at Bourn, Cambridgeshire, was put forward, the first windmill to be considered. It was discussed at length, but turned down. In May 1936 the scheduling of the Pinhole Cave, the Langwith Cave and Mother Grundy's Parlour at Cresswell, Derbyshire, were requested by the British Archaeological Association and considered by the Board. Caves could become scheduled monuments where they retained evidence of human occupation,[5] and all were approved, as was the 'general principle of scheduling such caves'.[6] At the same meeting the Board con-

Bourn windmill, Cambridgeshire, put forward for protection but eventually rejected.
© Francis Frith Photographic Collection

sidered 'monuments discovered by Air Photography but invisible from the
ground' (i.e., crop marks). They decided to take each case on its merits but
to leave it to the discretion of the Chief Inspector to decide which were of
most importance.

In November 1938 the Ancient Monuments Department received a strong
letter from the Council for the Care of Churches deprecating the listing
of monuments in churchyards.[7] The Inspector of Ancient Monuments for
England, Paul Baillie Reynolds, spoke before the Ancient Monuments Board
stressing the vital importance of the preservation of early medieval crosses in
graveyards. It was decided that it was perfectly legal to schedule in churchyards, but if any action was required over a scheduled monument it was best
to report it first to the church authorities. At the same meeting, on 15 February 1939, a discussion on scheduling Martello towers widened to a discussion
on what actually constituted an 'ancient' monument:

> Mr Clapham . . . also suggested that one or two of the pill-boxes of the last
> War should be considered for scheduling – they are valuable as histori-

cal documents of Military History, and if Martello Towers were included, the series would be continued right through. Neither Sir Lionel Earle nor Sir Charles Trevelyan could see any harm in scheduling the Martello Towers but they wondered if the pill-boxes of the last War were worth it, and the question arose as to what constituted an Ancient Monument. The pill-boxes were not historically interesting at present but they may be in another 100 years and there are full records, photographs and drawings, etc., in the War Museum. It was recommended that all reasonably good Martello Towers should be scheduled, but that the scheduling of pill-boxes should be left to later generations.[8]

The first pillboxes were in fact scheduled in 1998.

By 1939 there were 2,998 scheduled ancient monuments on the list.[9] The work was in set aside during the Second World War, with fifty monuments on hold, but the process resumed in 1946.[10]

PRESERVATION ORDERS

The first test of the 1913 Act as a measure for the protection of inhabited buildings came in the first full year of its operation. In January 1914 Charles Peers addressed a memorandum to Lord Beauchamp alerting him to the imminent destruction of an empty seventeenth-century house at 75 Dean Street in Soho, London: 'This house has been much in the papers lately, and is in imminent danger of destruction. I am informed that it will be demolished next week if nothing is done to save it.' Its importance was clear to Peers: 'It was originally Crown property, having been built about 1697, and was the residence of Sir James Thornhill, who doubtless painted the staircase ... the details of stair-balusters, panelling etc., are exceedingly good, and the connection with Thornhill, and possibly therefore with his Son-in-Law Hogarth makes the place of more than common importance.'[11]

The owner of the property had been unable to find a purchaser and wished to demolish it. Peers recommended scheduling the house. This would have required the owner to give the Office of Works a month's notice before demolition and this would buy time, Peers thought, to find a permanent solution for the place. If necessary, a Preservation Order could then be made. Yet Beauchamp was confident enough in the act to issue a Preservation Order straight away. The Office of Works solicitor was instructed to prepare one

75 Dean St, Soho, London, before it was demolished. Reproduced by permission of English Heritage

for the following day. It was put before a Select Committee of the House of Lords for confirmation in May 1914. Giving evidence, Peers emphasised the architectural and artistic interest of the building, but the House of Lords did not confirm the order and awarded costs to the owner. It was a major setback for the Office of Works.

The reaction of staff within the Ancient Monuments Department was one of despair. Just a year after the passing of the first act with compulsive measures, it had been comprehensively undermined by Parliament. Lionel Earle wrote in a note to Lord Beauchamp:

> I should like to ask how a Committee of five peers, not to my knowledge specially qualified to judge of the merits of Ancient Monuments, can set themselves up to override and disregard the evidence of men such as Lord Crawford, Sir Edward Poynter, Professor Lethaby, Sir Cecil Smith, Sir Charles Holroyd, Mr. Warren, etc., and also the entire body of the Ancient Monuments Board. It appears to me that, if Parliament accept this present situation, the Ancient Monuments Board might just as well be done away with ... Would it not be possible, when the House meets again, to raise in some form or other a debate ... as regards the paralysing effect which this decision will have on the future working of the Act?[12]

The Select Committee did not release a report and the Office of Works was left to guess whether the Lords considered the Preservation Order to be against the rights of the proprietor or that they thought the house was not of national importance.[13] The advent of the First World War forestalled its demolition. In May 1919, however, Charles Peers reported that 'The Select Committee delivered this house into the hands of the furniture dealers, and the inevitable consequences are now taking place.' The staircase was shipped to the United States to be reconstructed in the Chicago Art Institute, Illinois, while other rooms were re-erected in a house in Ipswich, Massachusetts.[14]

Shortly before the Select Committee's decision not to confirm the order on the house in Dean Street, the Ancient Monuments Board had recommended a Preservation Order be served on Nunney Castle in Somerset.[15] It was suffering from neglect and the owner had refused either to carry out repair works or to hand it over to the county council in 1912. Following the decision on Dean Street this plan was dropped. At the next meeting of the Ancient Monuments Board it was decided that a decision to issue a Preservation Order for Wolverhampton Deanery would also be 'useless'.[16] The Board were now hesitant to recommend the scheduling of recently occupied buildings. In March 1915 local people made a case for scheduling the 'old house' in Palace Yard, Coventry, since it was unoccupied and likely to become ruinous. The Board thought the building 'extremely interesting' but resolved 'that it would be inadvisable to Schedule as a Preservation Order would not be likely to succeed'.[17]

After the First World War the mood was different and the scars left by the Dean Street case had healed. In the 1920s the Office of Works were ready again to resort to preservation orders, especially in cases where they recognised the monument to be of outstanding importance. At Buildwas Abbey a final warning to the owner threatening that a Preservation Order might be served tipped the monument into guardianship.[18] In the similar case of Netley Abbey, Hampshire, an ancient monument suffering from neglect and falling into rapid decay, the First Commissioner, Lord Crawford, took his proposal for a Preservation Bill to the Cabinet. He referred to the earlier decision of the House of Lords:

> In 1914 a preservation order was issued by Lord Beauchamp which Parliament refused to confirm. I was called as witness before the Lords Committee, and felt no surprise at the Department's failure, as the threatened building was a second rate residence in Soho. In this I am dealing with a monument of the greatest historic importance – a royal foundation and a building of supreme architectural merit.[19]

The mere threat of compulsory action drew the owner to a guardianship agreement on 14 April 1922.

By 1924 the Department was confident enough to issue a Preservation Order for some fragmentary earthworks at Lexden Straight Road, Colchester. These banks and ditches were the remains of a series of late Iron Age defences protecting the western side of Camulodunum – pre-Roman Colchester.[20] They were certainly less impressive than the great ruins of the Cistercian monastery at Netley. In fact, the owner, H. G. Papillion, claimed that they were part of an old lane and some local gravel workings.[21]

Papillion proposed to build houses to the east and then cut driveways through the earthworks in order to provide access to a main road in the west. His view was that if he were not permitted to do this a new road to the east would have to be built, necessitating an outlay of thousands of pounds. If the Government wished to save the earthworks, he felt he ought to receive compensation. Unfortunately, there was no provision to compensate under the 1913 Act, only provision for purchase. Charles Peers was determined that the earthworks should be saved. The Department had already sanctioned the destruction of a nearby barrow, stipulating that excavation was required beforehand.[22] But this case was different and it was felt it would mark a precedent: 'We have already allowed the destruction of a tumulus,' Peers wrote,

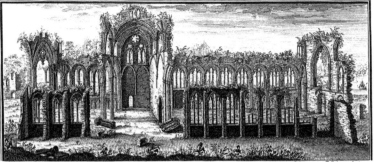

The overgrown ruins of Netley Abbey, Hampshire, in an engraving of 1733 by Samuel and Nathaniel Buck. © English Heritage

This, however, was an isolated monument, and its site is easily recorded. The other earthworks here are all part of a system of defence . . . Every part that is left must be preserved – it is not possible to say that any one piece is of less importance than any other . . . Local opinion in Colchester must be kept in mind. Our decision to allow the removal of the Lexden tumulus was unwelcome to many . . . if we now give way at the very next attempt of an owner to make money by destroying a scheduled monument, the country will lose all confidence in the Board [of Works] – it will consider that our action in scheduling is so much bluff and that we have no serious intention of protecting by the powers of the Act, monuments which have been declared of national importance.[23]

The owner of the site made a strong case against the Preservation Order, petitioning the House of Commons in February 1925.[24] He argued that the cost of preserving the monument for the nation should not fall to one individual. The Office of Works accepted the point and offered to purchase the earthworks. Papillon consented and the Government bought the earthworks for £2,000 in December 1925.

Despite the limited success of the Office of Works with preservation orders, it was determined to try and find a way of closing the legal and procedural loopholes that had resulted in the defeat of the order for Dean Street. In

1920 Lionel Earle succeeded in persuading Sir Alfred Mond to set up an Ancient Monuments Advisory Committee to recommend what might be done. Mond was a millionaire industrialist appointed First Commissioner by Lloyd George in 1916. He was not a traditional appointee but a hard-nosed businessman put into the Office of Works for managerial reasons. The war had vastly expanded the Office's wider works, taking in hospitals, clinics, training centres and housing estates and this was Mond's focus, not the Ancient Monuments Department. Yet things had quietened down by 1920 and he agreed that the committee should be chaired by his predecessor, Lord Beauchamp.

Beauchamp's committee comprised Charles Peers, Sir Lionel Earle, Sir Hercules Read and several MPs; they published their report the following year.[25] Given the weight of preservationists on the committee, it is not surprising that it reported that legislation was still far short of that in other countries such as France, which was considered the benchmark for ancient monuments protection. Nor did they recommend that inhabited buildings should be protected and that grants should be given to encourage owners to manage their monuments better. What was more of a development was that they widened their perspective to country houses and manor houses that they thought were of 'first-rate importance'. Country villages they saw as having 'incontestable influence' upon their surroundings, whilst ancient colleges, almshouses and hospitals were of especially 'high architectural merit'. In addition, cathedrals were still liable to damage from the whims of an architect appointed by the Dean and Chapter and needed policing through proper advisory boards.

In 1921 Mond was replaced as First Commissioner by the Earl of Crawford and Balcarres, probably the most cultured member of the Government (above, p. 55). As the report lay on his desk expectations were high, but, to the horror and frustration of Earle and Peers, he was unwilling to sanction such 'a grave an inroad upon private rights and the development of property' and set the whole thing to one side. The Government fell the following year and the matter was dead.

The overall conclusion was that a Fine Art Commission should be established to consider preservation orders, as well as 'all questions of taste' relating to the arts in England. The arguments generated by the Advisory Committee continued for several years but successive governments declined to implement them. In 1924 a Royal Fine Art Commission was established but its duties were limited; it merely had powers to enquire into questions of artistic importance and provide advice.[26]

SAVING HADRIAN'S WALL
THE ACT OF 1931

In October 1929 George Lansbury, the First Commissioner of Works, wrote:

> In order to estimate what has been achieved by the Ancient Monuments Department up to the present time, it must be remembered that it hardly came into fully effective operation until after the War. When that fact is considered and the smallness of the organisation and of the funds available, the amount and quality of the work actually done is, in my own view, a considerable achievement.

It was a fair assessment, but the Office still felt it was hampered in carrying out its duties by the powers at its disposal. This was to change, at least in theory, by two measures executed in 1931 and 1932.

Just as the case of Tattershall Castle was the background to the 1913 Act, so its amendment in 1931 was triggered by another cause célèbre, the destruction of parts of Hadrian's Wall. The great Roman wall had been under almost constant threat since the Middle Ages. Parts near settlements had long been plundered for building materials and more distant stretches dismantled to build field boundaries and farm buildings. But it was the construction of the Military Way by General Wade in 1746 that really accelerated its destruction. The Roman wall comprised three sections: the stone wall to the north, a Roman military road behind it, and a series of deep ditches, the vallum, to the south. Wade's new road, whose foundations were of Roman stone, was to run the course of the Roman road between the wall and the vallum, serving to move troops rapidly from Newcastle to Dumfriesshire in response to possible future Jacobite uprisings. Its construction was the single most destructive incident in the wall's history.

By the early nineteenth century the wall increasingly acquired friends, the most important of whom was John Clayton (1792–1890). His family owned Chesters Roman Fort and had shown growing concern over the gradual dismantling of the monument. In 1838 Clayton began to purchase land in the central sector of the wall, including Housesteads Roman Fort. This began to preserve important stretches and opened them to public inspection.[1] Yet the efforts of the Claytons could only safeguard small sections of the 73-mile-long monument, and in the late nineteenth century quarries at Cawfields and Walltown were causing irreparable damage. General Pitt-Rivers seemed not to have been aware of what was going on, or, if he was, chose not to get involved, although he was consulted by the National Trust, which was attempting to preserve the Antonine Wall in Scotland.[2] The first known involvement of the Office of Works was when Charles Peers, shortly after his appointment as Inspector of Ancient Monuments, spent two days inspecting Hadrian's Wall in September 1910. He was dismayed to find that several parts continued to be destroyed by whinstone quarries.[3] Whinstone was the local name given to the black basalt that formed the great ridge running east–west across the country, with a precipitous face towards the north forming a natural rampart upon which the Roman wall was built.

By 1910 several of the Roman forts near the wall had been excavated and consolidated, including Chesters (*Cilurnum*) and Great Chesters (*Aesica*), and digging was ongoing at Corbridge.[4] Peers found the wall standing four to five feet high in parts, serving as a boundary between various estates. Elsewhere, it had been reduced to a heap of stones. Most worrying, though, was the impact of quarrying. 'The destruction is not now rapid' Peers wrote,

> but may at any time become so, and the whole character of the country, apart from its historical and archaeological value, would be entirely ruined in the course of time . . . The maintenance of these most valuable remains cannot be considered assured, as long as it depends on the interest taken in them by private owners, and it would be most desirable that they should be placed under the Act, as the opportunity occurs.[5]

In 1928 even those parts of the wall that had been protected through the altruism of the Claytons suddenly became vulnerable when their estate was thrown onto the open market. In April 1928 the estate passed to John Maurice (nicknamed 'Jack') Clayton who had run up huge gambling debts and was forced to sell the estate in 1929. Divided into lots, it was auctioned that July. Some parts found benign new owners, such as the archaeologist Eric Birley (1906–1995), who purchased Vindolanda Roman Fort. He could not afford to buy Housesteads as well, but happily it did not sell at auction and was donated to the National Trust. At the same time an agreement was signed between the landowner, Sir Hugh Blackett, and John Fred Wake, an engineer and machinery merchant, giving Wake the mineral rights between the wall and vallum in one of the most impressive 5-mile stretches of the wall. He was entitled to quarry so close to the wall that it would leave it on little more than a knife edge.

The news reached the Office of Works by a letter from John Fred Wake in January 1930.[6] Charles Peers was appalled, regarding this as one of the greatest threats to a monument he had ever seen. He informed the Board:

> ...I consider that the Board should take it as a general principle that no quarrying should take place in the area between the Wall, the [Military] Way, & the Vallum...This is not only on historical grounds: the whole significance of this notable memorial of the Roman occupation of Britain is greatly heightened by the wild and beautiful scenery through which it passes...We must defend the amenities of the Wall, as well as its actual remains, with all the power which the Act gives us.[7]

Fear of what might happen when the estate was broken up had prompted the scheduling of the wall in December 1928, but the power that scheduling gave under the 1913 Act was strictly limited in cases like this. While Peers could protect the wall, he could do nothing about its surroundings. John Wake was informed, by letter, that not only was the wall safeguarded by being on the schedule, but that the Military Road and the vallum were also protected. Peers included a map showing the area that should not be touched. Unfortunately, the whole of Wake's quarry lay in Peers's protected zone, and not only had Wake spent a great deal on planning the work, but also in the midst of the Depression he would provide jobs for 200 men. He stated that his quarrying operations came totally within the area and that he had spent thousands of pounds drawing up the scheme.[8] Peers went back to Lionel Earle:

Mr. Wake relies on the scale of his operations and the number of men he may be able to employ to justify his Scheme. It cannot possibly be agreed to by the Commissioners. To retire before such an attack on a monument whose long overdue scheduling was last year greeted with a chorus of approval would utterly discredit ourselves and the Act. We must aim at a complete negation of the scheme – no compromise or half measures are possible.[9]

This was very difficult for the Board. The First Commissioner, George Lansbury, was, as has been seen (above, p. 111), committed to unemployment relief schemes and to prevent this large quarry from opening was politically tough. Nevertheless, Earle asked him to promote an amendment to the 1913 Act that would protect the setting of the wall and stop the quarry.[10] Lansbury consulted both the Prime Minister and the Chancellor of the Exchequer and also arranged a visit to Hadrian's Wall. On 23 April 1930 Lansbury travelled to the wall with Charles Peers and Frederick Raby. He was a master of publicity and the visit was reported in the *Daily Mail* under the title 'Mr Lansbury Ponders. Can he save Hadrian's Wall?'[11] He heard the arguments of William Straker, of the Northumberland Miners' Federation, and R. J. Taylor, Chairman of the Haltwhistle Labour Party, who tried to persuade him of the benefits that quarrying would bring to the local area. These centred on the considerable employment that it would provide at the depth of the economic depression. He was also shown the plans for the quarry by Mr Wake, with whom he shared a picnic lunch overlooking the wall.

Lansbury was convinced by his visit that the environs of the wall must be protected and, after consulting the Prime Minister and the Cabinet, got agreement to a new bill to do so.[12] Initially, the Department had considered incorporating this in the Town and Country Planning Act (above, p. 89), but a decision was taken to press ahead with a separate measure. Whilst Sir Lionel Earle drafted the bill, preparations were in hand for a scheme for Hadrian's Wall that could be put in place as soon as the act came into force. 'The general idea,' the Department stated, 'is to cover all those stretches of country where the historic setting of the Wall is least altered, leaving out, so far as possible villages and areas where railway lines or other modern works have destroyed the significance of the surroundings of the Wall.'[13] Thus a blueprint for the Department's subsequent actions was put in place.

MR. LANSBURY PONDERS.

CAN HE SAVE HADRIAN'S WALL ?

First Commissioner of Works, George Lansbury, sitting by Hadrian's Wall in April 1930. Lansbury was a master at publicity and he was teased in the House for publicising his travels on behalf of the Ancient Monuments Department. © Daily Mail archive

The Ancient Monuments Act was passed on 11 June 1931. The first section empowered the Commissioners of Works to prohibit or restrict the construction, alteration or extension of buildings or structures in an area 'comprising or adjacent to an ancient monument'.[14] They could also prescribe the external appearance of new buildings in the area, as well as prohibit or restrict quarrying, excavation and the felling of trees. Any person whose property was 'injuriously affected' by one of these preservation schemes was entitled to apply for compensation, while the penalty for contravention was a fine of up to £20 for every day on which it occurred.[15]

The 1931 Ancient Monuments Act was important because it gave the Board – for the first time – the power to protect the setting of ancient monuments, a considerable step forward in their view. Yet it was not altogether the solution for Hadrian's Wall. Since the act was not retrospective the quarries still had the legal right to remove stone until their leases ended. This was a major problem, since John Wake's lease ran until 1949 and was renewable for another twenty years. As a result, during the passage of the bill, a separate agreement was drawn up with Wake whereby he could quarry a small area but was not to touch the wall, vallum or Roman Military Way between the two.[16]

The Preservation Scheme for Hadrian's Wall was drafted by Frederick Raby, but despite his work it was not implemented immediately following the 1931 Act. Neville Chamberlain, Chancellor of the Exchequer, argued that there were not enough Government funds available, given the economic depression, to compensate owners and businesses, and in the absence of any immediate threat expenditure was unjustifiable anyway. So its publication was delayed until December 1938. The scheme covered 15 miles of the central section of the wall from Walwick in the east to Thirlwall Castle in the west, with exclusion zones at Cawfields and Walltown, where quarrying could continue, and the area where Wake was to operate.

Unfortunately, the outbreak of war meant that the Preservation Scheme was not finally ratified, and in 1942 quarrying again advanced towards the Roman wall. This time the demand for whinstone was for surfacing RAF airfields. Raby, being informed of this new threat, pressurised the Government to take action. In 1943 the Treasury finally sanctioned the necessary compensation to allow for confirmation of the Preservation Scheme and a separate Preservation Order to stop quarrying in the Walltown exclusion zone. Compensation amounted to £78,000 for quarries at Walltown and Cawfields, whilst John Wake's lease was purchased for an additional £6,500.

The Office of Works saw the whole episode as a long, drawn-out and unsatisfactory saga. Although the Hadrian's Wall Preservation Scheme was actively used right up until the repeal of George Lansbury's Ancient Monuments Act in 1979, no other Preservation Schemes were ever made. What had by then become the Ministry of Works reverted to the best form of protection it knew: guardianship. It was decided, though not announced publicly, that it would aim to take the whole of Hadrian's Wall into guardianship piece by piece, thus protecting it permanently. Between 1933 and 1972 a total of thirty sites were taken into care.[17] As parts of the wall were taken into Government control, they were uncovered and consolidated together with many milecastles and turrets, completely transforming the appearance of the wall. This work not only preserved the wall and made it archaeologically legible, but also it made it possible to regard the wall, for the first time, as the major tourist attraction it remains today.

13

WHO SAVES COUNTRY HOUSES?

A PROBLEM IS POSED

The First World War had accelerated the collapse of the economic base upon which the country house existed; the Second World War made it doubtful to anyone that people could go on living in them. Wartime requisitioning of country houses left many in a terrible, even unusable, state. Income tax and death duties made it hard for even the richest landowners to maintain a big house. Younger owners had got used to living more comfortably in smaller houses during the war and were reluctant to return to live in the cold, echoing halls of their forebears. Domestic service was no longer seen as a career and the lack of staff made many houses completely impractical to live in.[1] But the effects of war and economic collapse in the late 1940s and 1950s were different from those in the 1920s; the huge land sales and resulting development of rural land for new housing after 1918 did not happen again. The watchword was now planning, and control of land usage and ownership was a priority for post-war governments, and the 1947 Town and Country Planning Act enshrined this in statute.[2]

The difficulty was to decide what to do with the great houses that had formed the centre of rural estates. Though Tudor and Stuart houses had long been admired, the Victorians thought Georgian houses dull and unappealing. After the First World War tastes began to change, and while the bourgeois love of the Tudoresque was still spawning miles of half-timbered houses in the suburbs, those with more cultivated tastes turned away from 'ye olde Worlde' of the Arts and Crafts movement and the world that produced the

Acts of 1882 and 1913. The 1913 Act had been in part a reaction against the visible plunder of the England of 'Olden Times' by Americans wanting to buy into the English 'look'. From the 1920s that look was no longer fashionable and it was replaced in urban high society by the apparently simpler, ordered life of the Georgians. It was a metropolitan aesthetic, restrained and well mannered, that created a stylish modernism with ancestry. This developing appreciation for the eighteenth century led to a reassessment of Georgian country houses, one that was promoted by the magazine *Country Life*.

Particularly influential in this change was Christopher Hussey (1899–1970), who had joined the magazine in 1921 and became its editor in 1933. At Eton and Oxford Hussey had made friends with a group of like-minded enthusiasts for architecture and landscape, all of whom were developing an interest in Georgian buildings. Under Hussey's influence *Country Life* articles, books and guides, from 1930, began to re-establish Georgian country houses in its readers' imagination and affection. *Country Life* also took up the role of mouthpiece and campaigner for the preservation of the countryside. It linked itself to other campaigning bodies such as the Council for the Protection of Rural England and the National Trust, and argued for protective and planning measures in statute. Its concerns were not limited to countryside matters, for it was at the forefront of arguing for the preservation of Wren's City Churches, Nash's Regent Street, Soane's Bank of England and Georgian squares. However, it was the country house that most concerned Hussey and where his energies were most influential.[3]

In 1930 Hussey went to Norfolk to write up the great Jacobean mansion of Blickling Hall for the magazine. It belonged to Philip Kerr, who had just succeeded to the estate (and several others) as 11th Marquess of Lothian. Kerr wanted, and needed, to dispose of Blickling and other estates because he owed the Government 40 per cent of the capital value of his inheritance. Lothian was not alone, and many other estate owners feared for the future of their ancestral possessions under heavy taxation. Lothian and Hussey consulted the National Trust, even though at that time it was not an organisation that was much associated with country houses. It was good timing because its new chairman, from 1932, was the Marquess of Zetland, a Tory grandee deeply interested in art history much in the mould of Lord Curzon. Its new Secretary, the Trust's first professional head, Donald MacLeod Matheson, was a friend of Lothian's. The two men were to help set the small charity that held land for public benefit in a new direction.[4]

Blickling Hall, Norfolk, as photographed for Christopher Hussey's 1930 article in
Country Life. © Country Life Picture Library

A SOLUTION EMERGES

Matheson invited Lothian to speak about the plight of country houses at the
Trust's Annual General Meeting in 1934, and Hussey provided him with a
list of approximately six hundred houses that it was felt should be exempted
from death duties in order to preserve them. With Lothian's speech in hand,
Zetland went to see the Chancellor of the Exchequer, Neville Chamberlain, only to be told that the Government had no intention of either giving
private individuals tax relief on old houses or of authorising the Office of
Works to take them on. Chamberlain did, however, consult Ormsby-Gore
at the Office of Works, who then set the National Trust a challenge. Speaking at the National Trust AGM the following year, the First Commissioner
started by making clear that the work of the National Trust and the Ancient
Monuments Department of the Office of Works were complementary and
not competitive. They worked together in the closest cooperation, he said,

inspired by the same ideals, and both were determined to make their limited financial resources go as far as possible without any overlapping or waste.

The minister then turned to the issue of country houses, and *The Times* report of what he said is worth quoting extensively, since this was the first public statement made by the Government acknowledging the cultural value of country houses. He said that the

> number of wonderful houses in their beautiful parks, houses which still contained the accumulation by many generations of successive occupiers of the utmost historic and artistic interest in almost every county, was a unique heritage of Britain. No other country could match possessions like Penshurst, Knole, Bramshill, Hatfield and Blickling. Each incidence of death duties, and the high cost of maintaining the ancient homes of England in their wonderful settings in the way of gardens and woodland, threatened both fabric and contents in all too many cases. No doubt some of them would become ruins, and a future First Commissioner of Works would be able to take them over when they were ruinous. It seemed a pity to have to wait for that. As he saw it, the cooperation of owners and the National Trust might prove the best solution of a problem ...

But – and there had to be a 'but' – the National Trust was a tiny organisation that enjoyed limited support and if it was to be successful in helping to find a future for country houses it had to increase its income and its membership.

This was quite a challenge, especially since it relied in getting agreement amongst estate owners as well as a groundswell of popular support. Even then, it would still need the Government's approval to make any scheme workable. Neither *Country Life* nor the National Trust really believed that consensus could be found. Nevertheless, the Trust formed a small Country House Committee in January 1936. This became a pressure group within the Trust chaired by Oliver Brett, Lord Esher, son of the former Office of Works' Permanent Secretary. His tastes had been strongly influenced by those of his father and his love of architecture drew him to both the SPAB and to the National Trust. His right-hand man was the committee's secretary, James Lees-Milne, one of the new generation of educated aesthetes enamoured with all things Georgian.

Their first task was to consult country house owners and to do this they needed a better list than Hussey's several hundred houses. A new list was drawn up with the help of the, by then, former Chief Inspector, Charles

Peers. On the basis of this James Lees-Milne started to consult the owners of 230 'first-class' houses. No consensus was found and, in the end, the National Trust decided to go it alone and establish their own scheme through a Private Member's Bill that would empower owners to transfer their houses to the Trust with a tax-free endowment and lease them back to live in. The National Trust Act became law in July 1937 and in the same year Wightwick Manor, Wolverhampton, became the first country house to be offered under the scheme (although ironically it was not on the list of 230). Two years later the Office of Works and the Trust agreed an expanded list of the 320 houses 'of first importance' most worth saving, and a further National Trust Act was passed that dealt with the problem of entailed estates. Under this act, the Office of Works was required to certify that a house was of 'national interest or architectural historic or artistic interest' before the Trust could accept it.

But by then the country was on the verge of war again. Lees-Milne was in the army until 1941 and the Office of Works became distracted by massive new responsibilities. The Ancient Monuments Department had done its best to protect historic houses by steering the military away from the most sensitive buildings and landscapes, and also by carrying out protective work in houses, for instance boarding over the main staircase at Audley End while it was occupied by the Polish Special Operations Executive. Nevertheless, it was plain to see that the war was going to result in the abandonment of hundreds of requisitioned houses damaged while in military use, such as Rufford Abbey, Nottinghamshire. Meanwhile, through the efforts of Lees-Milne and the Country House Committee, the National Trust managed to persuade a few owners to hand over their estates, although they had to compromise on public access, ownership of contents and the rights of the 'donors'; the Trust was even forced to contribute to the endowment for Knole House in Kent. Moreover, by 1943 there were signs of open hostility towards the Trust's scheme, which was seen, by some, as an aristocratic tax dodge with little public benefit. Reluctantly, in 1944 the Country House Committee agreed that they should ask the Ministry of Works for help.[5]

A RIVALRY DEVELOPS

Although during the 1930s there had been cordial relations between the Trust and the Department of Ancient Monuments, the acquisition of a dozen houses by the Trust in the 1940s raised questions about the Ministry's own

"It's a toss-up whether it goes to the National Trust or the Ministry of Works."

"It's a toss-up whether it goes to the National Trust or the Ministry of Works."
Cartoonist Michael Ffolkes parodies the competition between the Ministry of Works and the National Trust in this cartoon from 1948.

collecting policy. There were two problems: one of period and one of use. Officially, the eighteenth century was out of bounds for the Government. The Royal Commission on Historical Monuments had an end point in its activities of 1714 and this marked a sort of official cut-off point for State interest in historic buildings. In addition, because most eighteenth-century buildings were in use, or at least capable of habitation, they could not be accepted by the Office of Works under guardianship.

In November 1945 Lord Methuen, a country house owner himself, who as an army officer had been involved in the protection of historic buildings during the allied invasion of Europe, initiated a debate on increasing Government powers for the preservation of historic buildings. The Ministry took this opportunity to clarify their powers in relation to country houses. Lord Henderson, speaking for the Government, stated that it was able to accept inhabited houses 'as a gift, with or without an endowment, or to buy them'.[6] In January 1946 the Ministry received, with some excitement, its first (and only) approach from an owner of an occupied country house. Clare Sheridan, an eccentric sculptress, a cousin of Winston Churchill, offered her house, Brede Place in Sussex, as a gift to the Government on the condition that she would be able to live in part of it. Sir Eric de Normann responded that he 'certainly should like to see us taking over some of the finer old houses'. He believed that if they could come to an agreement with Mrs Sheridan it would encourage other owners to offer their houses on similar terms. Even better for the Ministry, the National Trust were under the impression that the house was going to be left to them on Mrs Sheridan's death. The Chief Inspector of Ancient Monuments, Bryan O'Neil, visited the house in May 1946 and noted 'it is *par excellence* the sort of inhabited house we had in mind, when Lord Henderson drew attention to our powers in the House of Lords'. After some negotiation, however, the offer was withdrawn, because of the conditions set by the Ministry, and on the advice of Mr Churchill.[7]

The Ministry's inspectors were bitterly disappointed, but they were soon angling for a much bigger catch, the outstanding Jacobean palace, Audley End, in Essex. Lord Braybrooke, its owner, unlike Mrs Sheridan, did not want to live in his house. His cousin had died in 1943, and both house and title passed to him together with a double set of death duties. Braybrooke approached Lees-Milne to ask if the National Trust might take the house over. After meeting him in May 1944, Lees-Milne described Braybrooke as 'embarrassed by his inheritance' and 'at his wits' end what to do with Audley End'.[8] Normally, the Trust would accept a house as a gift only with an accompanying endowment – in cash or in land – to provide for its future maintenance, but in the case of Audley End Braybrooke was prevented by his trustees from giving the house away and could not afford to provide an endowment. So to save Audley End it was necessary for the Trust to find both

Audley End House, Essex, as it appeared in the early days of Ministry of Works ownership. It was so obviously a big prize for the men from the Ministry. © English Heritage Photo Library

a tenant and the purchase price. Lees-Milne attempted to interest a number of potential users, but by 1946 he was forced to turn to the Government for help. Sir Alan Barlow of the Treasury gave a sympathetic response initially and wrote to the Ministry of Works asking for confirmation of the Trust's view that the house was in fair condition.

Sir Eric de Normann replied by putting in an unsolicited bid for the house on behalf of his ministry. If 'this extremely important house is to be acquired for the public, only if the Treasury put up the £30,000, we think that it ought to come to us to look after and shew to the public, rather than be given to the National Trust'.[9] 'One or two country houses of this supreme quality', de Normann continued, 'ought, we think to be available for full inspection by the public, like Hampton Court in London. Houses like Audley End are at present known to very few except from photographs and descriptions in books not readily available.' The Ministry now not only believed that they were better qualified to look after large buildings than the National Trust; they also thought that to make their collection of monuments typologically complete they should have the crème de la crème of houses themselves.

The Treasury were not convinced, anxious about using public money for maintaining 'white elephants'. Meanwhile, the National Trust informed them that they were in negotiation with Cambridge University to use the house as a residential college. This undermined their bid fatally, because, quite reasonably, Treasury officials thought it made more sense for the user of the house to be responsible for it and Cambridge University did, after all, have long experience of caring for ancient buildings. Moreover, it was also keen not to advertise its generosity in this matter at a time of austerity, and while purchase money could be wrapped up in the normal annual grant to a university, a grant to the National Trust would become public knowledge. This, it was feared, might undermine the willingness of other country house owners to give away their property for nothing.

Negotiations with Cambridge fell through, but, to general surprise, the Ministry of Education came forward to propose that they should use the house for residential education conferences with the house vested in, and maintained by, the Ministry of Works. The Chancellor of the Exchequer, Hugh Dalton, who had taken a personal interest in the case, approved this proposal 'with great satisfaction' and the Ministry was asked to proceed with the purchase of the house on behalf of the Government.[10] Negotiations nearly came to grief in 1948 over the financial value of the house, but they were saved by the intervention of Sir Edward Bridges, Permanent Secretary to the Treasury.[11] He argued that 'any valuation for a property such as Audley End at the present time is bound to be rather unreal' and it was more important to focus on the principle of whether the State 'should find means of preserving a limited number of the great country houses of the land'. To his mind, Audley End was certainly among the twenty or thirty greatest houses in England and it deserved the skilled attention that only the Ancient Monuments Department could give. 'All this, no doubt, is a very unorthodox minute for a Permanent Secretary to the Treasury to write; but it happens to be what I feel about the subject.'[12]

On 2 February 1949 the Ministry of Works took possession of the house, on the basis that they would open it temporarily as a 'show-place' until the work necessary for the Ministry of Education use could be undertaken. Ironically, since they had pressed hard for a beneficial use for the house as a condition of its purchase for the nation, the Treasury refused to release money for this scheme to start, and by the beginning of 1951 it had been permanently postponed. Thus Audley End House became a permanent, State-owned 'show-place', not the outcome that most of those involved in the process had intended, but a spectacular coup for the Ancient Monuments Department. Lees-Milne was devastated: 'I *am* sorry that the NT has not got it', he wrote, 'because I am convinced that they will present houses better than the tasteless Ministry of Works.'[13]

Here Lees-Milne was wrong; while some might have considered the Ministry tasteless, they were hardly novices at presenting historic houses. While it is easy to see the Office and Ministry of Works as custodians of unfurnished, unroofed ruins, it should not be forgotten that they had long opened to the public some of the most spectacular houses in the land. This had given them unrivalled expertise and experience in looking after exactly the sort of houses that the Trust was now acquiring. In particular, the Office was proud of its massive restoration of the state rooms at Hampton Court in the 1930s. Here from 1929 they started to re-hang the rooms in silk damask, but found that they were unable to make progress in improving the apartments because of the intrusive heating pipes. Although the Department's architects had devised an invisible under-floor system that would have transformed the rooms, it was unaffordable. In 1937 Sir Philip Sassoon was appointed First Commissioner. He was not only a politician and heir to his father's great fortune, but was also a considerable connoisseur; he realised that 1938 was the 100th anniversary of the opening of Hampton Court to the public and decided to undertake a major restoration of the rooms in celebration. Owing to the Defence Programme there was no money in the Office of Works for anything other than necessities, and so the philanthropist Lord Duveen was persuaded to donate £11,500 for the replacement of the heating.

The state apartments closed in September 1937. Furniture and paintings were removed while building work went ahead, and the following April Sassoon made an inspection of the completed spaces prior to their reinstatement. At this point he agreed with the Surveyor of the King's Pictures, Kenneth Clark, and Queen Mary a radical redesign, re-hanging all the rooms with silk and tapestry, bringing in some of the greatest paintings in the royal collection and making a logical arrangement of the furniture. For this to

The Audience Chamber at Hampton Court after the restoration of 1938, with one of Sir Philip Sassoon's chairs under the seventeenth-century throne canopy. Reproduced by permission of English Heritage

happen the presence chambers needed thrones, and since the royal collection had none of the right date Sassoon offered to donate two appropriate throne chairs of his own. On 14 July 1938 Queen Mary attended the formal reopening of the apartments and a garden party on the east front in her honour.[14]

THE MINISTRY ASCENDANT

With Hampton Court, Kensington Palace, Holyroodhouse, Osborne House and Walmer Castle in their care, not to mention the Government's private estate of residences and offices, no wonder the Ministry of Works thought itself qualified to take on country houses. Indeed, in 1948 it effectively took over two more houses, Ham House and Osterley Park. Ham House in Petersham, Surrey, was offered as a gift to the Trust in 1945, but the Tollemache family were unable either to offer an endowment to cover the cost of future maintenance or to give away the spectacular contents. The Trust therefore approached the Government for financial assistance. A scheme was devised for the freehold to be vested in the National Trust, which would in turn give a lease to the Ministry of Works to maintain the house, on the understanding that it was to be used as a museum; the Victoria and Albert Museum (V&A) would purchase the contents and administer the museum.[15]

It was an unusual step for the Trust to take, and if the Tollemaches had not been implacably opposed to the house going to the Government, the Trust

"This is my last warning, Charles. If you do not mend your ways I shall leave the estate to you instead of to the National Trust." This cartoon by Acanthus appeared in *Punch* on 22 January 1947.

"This is my last warning, Charles. If you do not mend your ways I shall leave the estate to you instead of to the National Trust."

would have been cut out of the deal as they were at Audley End. Sir Eric de Normann explained: 'the reason for the presence of the National Trust in the transaction is, I gather, simply to make it acceptable to the present owner'.[16] Nevertheless, it took another two years of difficult negotiation for the scheme to be agreed. On 9 March 1948 Lees-Milne wrote in his diary: 'An awful meeting at the Ministry of Works on the subject of Ham House. The Admiral [Bevir, Secretary of the National Trust] presiding over a baker's dozen . . . of dreary subfusc civil servants and attorneys. How I hate their guts. Little achieved owing to huffing, puffing, um-ing and er-ing.'[17] The Ministry meanwhile resented the Trust's insistence on controlling what was done to the house and gardens, since they believed themselves better qualified to do the job. Eventually, a deal was made and the V&A and the Ministry took over in June 1948. Problematic though it was, Ham became a template for the treatment of Osterley Park, another house offered to the Trust that had no future as a residence. This was also handed over to the Ministry on a long lease, the freehold with the National Trust, and the contents with the V&A.

Saving Audley End was made possible by the favourable attitude of the Labour Chancellor of the Exchequer, Hugh Dalton, who was also in at the start of negotiations over Osterley Park. He realised that the effects of his taxation policy could lead to a deluge of land sales as had happened after the First World War and wanted to find a way of turning the finest land into a public asset. His solution, in 1946, was the National Land Fund, a huge endowment of £50 million that could be used to 'buy some of the best of our still unspoiled open country, and stretches of coast, to be preserved for ever, not for the enjoyment of a few private land-owners, but as a playground and national possession for all our people'.[18] In this he saw the National Trust as a natural partner: he later told the Earl of Crawford, Chairman of the National Trust, that he regarded the Trust as a typically British 'example of Practical Socialism in action'. As such, 'a Labour Government should give it every encouragement greatly to extend its activities'.[19] Dalton did not care much for country houses; his scheme was about the countryside (he had a passion for walking and was later President of the Ramblers Association). Yet houses were on the land and this meant that because the Cotehele estate in Cornwall was bought by the Land Fund, the house would come with it. The National Trust turned up to a meeting in Whitehall to discuss Cotehele, to find the Ministry of Works assuming that it would take over the house. Lord

Mount Edgcumbe, in common with all aristocratic owners of the time, had no intention of handing anything over to the Government and, after a meeting with the minister, and with the support of Hugh Dalton, the house and land passed to the Trust in 1947.[20]

Dalton lost his job at the end of 1947 and was replaced as Chancellor by Stafford Cripps, who retained his former post as Minister for Economic Affairs, concentrating in one pair of hands huge influence over economic affairs. The fate of country houses might not have been expected to be high on his list of priorities, but within his first few weeks in office the Ministry of Works was being asked to provide the Treasury with a list of houses of notable historic or architectural interest that should be 'preserved at all costs'. A list was quickly compiled of fifty-two 'important country houses' in England and Wales that were not already protected by the National Trust, local authorities or the Government. It ranged from twelfth-century Boothby Pagnell to eighteenth-century Compton Verney.[21] Shortly after, another list was produced, of 'typical houses worthy of preservation', which, rather than concentrating on great houses, was aimed at giving a representative selection of the best domestic architecture. In this list of forty-one individual houses, there were, in addition to famous Tudor and Georgian mansions, manor houses (Hemingford Grey), castles (Stokesay) and town houses (44 Berkeley Square). The most recent house on the list was Dodington Park in Gloucestershire, a house by James Wyatt of *circa* 1800. More remarkably, nearly twenty years before protection for conservation areas, examples were given of streets (Broad Street in Ludlow) and groups of houses (the Royal Crescent in Bath, Bedford Square in London) that were worthy of preservation. The inclusion of these groups stemmed from an intimation by Treasury officials that they were prepared to consider acquiring for the nation houses, squares or even a village, if that was what the experts advised.[22]

In the late 1940s, as these requests from the Treasury show, the Government was moving towards a policy for preserving inhabited buildings by taking them into State care, but had not settled on the means of doing so. But one thing was certain: there was now intense rivalry with the National Trust. This is illustrated nicely by the case of Wall in Staffordshire. This small Roman site outside Lichfield, otherwise known as Letocetum, belonged to the Trust but had been neglected in the war years. Lees-Milne visited in April 1947 and wrote in his diary: 'Called at Letocetum which is a lamentable, tumbledown property. The sheds over the Roman remains have collapsed:

the exhibits consist of dusty, broken bits of Roman pottery. The whole place unkempt and uncared for. I would like to blow it up.'[23] As a consequence, the Trust offered guardianship to the Ministry. The Inspector, abrasive Baillie Reynolds, accepting guardianship on behalf of the Ministry, told his colleagues: 'On propaganda grounds, it would be quite a good thing that the National Trust, having had this site in its possession for 20 years, should in the end have to hand it over to us because it cannot maintain it.'[24]

THE GOWERS REPORT

Perhaps wary of being overly influenced by the Ministry, which had its own agenda, Cripps decided that an independent committee should be established 'to consider and report what general arrangements might be made by the Government for the preservation, maintenance and use of houses of outstanding historic or architectural interest which might otherwise not be preserved, including, where desirable, the preservation of a house and its contents as a unity'.[25] Established in December 1948 under the chairmanship of Sir Ernest Gowers, a veteran civil servant, the committee heard evidence from owners of country houses, from amenity societies, the National Trust and the Ministry of Works.

The Ministry moved quickly to establish a policy position, realising that 'the National Trust will make a determined effort to claim this [country house] work and ... we ought to make it clear in greater detail why we regard this Ministry as more qualified to take on the job'. The greater detail was twofold: the Ministry believed that the Trust did not have the money to save the houses and keep them repaired, but, more significantly, did not have the expertise. The Deputy Secretary, Eric de Normann, met Lord Esher to see whether some 'lines of demarcation' could be drawn. The obvious line, suggested by Esher, was between occupied houses that the Trust should take on and 'museum' houses, where there was no family, which should fall to the Ministry. Three days before the men from the Ministry were due to give evidence to the committee they settled their policy: 'it was agreed that we should claim all historic houses as our domain, leaving to the National Trust places of natural beauty', but, they went on, 'As it would be impossible to reach agreement with the National Trust on this basis, Sir Eric de Normann decided not to endeavour to agree a line of demarcation with Lord Esher in advance of consideration by the Gowers Committee.'[26]

De Normann told the committee that the best solution for county houses was continued private ownership and occupation. His department could advise owners, or take their homes into guardianship; as a last resort, the Ministry would be able to facilitate using its experience of providing accommodation for all parts of the public service. He was open-minded about new uses for country houses, for 'nothing ruined a house more than to stand empty'.[27]

The National Trust, which gave evidence at the Gowers Committee's third meeting:

> emphasised that the National Trust were the only National body qualified to hold and administer country houses, with their contents, as an integral unit. The Trust took the view that a house should not be a dead place, but should live and should show the continuity of history and the stratification of taste through the centuries ... Secondly the Trust felt that it enjoyed the confidence of the public and was in a position to do this work, in a way in which no other National body could.

Lord Esher felt 'that the task might become too big for any one body. It was for this reason that the Trust had suggested ... a division whereby uninhabited houses of the museum type might be administered by the Ministry of Works'.[28]

The Gowers Report appeared in June 1950.[29] It strongly asserted the claim that houses of outstanding importance were best preserved privately, occupied by families connected with them. This, the Committee recommended, should be facilitated by generous tax arrangements, in return for public access. Owners (including the National Trust and local authorities) would also be able to benefit from grants or loans provided by new independent statutory bodies called Historic Building Councils. Crucially, it failed to endorse the Ministry's ambition to add occupied houses to its collection of monuments.

Whitehall greeted the report with a chorus of disapproval.[30] The Ministry of Works disagreed with the assumption that the National Trust was the only body capable of preserving the country house as a home and opposed the idea of independent statutory councils. They were also unhappy about the concentration on country houses at the expense of town houses, which also faced problems. The Minister of Works, Richard Stokes, was unimpressed, feeling that his Ancient Monuments Department could deal with the main points of the Report without the need for a new organisation in the form of a historic buildings council. The Treasury, which had commissioned the re-port in the first place, found the taxation proposals unacceptable and rejected the idea of an executive council accountable to the Chancellor. Instead, they proposed their own scheme, in which the work would be handed over to the Ministry of Works, advised by a non-executive council that would deal with ancient monuments as well as historic buildings. 'Houses remaining in the occupation of owners', said the lead Treasury official Dennis Proctor, 'should continue to be dealt with by the NT, who would receive financial assistance from the Ministry of Works.'[31]

NEW LEGISLATION

Although the detailed recommendations of the Gowers Report were largely rejected, it nevertheless provided a stimulus for Government action. In April 1951 the Ministry of Works was asked to prepare a bill along lines decided by the Cabinet. After extensive consultation the Ministry drafted an ambitious and far-reaching set of proposals that sought to solve more than just the prob-lem of country houses (below, p. 201).[32] The bill was more or less ready by the time of the General Election of 1951, but the victory of the Conservatives brought a new minister, David Eccles, and he was not prepared to proceed with it. Eccles was a cultured man, a collector of books, paintings and sculp-ture and a member of the Georgian Group, who might have been expected to support preservation of historic houses but he declared the bill to be 'too Socialist for my liking'.[33] As a result, a simplified bill was introduced focus-ing on the creation of Historic Buildings Councils and new grant-making powers for the Minister of Works. Eccles said at the second reading of the bill that it was 'presented in the belief that half a loaf is better than no bread', asking MPs to see it as 'a start in the right direction'.[34] It had wide support and received Royal Assent in July 1953. Although the act fell a long way short of the ambitions of the Gowers Committee and the intentions of the Ministry, it nevertheless marked the start of a new age in heritage protection.

Crucially, the Historic Buildings Councils and the Ministry were able strategically to support the National Trust's acquisition of houses and, in a small number of cases, agree to subsidise long-term running costs not covered by endowments. Of the twelve taken on in the years 1957–61, for instance, nine were financially assisted through grant aid or acceptance in lieu of tax.[35] Increasingly, the Councils also gave grants to private owners enabling them to repair and re-inhabit their houses. The crisis of the country house was not quite over, but by 1953 a solution existed and the will was there to use it. The number of houses in the care of the National Trust rose rapidly from fifty-two in 1950 to seventy-five in 1960. As far as the Ministry of Works was concerned, a solution had been found but not the one it had expected. The fundamental problem was that it had hugely underestimated the deep hostility of private owners to any suggestion that the Government might take on their houses. The Ministry had assumed that owners would be grateful to have their estates taken off their hands, just as they had been happy to hand over their ruins. That assumption was wrong. In the event the Government did not take on another intact country house with contents as a permanent showplace until 1990, when the Ministry's successor, English Heritage, bought Brodsworth Hall in Yorkshire.

14

WAR AND AFTERMATH
1939–1953

BIG AMBITIONS

The Second World War brought both triumph and defeat for the Ancient Monuments Department. While its inspectors did a remarkable job, dealing ad hoc with the catastrophic effects of bombing and the impact of allied military installations on the home front, it lost the opportunity to become the national ministry for preservation. Instead, protection was split between two ministries, a failure that went on to dog British heritage protection until 1970. The Historic Buildings and Ancient Monuments Act of 1953, however, established machinery that would allow the Ministry, for the first time, to use financial muscle to solve the problems of important buildings rather than simply acquiring them.

In 1940 Winston Churchill appointed Lord Reith to his Cabinet as First Commissioner. Overtly ambitious, combative, autocratic, hugely energetic, the former first Director General of the BBC was never going to be an easy minister. The eccentric architect and conservation campaigner Clough Williams-Ellis, writing in *The Spectator*, observed that 'Hitler had inured the British to large-scale destruction; it was now for Reith to show what dynamite could do when selectively applied in the service of town planning and civic regeneration'.[1] Reith never really wanted to run the Office of Works but saw that its remit could be expanded to take over planning, an area that really interested him. Reith thus engineered a position as Minister Designate, and the Works ceased to be an Office and became a fully fledged Ministry of

John Charles Walsham Reith, 1st Baron Reith, drawn by Sir William Rothenstein. His big ambitions for the Office of Works failed to materialise after he fell out with Winston Churchill. © Estate of Sir William Rothenstein / National Portrait Gallery, London

State. Soon he was gathering around himself the most influential architects and town planners of the time, men such as William Holford. In 1942 he succeeded in transforming his ministry into the Ministry of Works and Planning.

Of course, the Ancient Monuments Department was a tiny part of this. Between 1939 and 1946 numbers of Ministry of Works staff rose from 6,000 to 22,000 and the number of buildings in their orbit of responsibility climbed to approximately 300,000. Yet Reith was interested in preservation and was willing to support his small department in dealing with problems that had never before been faced by conservationists. The bombing of London and provincial cities forced local authorities to make decisions as to which damaged buildings should be saved and which could be demolished, secure in the knowledge that they were not historically significant. The Ancient Monuments Department had not normally been involved with post-medieval urban buildings, but now was forced to organise a scheme that would allow the rapid assessment of thousands of buildings in towns up and down the land.

THE SALVAGE SCHEME

The answer was their Salvage Scheme, which was intended to be a complete survey of the nation's historic building stock, something that had been argued for, in some quarters, since the beginning of the century (above, pp. 60–3). Now it was to take place in the most extreme and pressurised of environments. With the help of the Royal Institute of British Architects (RIBA), the Ministry gathered together 300 architects who were issued with a set of criteria and then asked to tour their localities and assemble lists of the buildings that met them. Lists flooded into the Ministry and, in the space of a year, the whole country had been assessed. The lists were highly variable in quality but they allowed local authorities to notify the Office of Works if a listed building had been damaged. Mostly, notification resulted in the local architect who had compiled the list attending, but in extreme cases one of the Department's specialist architects would attend and give advice.

Where buildings were either completely destroyed or thought to be incapable of repair, the Ministry argued that historic fixtures and fittings, especially fireplaces and decorative woodwork, should be removed and stored. Those that were on a list or in their damaged state revealed greater historic interest or antiquity were repaired or, at least, shored up by local authorities. In a small number of cases the Ministry itself intervened. These were buildings of importance that were badly damaged and on which the owners and the local powers wanted centrally directed expertise. This salvage work was extremely important and saved major historic buildings in Exeter, Canterbury, Bristol, Norwich, Ipswich and elsewhere. The Ministry was heavily involved in the row houses in Great Yarmouth, to their delight discovering the cloister of

The façade of Southernhay West, Exeter, Devon. Margaret Tomlinson, an architect and skilled amateur photographer, was the National Building Record's representative in the south-west in its early days, and took this photograph of a Georgian terrace almost destroyed by bomb damage in 1942. The ruins were later demolished. Reproduced by permission of English Heritage

Greyfriars embedded in later buildings. After the war they were to take on two row houses and a huge quantity of salvaged fittings and open them to the public. Similarly, work in Southampton revealed a spectacular medieval merchant's house, which the Ministry was eventually to turn into an attraction.[2]

The Ministry's inspectors were also heavily involved in rescue excavation. Even before the war, as rearmament ramped up, Government departments wanting to build new facilities were required to check with the Ancient Monuments Department that there were no archaeological remains before work began. From 1940 this became a major strand of work, especially investigating the sites of proposed airfields. The early wartime rescue digs were largely in the west of Britain on prehistoric sites, but by 1942 the Ministry was busy in central and eastern England. At Heathrow, for instance, the laying out of a runway uncovered a Celtic temple, a unique discovery at the time. At least fifty-five rescue excavations took place during the Second World War, setting the precedent for continuing rescue archaeology by the Ministry afterwards. As the bombs dropped Bryan O'Neil, the Chief Inspector, wrote: 'When it is possible to make known to the archaeological world the extent and the results of this work, I am convinced that we shall be universally praised, just as, had we done nothing, we should have been universally criticised as blind to our duty and opportunities.'[3]

Closely aligned to the Salvage Scheme was the creation of the National Buildings Record. This initiative, to make a photographic record of significant urban buildings by the Royal Institute of British Architects, was promoted by the Georgian Group, the SPAB and a number of distinguished architects and historians. They succeeded in persuading Reith to contribute to the project. The Ministry stumped up and, with additional charitable funds, the Record started to take pictures. Photographs were taken on the basis of lists of buildings thought to be important and, by September 1942, 172 towns had completed lists; of these, sixty-seven had already been photographed and twenty-one were in progress. For many places this was too late: the Record managed to capture the interior of only one of the City of London parish churches before so many were gutted in 1940. For those that were photographed, no protection was guaranteed; this was a record, not a route to preservation. Nevertheless, a huge amount was achieved and the Record was transferred, in 1963, to the Royal Commission on the Historical Monuments of England.[4]

LISTING BEGINS

In 1942, having fallen out with Churchill, Reith lost his job and was replaced by Lord Portal of Laverstoke. Almost immediately his department was carved up, and planning was extracted and placed in the new Ministry of Town and Country Planning. This meant that when, in 1944, the Town and Country Planning Act established the listing of buildings of special historic interest as a statutory activity, it was not within the Ministry of Works. The new listing system of 1944 should not be confused with the system that is now called scheduling and which had begun in 1913, described above (pp. 162–3). Scheduling continued within the Ministry of Works, but there was now a parallel system of listing for inhabited buildings in another Government department.

The 1944 Act required an Advisory Committee to be established to give expert advice to ministers. One of its members was John Summerson, who was charged with drafting criteria for the selection of buildings for listing. These emphasised, in particular, completeness of survival of the original fabric and were heavily weighted towards pre-Victorian architecture, giving little weight to vernacular buildings. As a result, although some urban centres were quite well covered, rural areas were severely under-represented.

S. J. Garton, a former Ministry of Works architect, was put in charge of the survey and, in 1947, armed with their instructions, approximately thirty-five investigators (to distinguish them from the Ministry of Works inspectors) embarked on a survey programme envisaged to last for three years. This was very optimistic. In June 1950 the investigators had surveyed around 700 local authority districts and it was estimated that the job would take another five years to complete. Various ideas were adopted to speed up the survey and by 1959 a total of 931 areas had been covered and 275 partly completed. This comprised 73,310 listed buildings.

This activity was seen as part of the planning system: baseline information required by local authorities to make effective decisions. In the 1950s it was not certain that listing would always remain in the Ministry of Town and Country Planning (which turned into the Ministry of Housing and Local Government in 1951) and there was a suspicion that it might return to the Office of Works once the intensive period of post-war reconstruction was over. In 1948 the report of a Government committee responsible for structural reform recommended that there should be a single code for protection administered by a non-governmental body answering to the planning ministry. Yet listing was still in the Town and Country Planning Department in 1950 when the Gowers Committee reported.[5]

The committee noted that it was 'absurd that the preservation of historic buildings should depend on two largely independent codes, overlapping at some points but differing in the departments responsible for them'. Of course it was, and the Ministry of Works, with ministerial support, moved to grab back listing and establish, in a single ministry, the whole apparatus for the protection of the nation's heritage. The draft bill prepared by the Ministry in 1951 thus sought to solve more than just the problem of country houses (above, p. 194). Instructions to Parliamentary Counsel asked that the legislation reduce to a single code the Ancient Monuments Acts and the appropriate sections of the 1947 Town and Country Planning Act. In other words, it proposed to abolish the legal distinction between ancient monuments and historic buildings – between scheduling and listing: 'Neither consolidation nor amendment is proposed', they said, 'It is intended to deal with the whole subject afresh.'[6] When the bill was published in July 1951 it allowed for all the preservation work of the Ministry of Local Government and Planning, including listing, to be transferred to the Ministry of Works so that there was one central authority for preservation.[7] A consent process analogous to planning permission was proposed that would be operated by local councils, except for buildings and monuments that were 'outstanding', or of primarily archaeological interest, which would be dealt with by the Ministry of Works.

As has been seen, the General Election of 1951 brought a new Minister of Works, David Eccles, who did not support the proposals in the draft bill. Fear of losing the legislation altogether meant that the Ministry of Works did not press either its claim to a transfer of powers from the Ministry of Housing and Local Government or the extension of guardianship powers to inhabited houses. A simplified bill was eventually introduced that focused on the creation of Historic Buildings Councils and new grant-making powers for the Minister of Works (below, p. 211).

NATIONALISATION

The Ancient Monuments Department had been relocated to Rhyl in north Wales for most of the war. Its return to London in 1945 marked the beginning of the most frenetic period of collecting in its history. In the few years between 1945 and 1953 its collection of monuments more than doubled; in England alone 101 new sites were accepted for guardianship. Despite this massive expansion, an economic crisis remained; owners were even less able to maintain monuments, many of which had rapidly deteriorated during the war. But there was a new factor, for the men from the Ministry found that, after 1945, they swam with the political tide. During the inter-war years there was still the prevailing assumption that the State should not intervene in private property rights. This view, which had so often held back the Office of Works in their desire both to protect and collect, was no longer dominant. The Labour Government of 1945–51 pursued a policy of nationalisation that brought the Bank of England, cable and wireless, civil aviation, railways and road haulage, health services, coal mines, gas and electricity provision into State ownership. There was no formal policy on the nationalisation of ancient monuments and historic buildings, but the prevailing mood was an assumption that the central government should take increasing control of Britain's heritage.

The model for nationalisation was one in which publicly appointed managers ran monopoly industries in the public interest, but largely autonomously. It was based on the principle of the 'public-minded expert' who could be expected to manage things in a professional and objective way.[8] The protection of the nation's ancient monuments was already in the hands of just such a body of experts. The Inspectorate of Ancient Monuments numbered fourteen in 1947, including the Chief Inspector of Ancient Monuments: eleven inspectors covering England and Wales based in London, and three in Edinburgh.[9] Alongside the Inspectorate was the Architects' Division, five of whom worked on ancient monuments and another two dealt with royal palaces and historic buildings in London. A direct labour force of skilled specialist workmen, mostly masons, worked for the architects. This workforce had been reduced during the war but built up again afterwards and, by 1952, numbered about 450 in England and Wales.

Bryan O'Neil (1905–1954) was appointed Chief Inspector, a post he retained until his early death in 1954. Previously, he had been Inspector for Wales, but had remained in London during the war to help conduct emergency excavations. Described as 'a forceful character and a tireless worker', O'Neil brought to the post a strong belief in the standards and traditions of the Office of Works. In 1948 he said: 'I have bent all my energy to re-establishing this work upon its pre-war basis . . . and also to extending it or at least to laying plans for its extension. It is indeed capable of considerable extension not only in quantity, but also in range.'[10] As will be seen, it was that extension in range that was to begin to characterise the Ministry's work after 1945 (below, p. 217). In this O'Neil was supported by the new Permanent Secretary, Sir Harold Emmerson (1896–1984), a career civil servant who acquired a passion for the Ministry and later wrote its history.[11] He believed that there were 'many other monuments which we should take over in the public interest'.[12]

ECONOMICS AND ACQUISITIONS

Taking a monument into care, whilst the surest way of saving it, was also the most expensive. Although the Department's budget more than doubled between 1945 and 1951, from £119,500 to £300,000, this was not enough to

Chief Inspector Bryan O'Neil, who developed investigative archaeology in the Ancient Monuments Department. Reproduced by permission of English Heritage

cover its rising liabilities. Outstanding commitments in England and Wales were estimated, in October 1950, as £2.3 million. A further increase in budget to £2.7 million had been agreed by March 1953. Such an increase in expenditure against the dark economic background of Austerity Britain was a remarkable achievement. One Mrs Johnstone, the principal Treasury official dealing with the Ministry throughout this period, wrote in reply to the Ministry's warning of additional expenditure on Chiswick House in 1948:

> This is all very well in normal times, but we are not likely to live in 'normal times' for many years to come. It is possible that very soon our first question on having a proposal to spend any money put up to us will be

that favourite question of the BBC's 20 Questions game, 'Can you eat it?', or, reduced to official jargon, 'Will it assist our efforts to alleviate our present economic difficulties?'

She felt that it was likely that the Ministry's inspectors would doubtless be happy to forgo eating for a few weeks

to preserve an obscure tumble-down 17th century hovel but, without wishing to seem a Philistine, it seems to me better that my grandchildren should enjoy a reasonable standard of life and see pictures of old buildings than that they should creep about undernourished, ill-clad and ill-housed scarcely able to appreciate the monuments we have so dutifully left for them.[13]

This was an extremist position taken, perhaps partly tongue in cheek, by a relatively junior official, but it represented concern that the vast influx of monuments that came into Ministry care, reaching its peak in 1950, would eat up huge amounts of money. It is no coincidence that the numbers of buildings entering care started to diminish after the establishment of the Historic Buildings Council in 1953. This enabled the Ministry's policy to switch to supporting owners rather that defaulting to acquisition.

Whilst the Ministry's financial position was remarkably rosy, the same could not be said of many owners. War and then high levels of taxation had extinguished the capacity of many to maintain ancient monuments (above, p. 178). Cecil Binney, the owner of the medieval Duxford Chapel in Cambridgeshire, whose father had bought it with the adjacent public house and repaired it, was delighted in 1948 to learn that the Ministry of Works wanted to take over the building. He had retained the chapel when he sold the pub, to try and save it, and had turned down offers from people who wanted to convert it into a dance hall and a bungalow. The Department were well aware of the predicament of private owners and were not above using their circumstances to force guardianship on them. In 1947 it was agreed that the Inspector of Ancient Monuments for England, Paul Baillie Reynolds, should write a sympathetic letter to the owner of Sawley Abbey in west Yorkshire, in an attempt to extract an offer of guardianship. He wrote to Mr Fattorini that 'it seemed to me possible that with high taxation and enormously increased costs of labour and materials you might not find it practicable to carry on the work however much you might wish to do so. If that were likely to be

Duxford Chapel, Cambridgeshire, was not an untypical ancient monument to be saved after the Second World War. Here it is seen before and during restoration works. Reproduced by permission of English Heritage

the case, would you perhaps consider handing the Abbey over to this Department?'[14] In the same year, Baillie Reynolds suggested in connection with Castle Rising Castle, Norfolk, that, when the Department was in a position to be able to carry out the necessary repairs, 'a detailed report of work required may be useful to frighten the owners into handing over to us'.[15]

Local authorities shared with central government powers under the Ancient Monument Acts, so the Ministry was reluctant to accept properties from them. Yet they had a low opinion of the ability of most authorities to care for monuments. When the Ministry heard that the Earl of Yarborough proposed to sell Conisbrough Castle to the local council, O'Neil thought it would be 'a calamity'. The local authority would be 'unable to do justice to this which is one of the finest castles in England. We should have it.' The council readily agreed to the suggestion of guardianship and effectively had been nothing more than a conduit for the transfer from a private owner to the State. Temple Manor in Strood, Kent, was acquired by the City of

Conisbrough Castle, Yorkshire, as it appeared in its pre-guardianship days. Reproduced by permission of English Heritage

Temple Manor Strood, Kent. A rare example of a Knight's Templar grange built in the 1220s. In a state of utter collapse in 1949, it was willingly given to the Ministry by the local authority in 1950. Reproduced by permission of English Heritage

Rochester in the early 1930s by accident, because it happened to be on land wanted for industrial development. They failed to find any use for the house before the war and a combination of bomb damage and vandalism had reduced it to virtual ruination by 1949. The Ministry had been involved in attempts to find a use for the building in 1934 and had witnessed its decline for fifteen years. 'This is another example of the inadequacy of a local authority,' wrote O'Neil, shortly before an offer of guardianship arrived. The council was not prepared to spend any money on the monument, even with grant aid, and with the threat of a Preservation Order hanging over them guardianship was the easy way out.

Most private owners who gave their ancient monuments to the Ministry genuinely wanted to save them and offered them so that they could receive the right treatment, not simply to relieve themselves of a liability. In some cases this was straightforward pride in their own property, which may have been a family possession for centuries, but there were also owners who had serious antiquarian or archaeological interests. Lord Ilchester, who gave the

Ministry guardianship of Abbotsbury Abbey in Dorset in 1948 (and before the war had given nearby St Catherine's Chapel), was a historian, a trustee of the British Museum and Chairman of the Royal Commission on the Historical Monuments of England. Lord Harlech, the donor of the spectacular Old Oswestry Hill Fort, Shropshire, in 1945, had been First Commissioner of Works from 1931 to 1936 and was later Chairman of the Ancient Monuments Board for England.

Of course, not all owners were benign and altruistic and, in some cases, the Ministry had a full-scale battle on their hands. Their powers were still relatively limited, but *in extremis* they could carry out repairs on behalf of an owner at their own expense. So sometimes work began before guardianship was agreed, as at Bishop's Waltham Palace, Hampshire, and Appuldurcombe House, Isle of Wight, where the Ministry of Labour demolished the roofs and floors to make it safe. The exquisite and beguiling Elizabethan folly Rushton Triangular Lodge, Northamptonshire, had been utterly neglected by its owners, who claimed that any work to the structure, which was in terrible condition, would encourage visitors and disturb birds that they reared for shooting. The case was described as one of 'persistent and deliberate neglect'. The owners did make an attempt to carry out repairs in 1942, but after two more years of decay the Ministry sent their own men, with the approval of the owner, to carry out first-aid work at the Ministry's expense. Voluntary guardianship was finally agreed in 1950.

Where owners could not be won round by any means, the Ministry was still forced to consider a Preservation Order, which is what happened at Horne's Place Chapel, Kent. This is a rare survival of a small domestic chapel of the fourteenth century, attached to a farmhouse on a working farm. When the farm was put up for sale in March 1948, an architect from the Ministry visited the chapel and as a result it was scheduled. This gave the Ministry a stake in its future and, after long deliberation, they wrote to the new owners at the end of 1949, suggesting they carry out repairs costing about £750. The response from Nellie Daines, the owner, was negative. She thought if it were a national monument, the nation should pay for its upkeep. For good measure, she reported that she had considered stripping the roof because tiles were falling off and landing in her yard. She did, however, offer to sell the monument to the Ministry. The Ministry tried to negotiate guardianship, but the owners would not cooperate and gave notice that they were going to strip the roof in June 1950. Three months later a Preservation Order was

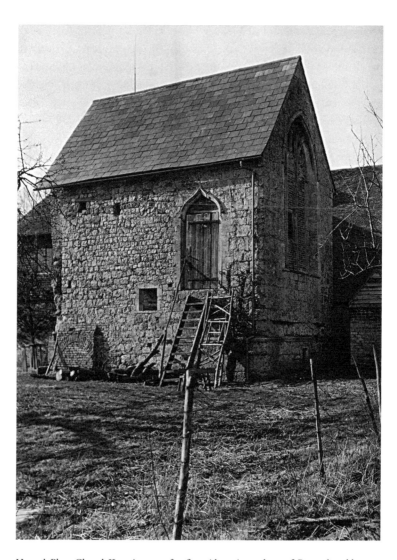

Horne's Place Chapel, Kent, in 1952 after first-aid repairs to the roof. Reproduced by permission of English Heritage

signed by the minister, and on the following day it was delivered by hand to Mr Daines and a copy nailed to the door of the chapel.[16]

Obviously, Mrs Daines wrote in furious objection and Sir Eric de Normann, the Deputy Secretary, recognised this as a 'test case'. 'We shall only look ridiculous, offend the Ancient Monuments Board, and generally encourage other owners to resist' if this case failed, he said. Yet it was going to be hard for the Ministry to press the case because Parliament was awaiting a ministerial response to the Gowers Report (see above, p. 194). For the Minister of Works to bring forward a bill for the preservation of a small, obscure and disused chapel at greater expense than the cost of purchasing it was thought to be highly embarrassing. The Ministry started emergency works on site and in the end persuaded the owner to accept both the Preservation Order and compulsory guardianship without the need for a special Act of Parliament.

In this case the Ministry had been quick to issue a Preservation Order, before any serious negotiation had taken place. The owners' attitude was equally confrontational, but at heart it was a refusal to be told what to do by the men from the Ministry. Mr Daines was quoted in the *Evening News* as saying: 'visitors to the district sometimes asked permission to look over the old chapel, and I always agreed. But having to admit people by Government order is a different matter.'[17]

THE HISTORIC BUILDINGS COUNCIL

The Historic Buildings and Ancient Monuments Act of 1953 gave new powers to the Minister of Works for grant aiding and the acquisition of historic buildings. This was a fundamental change of direction for the Ministry of Works, since it meant that in the future there would be less reliance on taking monuments and buildings permanently into care as a means of preservation.[18] The principal motivation behind the act was the preservation of country houses (above, p. 194), preferably in use and still occupied by their traditional owners. Legislation was needed because inhabited houses had been excluded from the provisions of the Ancient Monuments Acts relating to grant aid and to guardianship.[19] As in the Ancient Monuments Acts, the definition of eligibility in the 1953 Act was as broad as possible. It covered any buildings that appeared to the Minister of Works to be 'of outstanding historic or architectural interest' and, with country houses particularly in mind, 'any land comprising, or contiguous or adjacent to, any such building' or 'any objects ordinarily kept in any such building'.[20] Unlike the Ancient Monuments Acts, no exclusions were made, though churches would only be grant aided in exceptional circumstances.[21]

Ministers feared that setting up as a grant giver would result in a stampede of applicants, and so as 'a powerful buffer'[22] between ministers and owners the 1953 Act created Historic Buildings Councils, for England, Scotland and Wales. These were to advise on grants, the acquisition of buildings and on finding new uses for redundant structures.[23] The membership of the Councils came from the ranks of 'the great and the good', including MPs, aristocrats, architects and architectural historians. Members of the first Council for England included the Earl of Euston (later Duke of Grafton), Sir William Holford, Christopher Hussey and John Summerson. The first chairman was Sir Alan Lascelles (1887–1981), who had served the royal family since 1920, latterly as Private Secretary to Queen Elizabeth II. The Councils had no staff of their own and relied on the inspectors for expert advice on casework.

Remarkably, the Councils were given a new ring-fenced annual budget of £250,000 within the ancient monuments vote of the Ministry. This rose to £350,000 in 1955–6 and to £400,000 in 1959–60. When setting the original allocation, David Eccles had talked of the scheme as a pilot, which would lead to a bigger operation when money allowed. Although the budget continued to rise gently, reaching £700,000 in 1970, successive annual reports of the Historic Buildings Council bemoan the inadequacy of the fund.

In 1954, the first full year of the Council's work, 342 applications for grants were received and 287 grants were offered, to a total value of £268,054. They ranged in value from just £100 for the restoration of wall paintings in a medieval house in Hemel Hempstead to £17,000 for repairs at Gosfield Hall, Essex, the first building to be listed in 1946. The act also gave powers under which the minister could acquire a historic building, but this was seen as a last resort, and it was clear that the Historic Buildings Council cash was not going to be used for adding to the Ministry's collection. Buildings were acquired so that they could be repaired and passed onto a new user. To make this possible the Ministry set up a Historic Buildings Bureau with the role of 'finding new uses for [unoccupied] historic buildings and collecting information about organisations which might be able to use such buildings'.[24]

A house that tested this new system was Cobham Hall, Kent, home of the Earl of Darnley. His trustees were finding it increasingly difficult to maintain this very large Jacobean house and, in 1954, the Historic Buildings Council was informed that public acquisition of the house and contents might soon be necessary. Various options were considered: purchase of the house by the Ministry, conversion into flats and transfer to the National Trust. The financial projections, however, showed there would be an annual shortfall of £3,000 if the Trust were to take it on and the Council had no appetite for granting an annual subsidy. Instead, a repair grant of £25,000 was offered to Lord Darnley, which he rejected, because it committed his successors to maintain the house. So Cobham Hall was put on the market and the Historic Buildings Bureau was asked to look for a purchaser.

At first, a buyer was found who wished to turn the house into a school, but the sale fell through. The Bureau concluded that no one would buy the place, but if the Ministry bought and repaired it, there should be little difficulty in finding a tenant. This was an entirely new approach, one that was to be replicated many times subsequently and still forms one of the options that the Ministry's successor, English Heritage, occasionally performs. It was a course supported by the Historic Buildings Council, and in December 1957 the minister (Hugh Molson) agreed to proceed with the purchase of the house and contents, with a view to letting it, either for use as a school or to Mutual Households Ltd as retirement homes.

Cobham Hall was thought worth saving, yet not quite 'first class'. Dyrham Park in Gloucestershire, by contrast, was considered one of the fifty-two greatest houses in England and Wales on the Ministry's list of 1948. It was one of many houses offered to the Treasury in the 1950s in settlement of death duties, but its owner fell foul of the rule that the Treasury could not accept property that was more valuable than the duty payable. A potential solution might have been to sell some of the contents, reducing the value of the estate, but one of the main aims of the 1953 Act was to prevent the breakup of first-class houses and their contents. Dyrham had remained in the Blathwayt family since the end of the seventeenth century, and house and contents together were widely recognised as creating a uniquely important ensemble. So when a large part of the Blathwayt collection was put up for sale at Sotheby's in 1956 the Historic Buildings Council asked the Minister of Works to buy the house, its land and the most important contents. Treasury approval was secured on the basis that the Ministry of Works would repair the house, convert parts of it into flats (to provide an income in the absence of an endowment) and then hand it over to the National Trust to be shown to the public. In 1957 the house and 12 acres of land were bought for just £5,000 and the contents for £42,000; in June 1961 it was opened to the public.

Although hundreds of country houses were demolished during the 1950s, in the 1960s the rate slowed down. The economic fortunes of landowners picked up and due to a liberalisation of the planning system the capital value of estates soared. Bits of land were sliced off and lucratively sold to housing developers; farms were taken back in hand; and some houses abandoned after the war were refurbished and reoccupied. Enterprising owners began to open their houses to the public and, after 1950, increasing numbers imitated the National Trust and a handful of private owners who were making a commercial success out of tourism.[25] As a result, the Ministry's powers to acquire historic buildings went unused during much of the 1960s (although some contents were purchased for National Trust houses) and it was only in 1969 that the power needed to be exercised again, to save Heveningham Hall in Suffolk. Heveningham was designed by Sir Robert Taylor and completed by James Wyatt, who also designed furniture for the house; Capability Brown laid out the park. Together, the park, house and contents formed an important ensemble of late eighteenth-century design.

The owners, the Vanneck trustees, were unable to find a purchaser for the property as a whole, even with the help of the Historic Buildings Bureau, so they decided to sell the contents and sought permission to demolish the house. The Georgian Group started a campaign to save Heveningham and the Historic Buildings Council recommended acquisition by the Government as the last resort. The National Trust was asked to accept it, but declined, unless they could be guaranteed against financial loss (in the event of being unable to find a tenant). The Ministry of Housing and Local Government was therefore caught between the public outcry that would have resulted from demolition of the house and the risk of having an expensive 'white elephant' on its hands. Lord Kennet reportedly had strong views on the importance of Heveningham and in 1969 the decision was taken to negotiate for the purchase of the house, the Wyatt furniture and 477 acres of land. The sale was completed on 5 August 1970 for £300,000.

These cases demonstrate that, from 1953, the Ministry of Works began to be a very different organisation. Before 1913 the only real power the Office had to save sites was acquisition, but the 1913 Act had added the mechanism of scheduling and the power to issue a Preservation Order, yet State acquisition was still seen to be the most secure route to preservation. In 1944 the establishment of listing brought an entirely new route for preservation, albeit one exercised in another part of Government, and in 1953 grant schemes administered through the Historic Buildings Councils finally began to re-orientate the Ministry away from acquisition. The Ministry now could use targeted grants to save buildings and encourage responsible behaviour. This was not the only change; just as fundamental was a recalibration of their views on what was 'first-rate' heritage. In the years 1945 to 1970 the inspectors joined in with a general reassessment of what components really comprised the nation's history.

15

THE MINISTRY BRANCHES OUT
1953–1970

NEW FACES, NEW IDEAS

In the later 1950s the austerity of the immediate post-war years was left behind as the British economy boomed. Spending on the National Heritage Collection, however, was tightly restricted and the post-war expansionist ambitions of the Inspectorate were stifled. Whereas in the years 1945–53 the English collection of monuments had grown at an average of ten a year, the annual growth over the period 1953–70 was less than half that. Nevertheless, eighty-one new monuments were taken into care in the period.

The post of Chief Inspector was filled by two men with a record of long service in the Inspectorate, ensuring strong continuity of ethos: Paul Baillie Reynolds (1896–1973) became Chief Inspector on the sudden death of Bryan O'Neil in 1954. He was a Classical scholar and archaeologist who had joined the inspectorate in 1934 from a teaching post at Aberystwyth. He served with the Royal Artillery during the years 1939–45 but returned after the war to become Inspector of Ancient Monuments for England. When he succeeded as Chief Inspector, a new Assistant Chief Inspector post was created, and it was filled by Arnold Taylor (1911–2002). Taylor was a medieval scholar, archaeologist and architectural historian, an international expert on European castle building. He had joined the Inspectorate in 1935, becoming Inspector for Wales before assuming the title of Chief Inspector in 1961.[1]

In the immediate post-war years there was a surge of academic interest in cultural, social and economic history at the expense of more traditional spheres of political and constitutional history. Up until this point, in many senses, the Ministry had epitomised the official version of the national story, one dominated by castles, palaces, monasteries and churches. Guidebooks and official publications emphasised the grand, national narrative in which the Ministry's sites took the stage one by one. This is why the National Heritage Collection had been founded in 1913; it was the great outdoor museum of the national story, containing in 1945 the buildings of the establishment and the ruling classes.

But the interests of the young men and women coming out of the universities, and the more adventurous of their teachers, were now in local history, agrarian history, working-class history, historical geography and economic history. The book that sums up the change in historical orientation for so many younger scholars of the day was E. P. Thompson's *The Making of the English Working Class*, published in 1963, an 800-page narrative describing the creation of a self-conscious working class in England between 1790 and 1832. His range of sources was huge, diverse and unexpected. In the introduction he staked a claim for a new sort of history 'from below'. Changing academic perspectives in the libraries took place at the same time as fundamental changes in the archaeological trenches. At the very time when historians were broadening their range of sources and interests to include archaeology, archaeologists themselves were getting to grips with deep medieval stratigraphy in towns. From 1946 William Grimes was leading the excavation of bombed-out parts of the medieval and Roman city of London; this work was followed in other blitzed cities such as Exeter, Southampton and Canterbury. These digs, which revealed the complex multi-layered stories of these towns from the Romans to the nineteenth century, hugely raised the importance, interest and value of medieval archaeology. Though R.J.C. Atkinson's *Field Archaeology*, the best-selling archaeological text of its age, published in 1946, did not mention medieval archaeology, only a few years later it was where the exciting digging really was.[2]

The men from the Ministry shared in this thinking. Though grounded in the inter-war disciplines of standing medieval archaeology in castles and abbeys and the buried archaeology of prehistory, they now became intensely interested in medieval archaeology, post-medieval archaeology, industrial archaeology and landscape. Their interests, whilst rooted in the academic fashions of the day, were also responding to popular trends. During the 1960s there was a popular revival of interest in history. People started to appreci-

More than any other building, the Euston Arch in London represented the failure of Government policy to protect significant buildings in the 1960s. © English Heritage Photo Library

ate railways, gasometers, canals, warehouses, railway stations and old tractors. There was a genuine sense of public outrage when the Prime Minister refused to intervene and save the huge Victorian Doric portico that stood in front of Euston Station. People became fascinated by antiques, a trend epitomised by the long-running TV show *Going for A Song* presented by the antique dealer Arthur Negus from 1965. From 1960 there was also a huge surge in history publishing that was sustained through the 1970s and grew in the 1980s.[3]

These streams of thought and interest came to influence the Ministry's policies towards preservation during the 1960s and 1970s, most visibly in a change in attitude to medieval settlements and industrial remains.

Immediately after the war the Chief Inspector, Bryan O'Neil, felt that his department should take a more strategic approach to acquisitions, focusing on a small number of first-class sites. In 1949 he drew up a list of targets under four headings: Norman keeps, other medieval castles, pre-Norman churches and medieval monasteries. Progress on the last category was almost instant, three of the eighteen entries being taken over within three years, at which point O'Neil wrote that 'the day is perhaps not far distant when we shall be able to say that we have in our charge all the most important monastic remains in England and Wales'. But the Inspectorate recognised that this was increasingly regarded as a limited representation of national culture. As will be seen, attempts to widen the type of buildings taken into care were at first frustrated by politicians, but O'Neil's successors were increasingly successful at pushing the boundaries.

In 1956, because the Ministry's Scottish branch could no longer afford to take on new monuments, a review of the acquisition policy was ordered. It was to report to the Conservative Minister, Patrick Buchan-Hepburn (1901–1974), a connoisseur of art and architecture and a future chairman of the Historic Buildings Council (1963–73). He wanted to see firm criteria to steer acquisitions and so the Chief Inspector, Baillie Reynolds, was asked to create two lists, one of first-class monuments that were so important they would have to be accepted if offered to the Ministry, and a longer one of monuments that were regarded as desirable as having. In comparison to the list created a few years earlier by O'Neil, Paul Baillie Reynolds's first list was shorter and the second list broader. The first comprised only six monuments, all medieval: Fountains Abbey, Corfe Castle, Ludlow Castle, Wingfield Manor, Stokesay Castle and Bolton Castle. The longer list contained 116 monuments, broken down into categories: long barrows, round barrows, henge monuments, camps, settlements, Roman, linear earthworks, monasteries, chapels and churches, gatehouses, castles, city walls, other secular buildings, mills, barns and bridges. The two largest categories were still castles (forty-eight listed) and monasteries (twenty listed), and although the other half of this list contained a slightly wider range of types, no industrial monuments or medieval field monuments were included.

✳

Industrialisation had been one of the most significant factors behind the birth of the conservation movement and so for conservationists to want to preserve its monuments was, inevitably, going to take some time. The Newcomen Society was founded in 1920 to study the history of engineering and technology. It was named after Thomas Newcomen, who invented the first practicable steam engine in what was then a respectably distant 1712. The Royal Commission on Historical Monuments had also taken an interest in industrial buildings, but it took a very long time to make industrial archaeology more than what the *Economist* magazine called 'a hobby for harmless lunatics'.[4] The ancient mills expert Rex Wailes complained in the early 1960s of the difficulty of getting industrial archaeology taken seriously, writing: 'It usually takes two generations to get an idea of this sort across, and if we take the foundation of the Newcomen Society in 1920 as the start we can expect that our efforts, at present regarded as mildly curious by the uninitiated, will be enthusiastically accepted by 1970.'[5]

Bryan O'Neil was a member of the Newcomen Society and saw that one of the greatest post-war threats would be to early industrial equipment upon which he thought 'the Empire was built'. This was a very forward-looking point of view and he had to persuade the Ancient Monuments Board, in 1947, that industrial remains could be treated as ancient monuments and that they should, in principle, schedule the best examples. In 1951 the Board discussed industrial monuments and expressed the view that 'the Minister should use all his power to preserve important relics of this nature'.[6]

The first attempt to take over such a monument was Morley Park Ironworks in Derbyshire, where two blast furnaces were the surviving remnants of a large iron smelting works, abandoned in what was now a rural landscape. After visiting in 1949, O'Neil recommended acceptance if an offer of guardianship were made, but he could say only that such structures *seemed* rare (and therefore important) because, unlike more traditional types of monument, research on early industrial monuments had not yet been undertaken. When asked to rank the furnaces against other current possible acquisitions, he put them above Bury St Edmunds Abbey. While the civil servants were prepared to break new ground by accepting an ironworks, the politicians were not. The works were rejected for guardianship in 1951 after the intervention of Robert, Lord Morrison, the Parliamentary Under Secretary at the Ministry,

Morley Park Ironworks, Derbyshire, represented the scale of the problem of saving major industrial infrastructure. Reproduced by permission of English Heritage

who convinced the minister, Richard Stokes, that 'once we start making ancient monuments of old industrial buildings we are committing ourselves to a lot of expense in the future'. The following year the new minister, David Eccles, said that he liked 'the idea of preserving some of the best bits of the industrial revolution', but would not approve the necessary expenditure.

Although the monuments of heavy industry were politically unacceptable, the Ministry was successful in taking on a number of mills. Windmills were rapidly falling out of use and it was felt that some significant examples should be secured while still in working order. Yet, again, the Inspectorate found that they did not have the necessary research to determine priorities. They turned to the SPAB, who had founded a mills section in 1929 and had a considerable database. A list drawn up by the Mills Section for the Ministry put Berney Arms Windmill in Norfolk as number one because it had been offered to the society as a gift. Meanwhile the mills expert, Rex Wailes, convinced O'Neil of the importance of Saxtead Green Post Mill, Suffolk. A start was made by taking over these two in 1950 and 1951, respectively.[7] After O'Neil's death in 1954, consideration of Sibsey Trader Mill in Lincolnshire, the gift of which to the Ministry had fallen though at the last minute, was left to the new Chief

Inspector, Baillie Reynolds, to determine. He wrote that 'in general I do not want to take over any more windmills',[8] and then, in 1955,

> I think you know my views, which are not the same as those of the late Chief Inspector. I am in agreement with him in that I think it very desirable that certain early sites, which preserve in fair condition evidence of the beginnings of the Industrial Revolution, should be preserved. But I do not consider that the A. M. Branch of M.O.W. is the right body to undertake the preservation.[9]

Reynolds recognised that, while the Inspectorate was the leading body on medieval monuments, they had no expertise in industrial remains, particularly since so many contained working plant and machinery that nobody in the Ministry understood. Moreover, industrial remains were, he thought, expensive to maintain, especially if they were to be kept in working order.[10] As a result, the Ministry did not acquire any industrial building between 1953 and 1974.

In those twenty-odd years industrial archaeology was transformed to a proper academic discipline. In 1973 the Association for Industrial Archaeology was founded and thousands of people were mobilised, not only in academic institutions, but also in local societies, trusts and museums, to study, preserve and enjoy industrial monuments. Already in the 1930s the Science Museum was receiving 1.25 million visitors, and thirty years later the first of the open-air museums were being considered. The Beamish Museum of industrial life was proposed in 1958 and opened in 1970. The Ministry was not only aware of these developments but also encouraged them and participated in them. They gradually developed a strategy that scheduled threatened sites and then left preservation to local charitable societies to which the Ministry was prepared to grant aid. The ironworks of Wortley Top Forge near Sheffield exemplified this approach. When it was threatened with destruction, the site was scheduled, but the offer of guardianship was turned down. Instead, the Sheffield Trades Historical Society took over the ironworks in 1953 and was given advice on repair. The society struggled to maintain the site and later asked again that it be taken into guardianship. The Department responded with a 50 per cent grant of up to £6,250 to pay for the repairs.

By 1957 only six early industrial monuments had been scheduled and none was in guardianship.[11] Although the views of Reynolds prevailed, the Permanent Secretary, Edward Muir, was keen to take some action, and the

Science Museum and the Newcomen Society were invited to draw up lists of monuments that they believed should be considered for protection. The Science Museum's list comprised pumping engines, workers' cottages, an eighteenth-century industrial hamlet, a tide mill and a blast furnace. The Newcomen Society added beam engines, a gasworks and a railway station.

In 1959 the Council for British Archaeology (CBA), which had been founded in 1944 to campaign for better protection and promotion of archaeological remains, convened a conference on industrial monuments. Participants argued that the Ministry needed a proper published policy for industrial heritage. To set the ball rolling they agreed with Staffordshire County Council to start a pilot survey of industrial monuments in the county. This made slow progress and it was decided instead to set up a national survey using volunteers from their 300 affiliated organisations. Recognising the urgent need for such an exercise, the Ministry agreed to pay Rex Wailes as coordinator. Wailes (1901–1986), an engineer by training, was the foremost expert in watermills and a founder member of the SPAB Windmills Section, and under his guidance the National Survey of Industrial Monuments got under way in 1963. But it was all too late; ministers were agitating for a policy and questions were asked in the House of Commons.[12]

The Ministry, taking the early results of the survey, put forward a straightforward policy: henceforth, industrial monuments would be treated the same as any other monument class and £5,000 was earmarked for work on industrial monuments in 1966–7. This was announced in the House of Commons in May 1966 in response to an arranged question.[13] Dr Maurice Craig became the focal point in the Inspectorate for all industrial casework. This was not really a new policy – it was the formalisation of the approach that had begun in the early 1950s. The Historic Buildings Council had offered grants to industrial sites throughout the 1960s, including Holton Mill in Suffolk, the Dundas Aqueduct and Crofton Pumping Station, both on the Kennet and Avon Canal, a group of four Cornish engine houses and the Round House in Camden, London. The Ancient Monuments Board had also handed out cash to windmills, viaducts and the remains of heavy industry, nineteen industrial monuments in all.[14]

By 1974 more than 300 industrial sites had been scheduled, but none had been added to the National Heritage Collection. That year, Neil Cossons, Director of the Ironbridge Gorge Museums Trust, and a future chairman of English Heritage, writing in the *Museums Journal,* rightly observed: 'It is in-

The 'preserve as found' interior of Stott Park Bobbin Mill, Cumbria. © English Heritage

conceivable that the State could take into guardianship more than a handful
of industrial sites and even a small scale commitment would require massive
finance which does not exist.'[15] Yet that was the year that the Ministry took
on its only working industrial site (other than wind and watermills). Stott
Park Bobbin Mill, Cumbria, started producing wooden bobbins for the Lancashire weaving and spinning industries in 1835 and ceased production only
in October 1971. It was a trade that had once dominated the area, but Stott
Park was the last complete example of its type to survive. The mill first came
to the attention of the Ministry in February 1972, when the Lake District
Planning Board gave notice of an application to convert it into residential
use. To prevent the conversion, the Department scheduled the mill and ne-
gotiated purchase with the owners. The sale was finalised in June 1974 and

work began on repairing the buildings and refurbishing the machinery. Some of the former millworkers helped to compile a comprehensive manual for the operation of the mill and local people helped the Department to gather information on the history of the mill and its community.

The bobbin mill was acquired because, although it was not architecturally significant, it had remained virtually untouched since production ceased and so enabled the Department to present it 'as the men had left it on their last day of work'.[16] As such, it fulfilled Bryan O'Neil's criterion expressed back in 1953. 'I am always on the look out' for industrial monuments suitable for guardianship, he said, 'but find them desperately few and rapidly disintegrating ... I will not deal ... with scraps or with ruins. I want whole buildings with their gear, preferably just out of use for the last time, like Berney Arms Mill near Great Yarmouth.' Stott Park Bobbin Mill, complete and working, still shows to the public the processes and machinery of the industrial age.

MEDIEVAL ARCHAEOLOGY

As has been seen, investigative archaeology developed in the Office of Works in the 1920s and 1930s, but the Department's work during the Second World War had changed everything. The huge efforts directed to rescue archaeology had brought inspectors face to face with a much wider chronological spectrum of archaeological remains. Medieval archaeology was no longer seen as a poor relation, but rather as one of the prime areas for detailed investigation. So much progress had been made with documentary work, and in the collections of museums, that it was felt time that the archaeologists caught up. As a result, in 1957 the Society for Medieval Archaeology was founded. Amongst its founding members were a large number of inspectors, including the future Chief Inspector, Andrew Saunders, and John Hurst, who would go on to take the lead in medieval archaeology for the Ministry.

Hurst, together with Maurice Beresford of Leeds University, were the leading figures in the Deserted Medieval Village Research Group, one of the manifestations of the intense contemporary interest in medieval landscape and archaeology. In 1953 they estimated that there were about 1,300 deserted villages of all sizes in England, only thirty of which had been excavated, with another nine excavations in progress.[17] Many sites were threatened by housing, road developments and intensive agriculture. Rescue excavations were carried out at many sites, with help from the Ministry, which was also able to protect by scheduling. By the end of 1958 the number of known sites had increased to more than 1,600, and 109 had been scheduled.[18] In a memorandum to the Chief Inspector in 1965, the Research Group recommended that the six best surviving sites should be taken into guardianship as soon as possible; a further eight should be considered for eventual guardianship and forty more should be scheduled and some means of preservation found for them.[19] The sites identified as the prime targets for guardianship were Wharram Percy in Yorkshire, Gainsthorpe in Lincolnshire, Ingarsby in Leicestershire, Broadstone in Oxfordshire, Godwick or Pudding Norton in Norfolk, Gomeldon in Wiltshire and Hound Tor in Devon.

It was exactly this sort of prioritisation that had been concurrently attempted in regard to industrial sites. The Ministry and Arnold Taylor, the Chief Inspector, were very clear that the Group had done them a huge favour, first in identifying the problem and then in drawing up lists of sites for protection. In 1966 the Ancient Monuments Board agreed that the six most important sites should be taken into guardianship. Hound Tor and Wharram Percy came in 1972 and Gainsthorpe in 1974. From that moment the coffers of what had by then become the Department of the Environment were opened up. For twenty years excavation at Wharram had been undertaken without State funding, but from 1979 there began a formal partnership between the Ministry and Philip Rahtz of the University of York. This work and the sites, presented to the public, brought, for the first time, the lives of medieval peasants to the general public.

REDUNDANT CHURCHES

Ever since the 1913 Act had excluded any churches in use, the Office of Works had expected the Church of England to take responsibility for the maintenance of its own property, even where it was not in use for worship. The handful of church buildings that came into its care had been given by private owners, rather than the Church authorities, and their most recent use was more often agricultural than ecclesiastical. By the 1940s, however, there was a clear and growing problem, exacerbated by neglect and bomb damage during the war, of churches that could no longer be maintained by the parish and yet were of national importance.

In 1949 a report to the Church Assembly recommended that the Church of England should make the necessary legislative amendments to allow

John Hurst (seated in the centre right of the photograph) excavating on House 10 at Wharram Percy, Yorkshire, in 1955. Innovative open-area excavation – a technique borrowed from Scandinavia – produced one of the first exposures of an English medieval peasant house. © Wharram Research Project

churches of national significance to be offered to the Ministry, if no other future could be found for them. The Ancient Monuments Department were enthusiastic. Bryan O'Neil thought they should certainly take a choice selection of the best buildings, because 'the English-speaking world will be much poorer, since we shall lose a very large number of first-class medieval buildings'.[20] Fifty churches were selected from lists submitted by dioceses as definitely worthy of guardianship and another thirty-one were classed as 'undecided'. They were a mixed group, almost all medieval in origin, but including some that were thoroughly restored in the nineteenth century. Although active negotiations were taking place only with the Anglican Church, the Ministry felt that they would 'have to look with strict impartiality at the edifices of all denominations, having regard only to the historic and architectural importance'.[21]

Treasury officials, however, refused to make special provision for one particular building type and the Ministry would not take on the problem without extra funds. Instead of being able to embark on a new policy of acquiring the most important closed churches, the Ministry restricted itself over the next twenty years to taking on only ruined churches or non-parochial chapels.

Brinkburn Priory in Northumberland is one of the buildings that suffered from the Ministry's nervousness about setting a precedent for redundant churches. It was a well-preserved Augustinian priory church, which had been re-roofed in the nineteenth century. Although it had been a parish church up until the First World War and continued in occasional use into the 1950s, it had always been in private ownership. In 1950 it was offered to the Ministry, but because there was occasional use the Ministry steered clear of taking it on. After years of worsening condition, the Inspector Roy Gilyard-Beer visited the church in 1961 and wrote: 'the building is abandoned, the first windows have been broken and the time when it will become derelict is not far away'. This finally spurred the Ministry into action and an offer of gift was accepted in April 1962.

The larger problem had not, of course, gone away and it was inevitable that further attempts would be made to resolve it. In 1958 the archbishops of Canterbury and York established a commission under the chairmanship of Edward Bridges to enquire into the question of disused churches once more. Its conclusion, published in 1960 (and generally known as the Bridges Report), was that a new statutory system was needed to replace the existing patchwork of procedures, which dealt with important churches no longer needed for worship. The report estimated that some 370 Anglican churches were redundant and a further 420 might close in the next fifteen to twenty years. Of these, it suggested that between 300 and 400 churches might be taken over by a new body called the Redundant Churches Fund if no other use could be found for them. While the purpose of the fund was to be the upkeep of historic churches as monuments, it was recommended that the Government should also take over a small number of churches that were of 'such exceptional architectural quality as to deserve in particular the exquisite care for detail and surroundings which the Ministry of Works knows so well how to give, and in general a higher standard of restoration and maintenance than the trustees of the Fund might be able to afford'.[22]

It was recognised, as it had been in 1949, that guardianship would not be acceptable to the Church of England because it was irrevocable and precluded any return to regular ecclesiastical use. Instead, it was recommended

Brinkburn Priory, Northumberland. Reproduced by permission of English Heritage

that churches should be passed over as gifts since there was no legal bar to the minister returning a gift. The legislation was enacted in 1968 as the Pastoral Measure. It would not be until 1975 that the first transfer of a church under the Measure was completed and it was later admitted that the Department never really developed a satisfactory policy on redundant churches.[23] Nevertheless, in the second half of the 1970s, three outstanding parish churches came into the National Heritage Collection as gifts: St Mary, Studley Royal (1975), St Peter, Barton-upon-Humber (1976), and St Mary, Kempley (1979). In addition, the Nonconformist Goodshaw Chapel in Lancashire, which had been picked out by the Royal Commission expert Christopher Stell as particularly worthy of preservation, was given to the Government in 1976.

GEORGIAN BUILDINGS

In 1944 the section of the SPAB that had been campaigning for the protection of eighteenth-century buildings broke away and became a separate organisation: the Georgian Group. As the new planning system emerged the Group found that it did not have the resources to campaign on a wide front and decided to focus on individual cases. Appuldurcombe House was brought to the attention of the Ministry in 1947 when its owner announced his intention to demolish it. While this was saved by the Ministry, two other cases promoted by the group, Great Witley Parish Church, Worcestershire, and Dodington Park Chapel, Cheshire, were not. A partnership between the two bodies, however, saved Mistley Towers in Essex, which was offered to the Ministry in 1952, and came into guardianship after being repaired by the Georgian Group, with Raymond Erith acting as their architect.[24]

The big project, however, was Chiswick House. The Palladian villa of Lord Burlington that is now regarded with such reverence as one of the seminal buildings of the early eighteenth century was not in the nineteenth thought to be remarkable or important. Indeed, so far had it fallen from fashion that after the private lunatic asylum that had occupied it moved out in 1929, the 9th Duke of Devonshire contemplated selling the house and gardens for housing development. In 1929 the estate was bought by Middlesex County Council to prevent this, but neither they, nor Chiswick and Brentford Borough Council, to which it was leased, were able to maintain it. In 1938 they were looking to dispose of the house, but the war intervened. In 1947 the architect Claud Phillimore described the scene at Chiswick evocatively: 'The house is battered by bombs and corroded by dry-rot and disuse. The temples are crumbling, the statues decayed, while the walks and groves which they once graced and emphasised degenerate daily.'[25]

Phillimore, however, had a plan, which he promoted energetically to anyone who would listen, including the Ministry of Works. It was to remove the substantial wings that had been added by John White in 1788, in order to reduce the house to more manageable proportions and to restore it to its original state as left by Lord Burlington. It was felt that the importance of the original building could justify such a move, and since the villa was so well documented, it could be recreated where necessary, without resorting to conjecture. Phillimore compared the situation to that of the Queen's House at Greenwich, the restoration of which he believed no one could regret and which 'was achieved only by the ruthless removal of modern additions'.[26]

Inigo Jones's Queen's House had been the Office of Works' only important previous excursion into the world of iconic classical buildings. In 1934 the Office of Works had been responsible for preparing it for the new National Maritime Museum's occupation and later accretions were ruthlessly removed under the guidance of their Inspector, George Chettle, who was, like Sir Frank Baines, an architect from the office of C. R. Ashbee. Most significantly, the buildings that had blocked the original central roadway were demolished, reopening the east–west vista. The interiors were also radically

Chiswick House, London, showing the wings added to the house in 1788 by John White for the Fifth Duke of Devonshire. The wings were demolished by the Ministry with the support of the Georgian Group. Reproduced by permission of English Heritage

remodelled, returning them to their arrangement in the 1660s. The building was reopened in 1937 as a picture gallery for the new museum.[27]

The Queen's House was not really a parallel for Chiswick since that proposal involved the destruction of the fine 150-year-old wings to create a building that had never existed. Burlington's Chiswick House had always been joined to his Jacobean mansion next door, which was knocked down in 1788, when the wings were built. Chettle, though, was hugely enthusiastic: 'Burlington's villa, restored', he said, 'would be as perfect a gem of architectural beauty as Inigo Jones' miniature palace at Greenwich and could have its own perfect setting, which the Queen's House has lost. Its only rival would be the Petit Trianon at Versailles.' The plan, now supported by the Ministry, was supported by the Georgian Group, but opposed by the London County Council, the SPAB and the Royal Fine Art Commission. There were practical arguments about the usefulness of the rooms within the wings and their state of repair, but the fundamental issues were whether the wings had architectural and historical value in themselves and how important it was to preserve them as part of the building's historical development. The Ministry of Works, which was offered the house as a gift on 9 July 1947, came down in favour of a slightly modified version of the Phillimore plan. Demolition began before the transfer of the property had been completed.

The Chiswick project heralded a newly uncompromising attitude within the Ministry of Works, one that Charles Peers would not have condoned, and one born of assured confidence in their expertise and powers – and one that was to come to define their activities in the 1970s.

BOOM AND BUST
1970–1982

CONSERVATION AREAS

The growth in private car ownership that had facilitated the expansion of the Office of Works' portfolio of sites between the wars, and which had brought millions of visitors to them, turned, in the 1960s, from being the Ministry's friend to becoming its arch foe. As post-war reconstruction began in the 1950s towns were planned in a new way to facilitate the smooth and fast passage of the motor car; in the 1960s this process moved from the bomb-ravaged city centres of Coventry and Plymouth to historic towns that were now regarded as being out of date and unworkable. Ring roads, circulatories and bypasses, many with dual carriageways, and most with their roundabouts, flyovers and elevated sections, spread across Britain, followed by car parks, road signs and pedestrianised shopping centres.[1] The destruction this was causing to historic towns began to stimulate a vocal and passionate public response. One of the most important expressions of this was the foundation of the Civic Trust in 1957, a federation of local civic societies that wanted to encourage better urban design and protect historic buildings and places. By 1960, 300 societies were registered with the Trust, a figure that had doubled by 1967.

After winning the General Election of 1964, Harold Wilson appointed Richard Crossman, one of his cleverest and most loyal supporters, to the Ministry of Housing and Local Government. This was a big job, with which came the responsibility for listing. The number of listing investigators had been run down by the preceding Tory Government, from twenty-four to nine. This had stunted the progress of statutory protection: by 1962 of 1,474 local authority areas, 1,344 had been investigated, but only 1,020 lists had actually been issued. Most of these early lists contained few, if any, buildings dating later than 1800. Moreover, listing was not proving much of a bastion against destruction, since in 1959 there had been 505 notices to demolish, increasing to 584 in 1960. Preservation orders were not much help either, since local authorities were still anxious about the compensation clauses that made them liable for potentially big pay-outs.[2]

In May 1965 Crossman travelled to Newcastle upon Tyne and visited Eldon Square, perhaps the city's finest Georgian square, then earmarked for demolition and replacement by a shopping centre. He wrote in his diary: 'I blew up our regional staff in Newcastle and told them that they were vandals for giving my consent. But I knew that it was already a fait accompli and that when I get back to the Department I shall be forced to draft the directive letter saying that they should have permission.' This event convinced him of three things: first, that the fragmentation of preservation controls between his ministry and the Ministry of Works made it incredibly hard for his department to have an impact; second, that the lists of historic buildings compiled from 1944 were inadequate, especially in towns; and third, that the law needed changing to protect not just individual buildings, as listing did, but also whole historic townscapes. The civil servants did everything they could to stop him. In his diary he wrote that the Permanent Secretary Dame Evelyn Sharp proudly 'counted herself a modern iconoclast', believing that there was 'a clear cut conflict between "modern" planning and "reactionary" preservation'.[3]

In 1966 Crossman ordered a new listing survey focusing, at first, on a list of thirty-nine priority historic towns and cities supplied by the Council for British Archaeology and a supplementary list of other towns (especially London overspill towns) threatened by development. Rural areas were not considered a priority. Under the Chief Investigator, Anthony Dale (1912–1993), fifteen investigators set to work moving very rapidly – speed, not depth, was their brief; there was little background research and list descriptions were very short. Nevertheless, there was now visible political will behind listing.

His next step was to win, from the Ministry of Works, after a bloody battle, the £450,000 a year distributed by the Historic Buildings Council. The obvious next step was to get the Ancient Monuments Department itself transferred, but Crossman instead started work on considering a much

An aerial view of Eldon Square, Newcastle upon Tyne, in 1927. © English Heritage
Aerofilms Collection

wider reorganisation that would see the amalgamation of the entire Office
of Works with his Ministry. Meanwhile, he teamed up with the Conservative MP and former Housing Minister Duncan Sandys, who had instigated
the foundation of the Civic Trust. With the Trust he had developed the idea
of a bill that would preserve the history and harmony of whole areas that
might have few, if any, listed buildings, but as a whole were of great historic
interest, beauty and charm. Sandys had drawn first place in the ballot for
Private Members' Bills and this enabled the Civic Amenities Act that created
Conservation Areas to be passed in 1967 with the support of Crossman and
the Government.[4]

A NEW DEPARTMENT

After winning the General Election of 1970, Edward Heath followed through
with Crossman's plans and amalgamated the Ministry of Works, Ministry
of Housing and Local Government and Ministry of Transport into a new

super ministry – the Department of the Environment. Within this, in 1972, the Ancient Monuments Department was transformed into a new, largely self-contained, section called the Directorate of Ancient Monuments and Historic Buildings (DAMHB).[5] The old department that had existed since 1913 was now joined with the listed buildings section of the former Ministry of Housing, a desirable and sensible amalgamation. In 1969 administrative autonomy for Welsh and Scottish monuments had been delegated and, in 1978, a full transfer of staff and functions took place. By then, therefore, the DAMHB had become an England-only body; but it was also a much more specialised and autonomous one. Before 1970 mid-ranking civil servants had been involved in ancient monuments or historic buildings as part of a wider range of responsibilities; now they were dedicated solely to them. Most decisions, including the acceptance of offers of guardianship, could now be taken within the Directorate without having to go up to the Permanent Secretary and Minister. This gave the Directorate a sense of independence and confidence that it had not previously had.

Its new professional head was Andrew Saunders (1931–2009), who became Chief Inspector in 1973, succeeding Arnold Taylor, but with a job title that included historic buildings as well as ancient monuments. Saunders had joined the Inspectorate in 1954, becoming Inspector for England ten years later. He was an archaeologist, but had established himself as the leading authority on artillery defences. When the army abolished its Coastal Artillery Arm in 1956, Saunders had the opportunity to bring into guardianship a series of really important coastal forts, including Brockhurst and Cumberland and the colossal Napoleonic fortress on the Western Heights at Dover. His vision of the Directorate was an intensely traditional one in which he saw preservation being most effectively achieved through guardianship; writing in 1974, he stated unequivocally that 'the most effective way' of preserving monuments and sites was for the Secretary of State to take direct care of them. Grant aid to the owner of the monument was definitely the second option.

It was in this self-assured mood that the DAMHB regarded its new state. As has been seen, during the 1960s there had been a huge diversification in what the Department regarded as being important and this led to a vast increase in the numbers of owners applying to the Government for guardianship. During the 1970s the pace of additions to the collection quickened markedly, with monuments being collected at a rate of around eight a year, a significant increase on the 1960s, and in the peak year of 1975 thirteen monuments were added. Industrial sites such as the Iron Bridge at Coalbrookdale (1975) and Stott Park Bobbin Mill (1974) came into State ownership, as did a host of archaeological field monuments, a smattering of chapels and churches, artillery forts and much more besides. While the Ancient Monuments staff did not believe they could save everything, there was a palpable sense that they could or should try to save something of everything.

A nice illustration of how the Department's attitude to acquisition changed in the 1970s is the case of two houses that it had long ago turned down and now accepted. While the National Trust could now be looked to as a solution for occupied country houses, the ruined carcasses of abandoned houses that neglect and misadventure had created were beyond their interest. This left a category of building with which the DAMHB now felt they needed to become involved. So while Sutton Scarsdale, a great Baroque mansion in Derbyshire that had been roofless since 1920, was turned down flat by the Ministry of Works in the mid-1950s, in the late 1960s the view was that 'Sutton Scarsdale is too important to let go, and this being so we shall have to expect to bear the major part in saving it'.[6] Its owners, the Sitwell family, who had over two decades 'tried to beg, badger, encourage and cajole first one Ministry or public body after another' into taking it on, were delighted finally to have succeeded.[7] The Grange in Hampshire was another building that had been refused outright in the past, Frederick Raby remarking in 1936 that 'The Grange belongs to a type of building which is hardly within the intentions expressed by Parliament in the Ancient Monuments Acts'.[8] But when in 1969 its owner, John Baring, applied to Hampshire County Council for permission to demolish the dilapidated house under the newly introduced system of listed building consent, there were howls of anguish. After the DAMHB had initially refused it on the basis of cost, the scale of protest that the preparations for demolition raised was such that they felt they had to act, and in 1975 the house was taken into guardianship.

THE NATIONAL HERITAGE COLLECTION IN THE 1970s

In 1970 the English part of the National Heritage Collection stood at more than 300 monuments, and under the leadership of Andrew Saunders the Inspectorate, in expansionist mood and free from political interference, became determined to make its geographical spread and typological coverage more complete. This would be achieved through all the traditional means of

Northington Grange, Hampshire, as it now stands. Its rescue and reuse as an opera house was a happy ending to a long and difficult saga. © English Heritage

guardianship, transfer from other Government departments and, increasingly, outright purchase. One such 'opportunity purchase' was that of Bowhill in Exeter, one of the best examples of a medieval manor house in the West Country. It had been engulfed in suburban development in the twentieth century and when it came onto the market in 1976 had been in use as a restaurant for several years. Its 'fabric was ... in serious decline, the roof structures were in poor condition and the house had no safe, demonstrable future in private hands', the Directorate thought.[9] More importantly, it saw a chance to fill a gap in their collection by acquiring a high-status medieval house in western England. There was enough evidence to allow for considerable reconstruction of Bowhill to its earlier state, so it was purchased and a lengthy and exhaustive programme of restoration begun. In a similar spirit of looking for some sort of completeness of coverage, Clifton Hall, near Nottingham, was accepted in 1970 and Halliggye Fougou was accepted in 1979. Clifton Hall is a good example of a later medieval pele tower, and Halliggye Fougou was considered to be a finer example of its type than either of the two other Cornish monuments already in the collection at Carn Euny and Chysauster.

Expansion begat expansion, as owners saw buildings once considered outside the remit of guardianship now being accepted and so applied or reapplied to the new Directorate. As a consequence, a raft of sites refused in the mid-century were accepted in the 1970s, among them Bushmead Priory, Piel Castle, Chisbury Chapel and Edlingham Castle.[10] As ever, the research concerns of the senior officials influenced acquisition and Andrew Saunders's own interest in artillery forts, combined with changing use of sites by the armed forces, brought a series of such buildings into the DAMHB's hands, including the extensive garrison walls on the Isles of Scilly – where Saunders himself had dug – and Fort Cumberland and Landguard Fort.[11]

As the collection expanded repair and maintenance costs increased, while, at the same time, the suitability of some of the new sites as places for the public to visit, and therefore to generate a revenue, was unclear. Archcliffe Fort, part of the chain of post-medieval fortifications protecting Dover harbour, is an example of this. It was one of the sites of which the army announced its intention to dispose in 1977. 'In isolation,' wrote Andrew Saunders, 'I would not regard the fort as suitable for guardianship but I think it important to see the fort in the context of the long pattern of fortification at Dover.'[12] He recommended acceptance, with little concern for the cost of conserving such a large structure and the almost total unsuitability of the monument as a visitor attraction. It is located in a road-bound industrial area, with no off-street parking and most of the historic portions can best be seen from outside the fort itself. Nevertheless, the transfer took place in August 1979, and two years later Maurice Mendoza, the relatively new director of the DAMHB, visited Dover and saw the fort. He was clearly appalled: 'This is one of the monuments it would have been better not to have taken on. We are now bound to spend a substantial amount of money on consolidating the remains of the fort but I doubt whether anybody will ever pay money to see them.'[13]

The expense of repairing and maintaining the collection, particularly building types of which the old Ministry of Works' staff had little experience, was becoming horribly apparent. A test case was the lifting mechanism at a coal mine. The 'Isabella' Winding Engine at Elemore Colliery, north-east of Durham city, was scheduled in 1969, and in 1975 a larger area of the pit complex followed. It stood in the mid-Durham coalfield, which was largely developed during the first quarter of the nineteenth century. The shaft at Elemore had been sunk in 1825 and still had its original winder, the only machinery of its type left in the North-East. When the pit became redundant, the National Coal Board discussed preservation of the winder and surrounding parts of the colliery with the Directorate and eventually offered to

Archcliffe, Kent, is now sited in close proximity to a road in an industrial estate.
© English Heritage

sell the freehold of 3 acres with buildings, machinery, fixtures and fittings for a nominal sum of £5. Conscious that this acquisition might raise eyebrows, the officials of the DAMHB were keen to emphasise that this was a rarity: 'As part of the Department's highly selective strategy for preserving key examples of industrial archaeology Elemore would be the sole representative in England to be taken into care of the coal industry on which the rest of the Industrial Revolution was based.' By 1980 the costs of conservation work, originally estimated at £50,000, had risen to a monumental £330,000. In addition, restrictions on public sector staffing made it uncertain that the Directorate would be able to provide custodians to open it to the public. As a result, it informed the Coal Board, in March 1980 that it no longer wished to acquire the monument. The Ancient Monuments Board urged the Directorate to offer grant aid to enable an alternative guardian to take it over, but the Coal Board decided to demolish the 'Isabella' winder rather wait around for a solution.[14]

While this was a grievous loss to industrial archaeology, it was probably a mercy for the Directorate, since its resources were now totally inadequate to

The winding engine at Elemore Colliery near Durham. © Crown copyright.
English Heritage

meet its liabilities. Restrictions in public-sector manpower instituted in 1976
were having a progressive effect on the directly employed labour force, who
undertook much of the repair work. A workforce that had numbered approximately 1,000 in 1970 had shrunk by February 1980 to 627. At the same
time, the size of the collection had grown by around eighty monuments.
In 1980 it was reported to the Ancient Monuments Board that the policy
of the Department was to reduce the directly employed labour force by
natural wastage to an 'essential minimum'. It was intended that they should
withdraw from all new-build construction, all maintenance to non-historic
structures and maintenance to historic structures that did not require specialist skills, or where the monument was of the seventeenth century or later.[15]

PRESENTING THE COLLECTION

The sheer range of building and monument types that the staff of the Inspectorate was now dealing was bewildering and a challenge for even the most
accomplished generalist. Yet inspectors tackled the presentation of everything

from prehistoric standing stones to nineteenth-century interiors. In 1961–2 in a pioneering venture the Ministry had stripped the ground-floor rooms in the south wing of Audley End House of their nineteenth-century accretions, demolishing walls and moving partitions. This revealed the great apartment created by Robert Adam in the late eighteenth century.[16] In the following decade their approach became more scientific. Working closely with the Victoria and Albert Museum at Ham House and Osterley Park (see above, p. 189), they were able to observe at close quarters the pioneering work of Peter Thornton and John Hardy, curators in the furniture department. Their radical approach to arranging furniture, based on the evidence of inventories, created publicly accessible interiors that were, for the first time, historically based. At Ham they recreated wall hangings, and even beds, in order to capture accurately the seventeenth-century appearance of the house.[17] The DAMHB did a similar thing at the Banqueting House in Whitehall in 1975, where, for the first time, scientific techniques of paint sampling were used in order to determine a new decorative scheme. With the advice of the expert on the Stuart court, Roy Strong, they also recreated a throne canopy at one end of the hall.

At Hampton Court the DAMHB produced a master plan in 1974 to guide a £250,000-a-year restoration to improve the palace for visitors. This included shops, a ticket office and a new picture gallery for royal collection paintings. It also embraced an approach to the arrangement of the state apartments based on research in the national archives. In 1972 the DAMHB appointed a former theatre designer, Pamela Lewis, to be the in-house designer to research historic paint schemes and design soft furnishings in order to produce historically accurate interiors for furnished properties.[18]

While the DAMHB was unquestionably the leading body in the accurate presentation of furnished historic interiors in the 1970s, its activities in its monumentalised sites was more questionable. The vicious reduction of Chiswick House, which has already been described (pp. 230–1), was not an isolated case. Medieval monuments acquired from the mid-1950s were subjected to radical remodelling, tearing away later layers to get to an agreed medieval core date. At Framlingham Castle, Suffolk, the interior of the Poor House was dismantled in an attempt to recreate a convincing medieval space, while at Denny Abbey, Cambridgeshire, a post-medieval farmhouse was stripped out to reveal the monastic remains, leaving a tangled mass of timber framing and half-demolished walls to keep the place standing.

Of all the sites where this radical approach was adopted, Blackfriars in Gloucester was perhaps the most thoroughgoing. It was acquired in sections from 1955, and in 1962 work started on the removal of the handsome and important sixteenth- and seventeenth-century merchants' houses that had been built inside the priory church to reveal its remains. All the internal structure was removed, floors, staircases and panelling, leaving a medieval shell but containing much mid-sixteenth-century masonry. In the north wall of the church it was felt it would be unacceptable to remove the late eighteenth-century full-height bow window, so it was rendered in a neutral coloured mortar on the inside, blocking the windows, maintaining the external appearance. The north wall of the north transept was similarly treated, leaving the attractive eighteenth-century sashes with their Gothick heads *in situ* but concealing them internally. The south wall of the nave was entirely rebuilt in the eighteenth century and so was demolished and replaced with a glazed steel frame, an 'honest' solution to providing a new wall.[19] By today's standards all this was a terrible act of vandalism, and once completed the DAMHB did not follow through, and the place was never a successful visitor attraction.

This same uncompromising approach was applied to the DAMHB's visitor facilities in the 1970s. The gentle, Arts and Crafts ticket offices of the inter-war period were replaced with modern box-like huts that were designed to speak their age. A standardised design was adopted, green-painted with an overhang at the front supported by white steel columns to keep visitors buying tickets dry. An equal degree of 'honesty' was applied to the necessary staircases and supports introduced into the monuments for visitor access. Until then, these had been robustly, but elegantly designed in oak. But new staircases at Peveril Castle and Conisbrough were built in crisp reinforced concrete to geometric designs. It could be argued that such interventions were visually less intrusive since they required fewer supports, but for many raw concrete contrasted unfavourably with gently weathered medieval stonework. At Cleeve Abbey an undercroft was rebuilt with white painted reinforced concrete support in an abstracted vault pattern, a spectacular and modern solution to a structural problem, but one that could hardly be called sympathetic.

But these aggressive interventions passed by the critics. The Ministry's sites had never been more popular with the public. In 1962 the Ministry admitted 5.5 million paying visitors in England, 7.55 million in total in Britain. At the time the National Trust was attracting only 1.2 million in England and Wales. Private owners in total were reaching around 4 million. The Ministry was

A typical modernist ticket office from the 1970s, here at Barnard Castle. Modern materials and lines clearly spoke the building's age. © English Heritage Photo Library

by far the largest operator of tourist attractions in Britain. Of the top twenty largest historic attractions, eleven were the Ministry's, seven were private and two belonged to the National Trust. Annual visitor income rose from £1,988,000 in 1974 to £4,213,853 in 1977 – the following year it reached £5 million. Part of this was increased numbers, but part was price inflation. The Ministry realised, in the late 1960s, that they were under-charging for their attractions. While the National Trust was charging three shillings on average at their houses, Dover Castle was still charging sixpence. The Ministry season ticket was ten shillings for an adult.

Although the Office of Works had been publishing lists of Ancient Monuments since 1921, there was, at first, no specific list for the sites open to the public. In 1956, in collaboration with *Country Life*, the first handbook was published giving details of each site, its opening hours and admission charges. This guide, which even had a few photographs, was a Rolls-Royce affair compared to the Ministry's first in-house handbook published in 1961. In twenty-nine terse pages the monuments were listed by county, complete with individual Ordnance Survey grid references.

The staircase put in place to give visitor access to Conisbrough Castle, Yorkshire and the concrete additions in the Warming Room at Cleeve Abbey, Somerset. © English Heritage

In some ways this first handbook was untypical of the Ministry's publications in the early 1950s, since several of the most popular sites had new guidebooks, with more photographs, more accessible text and attractive covers. After the establishment of the DAMHB, the Department of the Environment's Publicity Office asked Arnold Taylor to produce a range of souvenir guides of a much more popular nature. Taylor refused, on the grounds that this would dilute the scholarly content, and so the Publicity Office went ahead, independent of the inspectors, producing its own parallel series of guides. At the same time, many of the old 'official' Blue Guides were given covers with colour photographs.[20]

ANCIENT MONUMENTS ACT OF 1979

Ever since 1882 guardianship had been seen as the surest way of achieving the preservation of the nation's heritage, but the crisis that existed in the DAMHB by 1977 left few in any doubt that, while the National Heritage Collection might occasionally be added to, it was now entirely inadequate as the Government's principal preservation tool. A consultative document was published in March 1977 setting out proposals for new legislation. The bill that was eventually passed in 1979 reflected these very closely, with some procedural changes. It set out to modernise a fragmented body of legislation, but also to extend its scope to take account of 'the increased pace and scale of modern development and the destructive capacity of modern agricultural methods, which together have resulted in the loss of a large proportion of our archaeological inheritance'.

The change brought in by the act was technical, from one perspective, but fundamental from another. Two points are critical. The first was the new requirement for Scheduled Monument Consent that replaced the antiquated system of interim preservation notices and preservation orders. This meant that the ultimate sanction was no longer purchase of the monument by the State. The second was power to enter into a management agreement in which an owner or occupier would maintain a monument on their land, or refrain from damaging it – by ploughing for instance – in return for a suitable payment.

The case of Bardney Abbey, Lincolnshire, illustrates the change of thinking that took place as a result. The monument had been rejected when guardianship was offered in 1928, but in 1974 a newly formed Friends Group renewed the offer. The Department were minded to accept, although they had misgivings about the lack of any high standing remains on the site, and the fragility of the buried stone that might be exposed. In January 1975 the offer of guardianship was accepted in principle, but on the basis that nothing would be done with the monument until stone treatment techniques had advanced sufficiently to ensure preservation of the then buried stone. More than usually protracted negotiation over access and boundaries meant that the case was still live in 1979. After the passing of the act the case was reassessed and it was agreed that there was no threat to the site, which was scheduled, and that it was now possible to protect it without guardianship. The Principal Inspector, Christopher Young (b. 1947 and at the time of writing still working for English Heritage), advised the Chief Inspector that 'this site can . . . be dealt with adequately by the route of management agreement under the 1979 Act and by grant-to-owner as necessary'. He also advised looking at the wider picture:

> We should not, I think, look at this case in isolation but use it as a starting point for a general review of our attitude towards means of preservation of field monuments, when our intention is to preserve a site as earthworks, not to excavate and display masonry. It seems to me that the new Act gives us a number of more flexible options for achieving preservation, including management agreements or grant to other bodies (e.g. local authorities, National Trust) for the purchase by them of ancient monuments.[21]

In his report on the DAMHB's work in 1982, Andrew Saunders was able to describe advice and grants to owners as 'an extremely important part of the Department's work', a radical change to his opinion of a decade earlier.

LISTING

Equally important were the DAMHB's listing activities. These had got off to a rocky start. The shotgun marriage that was intended to bring the Ancient Monuments inspectors and listing investigators together in 1970 was not a success. Anthony Dale, the Chief Investigator, was very hostile to the change and, when eventually they co-located in Fortress House in Savile Row, London, in 1972, the Ancient Monuments Inspectors were unwelcoming and superior, regarding their more recently constituted colleagues as a lesser breed. Arnold Taylor's retirement in 1972 presented an opportunity for greater integration and Andrew Saunders offered Dale the title of Deputy Chief Inspector. Dale said that he 'would rather be called Chief Rat Catcher than Deputy Chief Rodent Operative' and remained as Chief Investigator until his retirement in 1976.

Dale had been an investigator since 1947 and had led Crossman's resurvey since 1966. He had overseen a gradual widening of the criteria for listing: in the late 1950s the lists had started to include Victorian buildings, and in 1969 fifty inter-war buildings were added. With the merger, in 1970, there were more changes, in particular the selection criteria were revised and the concept of group value was strengthened. But things were not getting easier. In 1974 local government was reorganised, reducing the numbers of local authorities from 1,210 to 440. This, at a stroke, made all the existing lists of historic buildings very difficult to use, because they had, of course, been compiled under the old administrative units.

By 1977 there were only four investigators in the field and the junior minister Baroness Birk, one of Harold Wilson's life peers, wanted them to switch their efforts to grant cases, believing that 'too many buildings have been listed' and that in the future 'we shall not be giving so many buildings the benefit of the doubt'. In 1977, the year that the Department was to be cut, 246,000 buildings had been listed.[22] Yet the list was geographically patchy; entries were poor and inaccurate; and staff shortages meant that many buildings that were notified were never investigated and subsequently lost. The Department faced criticism from developers and conservationists alike.

In August 1980 the crisis came to a head when the Art Deco Firestore Factory in Brentford, built in 1928, was demolished over a bank holiday weekend to prevent a listing order being served. In reaction to the storm of protest, the Secretary of State, Michael Heseltine, ordered, in 1982, that the listing survey be accelerated and completed within ten years. Later he decided that this was too long and ordered it to be complete in only three years by a team of 110 fieldworkers. This was hugely ambitious, and in 1984 work was handed over to English Heritage to complete.

In the end this modern doomsday took more than seven years to complete, consuming 1,000 man years of time and costing £4–5 million. But Britain got the first and only complete and scientific list of historic buildings, numbering some 500,000 entries. It was an astonishing achievement, an inventory that few other nations can rival.[23]

In April 1980 a process began of reassessing all guardianship cases in the pipe-line to decide if they should continue. In a memorandum to the Chief Inspec-tor, Maurice Mendoza explained the reasons for the review. The human re-sources of the Directorate were, he stated, 'seriously overstretched'. Indeed, the resources were so scarce that 'we have to defer any conservation work on some monuments . . . even though we know that deferment will inevitably entail further deterioration and higher costs in the future'. In these circumstances 'for us to take on more liabilities would, to say the least, be imprudent'. Men-doza conceded that it was possible for a case to arise in which an outstanding monument was falling into ruin and guardianship was the only way to save it, but in such an instance he expected his approval to be sought before the owner was given any indication that the Department was open to negotiation.

In May 1981 the results of the review were reported to the Ancient Monu-ments Board. A total of twenty-two cases were to be terminated, twelve were to be continued (of which four were additional areas for existing monuments in care) and four required further consideration. The following November Andrew Saunders presented a paper on the future of guardianship to the Ancient Monuments Board. He told it that until the 1979 Act guardianship was the only secure means of preservation outside the use of compulsory powers. In the light of the new legislation, he said that the Department must look at the protection of antiquities in a new light. Since scheduled monu-ment consent and management agreements had been introduced as means of preservation, 'it could be said that to a degree all scheduled sites were now in care'. Saunders proposed that in future monuments should be considered only if a monument was deteriorating and the Department's expertise was essential to ensure its preservation. But old habits died hard. Having made the case for practically abandoning guardianship altogether, Saunders ap-pended to his paper a long list of monuments that were 'outstanding in their class and which qualify for consideration for guardianship should they become available'. Whatever the unrealistic ambitions of the Chief Inspector, the brakes had well and truly been applied, and in four years after 1980 only ten monuments were taken into care.

In 1981 the DAMHB was at its lowest ebb: it was unable properly to main-tain its sites, with a virtual freeze on acquisitions, and an inability to man even its largest and most popular monuments; it had disaffected staff and a faced a mounting barrage of external criticism. On 25 January 1981, eighteen months into the new Conservative Government, the former Chief Inspector of Ancient Monuments, Arnold J. Taylor, wrote an embittered letter to *The Times* in which he attacked the Secretary of State for the Environment, Michael Heseltine, for failing in his duties as guardian of the nation's ancient monuments.[24] There were three main accusations: first, that important monuments such as Furness Abbey, St Augustine's in Canterbury and Castle Rising had been closed or left unguarded; secondly, that the specialist labour force was being deliberately run down; and thirdly that the Department was seeking to divest itself of Battle Abbey and Fountains Abbey. The letter was published on 31 January 1981 and the debate that followed threw into sharp focus how the world had changed since the 1960s, when Taylor was Chief Inspector. Perhaps the most prescient response, of many, was that of Andrew Selkirk, the editor of *Current Archaeology*. He put it starkly:

> we must all realise that a fundamental shift in economics is taking place. Since the first Ancient Monuments Act in 1882, the list of ancient monuments has grown larger and larger, with new ones added every year. This cannot go on *ad infinitum*. The party's over, and we must face a future in which government spending will at most remain stable, but is rather more likely to decline steadily for the rest of our lifetimes. This means that those of us who wish to conserve the past must do something about it ourselves, and local archaeological societies up and down the country must be prepared to take over ancient monuments, as they so often did in the 1930s.[25]

ENGLISH HERITAGE

By this time the Government was already developing a rescue package. Maurice Mendoza first suggested to the Secretary of State, Michael Heseltine, in 1979 that the work of the DAMHB could be done better by an agency. Given the public attacks on the Directorate in the early part of 1981, the publication of a consultation paper on reorganisation of ancient monuments and historic buildings work in October that year was timely.[26] The proposed transfer of functions from the Department of the Environment to a new agency was presented as part of the Government's wider programme to reduce its responsibility for functions that could be more effectively carried out by non-governmental bodies. There is a hint of criticism in the suggestion that 'an organisation devoted entirely to the heritage would . . . be better able to focus single-mindedly on the functions currently being carried out by the Department' and would 'command a greater respect in the heritage field'.[27] The emphasis in the proposals, however, was for a more engaging and imaginative presentation of monuments in care to maximise their educational and commercial potential. This would require 'commercial and entrepreneurial flair', best located outside Government.[28] A parallel was drawn with the museums and the arts and the way they related to Government. More than 300 responses to the consultation were received, and the Government's conclusions were published the following year in *Organisation of Ancient Monuments and Historic Buildings in England: The Way Forward*.

This document stated that the present system worked well and reported that many respondents had praised the skill and dedication of the staff of the Department. Yet the Government was convinced that the expert nature of much ancient monuments and historic buildings work made it suitable for transfer to an agency. It was also thought that an agency would have the advantage of being able to tap into private funding and voluntary help. A new agency could also, the Government believed, bring innovation and imagination to the way that monuments were used in education. It was created by the National Heritage Act 1983, which received Royal Assent on 13 May,[29] and given the statutory title of the Historic Buildings and Monuments Commission for England (HBMC), but it adopted the name 'English Heritage' at the suggestion of its first Chairman, Lord Montagu.

Creation of the HBMC entailed the dissolution of two long-established institutions, the Historic Buildings Council and the Ancient Monuments Board, but the Commission retained the directly employed labour force first created in 1912. In order to ensure a smooth transition, the staff of the DAMHB were asked to work in the Commission on a two-year secondment, after which time they could choose to commit to it or return to the Department. Continuity was also aided by the appointment of Peter Rumble, Director of the DAMHB from 1981, to the post of Chief Executive of the Commission.

A DIFFICULT DECADE

The 1970s have been characterised as the Heroic Period of Conservation.[30] It was a period when the focus in conservation moved from the State to the individual. The initiative shifted from a small number of specialist campaigning societies, passionate but with limited support, who got governments to change the law through their friends in Parliament, to bodies enjoying massive popular support that could not be ignored by politicians. The story of conservation has been well covered elsewhere,[31] but its effects on the DAMHB were huge. It would be easy to blame Andrew Saunders for being completely out of touch and letting the Directorate get carried away with unrealistic acquisitions with no regard to the financial or managerial realities. It would be easy to blame him for not using grants earlier and more decisively and for not integrating the listing investigators into the Directorate effectively.

Yet that would miss the intoxicating background. The DAMHB was a department supremely confident, not to say arrogant, about its abilities and achievements. It was one recently liberated from political control that felt it could now make decisions based on its professional judgements alone. It was also one working against an external environment, on the one hand economically catastrophic, but on the other filled with the rousing noise of popular support for conservation. The DAMHB was the crest of the wave, the most exciting, varied and ambitious period in the history of the old Ancient Monuments Department, but when the crisis came the men from the Ministry were completely ill prepared to cope with it.

MEN FROM THE MINISTRY

THE NATIONAL HERITAGE COLLECTION

By 1984, when central government delegated the last of its responsibilities towards the National Heritage Collection to English Heritage, the British state had accumulated more than 880 monuments nationwide. These places had been acquired to save them, but, in accordance with the original intention in 1913, they were also acquired to inform and educate the public. As an example of State investment in education and preservation it was a really remarkable achievement. Unlike municipal collections, gathered together for the populations of provincial towns and cities, or the great national collections financed by the Treasury and located in London, the National Heritage Collection was dispersed across the nation. Whilst its geographical spread is uneven, its sites and monuments can be found from the Scilly Isles to the Orkneys.

The estimated 17 million people who visited these places in 2012 were only the most direct beneficiaries. For the innumerable hikers on Hadrian's Wall, picnickers at Hadleigh Castle, dog walkers at Kenilworth, motorists passing Stonehenge, North Sea sailors off Dunstanborough Castle, city workers passing London's Roman wall, these monuments mark people's place in time and space. They give places character, interest, beauty and history. The residents of Pickering, Castle Acre or Totness may rarely decide to visit their monuments but inescapably they make the places they live special.

This book has demonstrated that the collection is not accidental. As early as 1913 it is known that the Ancient Monuments Department started keeping lists of what they would like to acquire. At first, the monuments they took over were, to modern tastes, conventional: castles and abbeys. They represented the two great narratives of British history: Protestantism as captured in the spectacular remains of Henry VIII's suppression, and parliamentary democracy as preserved in the shattered fortresses of the Civil War. As perceptions of history widened after 1950 so the lists got longer and more ambitious in monument type and date. Always there was a strong sense of it being a collection. Like all national collections, such as paintings in the National Gallery or Portrait Gallery, acquisitions are conditioned by availability; and the Ancient Monuments Department often had to wait for many years until long-coveted sites became available for acquisition.

COLLECTING CULTURE

The process of building up a comprehensive collection of old masters in a gallery in Trafalgar Square and assembling a representative sample of historic monuments illustrating national history is very similar. Both involve a cadre of expert curators who have the knowledge that underpins acquisitions. Both aim for representative coverage and both do their best to explain the collection to the public.

There, perhaps, the similarities break down. Paintings in the National Gallery are not saved in the literal sense that the Ancient Monuments Department's monuments were. In most cases sites were given to the Government to rescue them from destruction: many had reached a point when private means were insufficient or unavailable to keep them standing. Unquestionably, the actions of the State saved many hundreds of internationally important sites from dereliction and collapse. Quite simply, had the Ancient Monuments Department not intervened they would not be there today. Objects acquired for museums are 'saved' only in the loosest sense. They are saved from private custodianship and private delectation in favour of public ownership and enjoyment. That is an entirely different thing.

The second significant difference between collecting monuments and museum artefacts is that whilst objects in museums do sometimes need expensive conservation work, monuments need repeated and continuous investment to stabilise them. Ruins are preserved in an unnatural state. Structures designed to have a roof, now preserved without them, are disproportionately expensive to maintain. This was recognised soon after the First

World War and charging for entry was seen as the legitimate response to the need to defray the costs of maintaining structures inherently unsustainable. Few question the right of heritage bodies to charge entry or begrudge the cost of paying for what is blatantly an expensive attraction. Remarkably, just before the Second World War, the cost of the National Heritage Collection and its income were more or less in balance. After the war that was upset by the acquisition of many non-commercial sites and many with very high defects. As a result the Government subsidy to the National Heritage Collection rose dramatically in the 1970s. Now, however, the English part of the collection is virtually self-sustaining again. This must open up questions about its future management and governance.

The third point of difference is the sense in which the Ancient Monuments Department's collection is truly national. The point has already been made that the National Heritage Collection is dispersed across the country and enjoyed primarily by the people who live and work in Britain. It is uniquely accessible, vast amounts of it visible without charge, and hundreds of monuments free to visit. It is not a collection maintained by central government finance for metropolitan visitors and foreign tourists. It is part of the very fabric of the nation, of society, indeed. It is also British. This is a difficult concept to argue without sounding xenophobic or nationalistic; but what is represented in the National Heritage Collection is, by very definition, the product of the peoples who lived on these islands. Like the National Portrait Gallery, founded on a very similar premise to the National Heritage Collection, it is a unique illustration of our way of life. So though our buildings are the most visible expression of our cultural and civic values, though they encapsulate most vividly our history and have been at the heart of expressions of power and politics, their importance has been seen to be less important and less prestigious than museum collections. This is partly due to the collection's dispersed nature, being rooted in the places where it was made and not an assemblage of displaced works displayed in a single place.[1]

In the Introduction I explained that a prime motive for writing this book was to emphasise the achievements of the State over a hundred years of protection and collection. With the distancing of the collection from direct political control in 1982, it has become progressively harder for politicians to understand and appreciate the National Heritage Collection. The astonishing rise of easel painting as the supremely important expression of cultural achievement has left, until recently, even the British Museum panting to keep up. While there is greater cultural value now given to decorative arts and archaeological artefacts, painting is still regarded as the most important cultural expression, a notion that would have bewildered our ancestors.

The supremacy of painting has been reflected in the sums paid recently for acquisitions for the National Gallery. The Duke of Northumberland's painting by Raphael, the *Madonna of the Pinks*, was bought in 2004 for £34.88 million; in 2009–10 they were successful with the Duke of Sutherland's two Titians, which were bought jointly with the National Gallery of Scotland for £95 million. Despite the loose language about 'saving' these paintings, they were not, in reality, saved at all. Nobody was going to burn them, or hack them to bits. The very worst that could have happened is that they were exported to be enjoyed by people in a museum in another country. Thus 'saving' portable art is not about safeguarding its physicality; it is about national pride and status.

COLLECTING AND NATIONAL PRIDE

This is why the purchase of the Titians was made possible by £12.5 million from the Scottish Government. The nationalist government in Scotland saw safeguarding the quality of the National Gallery of Scotland as an integral part of nation building. This goes for Scottish monuments too, the lavish restoration of Stirling Castle and other sites, such as that of the Battle of Bannockburn, form part of a strategy to build national identity. Money follows political will. In Scotland heritage funding per head of population in 2011 was around £10; in Wales, which had a similarly focused use for heritage, it was £5.50 a head; England spent £2.[2] Political interest in national identity and State heritage spending are closely related. This book has argued that the establishment of the collection between the wars owed much to a need to express and defend national identity and a desire to connect people in a more immediate way with their national story.

In the Introduction I referred to the divorce between Britain's built heritage and national pride in the late 1990s. In a book by Mark Leonard called *Britain: Reviewing our Identity*, published in 1997, Britain was characterised as 'a backward-looking has-been, a theme park world of royal pageantry and rolling green hills, where draft blows through people's houses'; it was a country that needed re-branding as more forward-looking and modern.

The Ancient Monuments Department of the Office of Works; the Department of
National Heritage; DCMS, abandoned in 2013 in favour of Crown branding.

This rapidly took place as the former (backward-looking) Department of
National Heritage, established by John Major's Conservative Government in
1992, was renamed snappily as the (forward-looking) Department for Culture Media and Sport. One of Mark Leonard's recommendations was for just
such a move accompanied by re-branding, and so the old royal coat of arms,
formerly the standard logo for Government departments, was replaced by an
unintelligible 'creative' blob.[3]

By 2010 the outright hostility to heritage had been forgotten. The London
Olympic Games, for which Britain was preparing, led to a worldwide advertising campaign based on Britain's greatness in everything from shopping
to the countryside and including 'Heritage' as the core theme.[4] Meanwhile,
the Cabinet Office issued instructions to abandon expensively designed cor-
porate logos and establish Government departments under the royal arms,
so-called Crown branding. This swing in the pendulum of political fashion
could have implications for perceptions of the National Heritage Collection.

What then is the role of such a collection in England today? The Scots
and the Welsh see a place for a collection of monuments in a programme of
national definition, pride and identity. Whilst the Department for Culture
Media and Sport in Whitehall has the air of being the national culture ministry, it is, in fact, the English ministry. What then is its policy? It is an economic one. Built heritage is seen as one of the most important assets the
nation has in terms of tourism. It recognises that this is why most people
come to the UK on holiday from abroad. 'Culture and heritage is the most
important part of Britain's tourism offering as at some point it touches every
visitors' trip to Britain', we are told.[5]

English identity is very closely bound up with the physicality of England: the patterns of fields and villages seen out of an aeroplane, red phone and post boxes, the mills of Manchester, Victorian civic buildings, the great cathedrals, seaside towns with their piers and amusement arcades, Blackpool Pleasure Beach, parish churches with their graveyards. This, of course, changes at the edges as new places develop. The Regent's Park Mosque, built in 1978, the *Angel of the North* finished in 1998, and the London Eye, erected in 2000, are all now part of the identity of the places were they stand. The bones of our heritage are the tangible and visible remains of our ancestors, their achievements, their industry and their ideas of beauty. This is what makes up our common visual understanding of our country. They are the clues that let you know that you live in England, not France or Italy.[6]

That sense of distinctiveness has been protected and is sustained by the second great collection described in this book. Since 1913 the Government has made lists of sites that are to be given legal protection. There are now approximately 532,000 of them in Britain, of which around 350,000 are in England. This second collection was formed, after 1944, with the knowledge that listing a site would not necessarily lead to its acquisition by the State. This freed the listers to create a larger and more diverse collection that captured what was special about Britain's buildings and landscapes. As a collection it is a mix of public and private ownership built on the national acceptance that it is possible to recognise the public interest in a privately owned place.

The establishment of listing has changed the job of bodies set up by Government to take into ownership historically important places. The National Heritage Collection, the National Trust and the Churches Conservation Trust, the three bodies established in law to care for the most valuable parts of our heritage, are no longer the first line of defence; they are the safety net, the social security of the system. In the vast majority of cases it is now possible to protect places in private hands and not add them to any of these three collections. Yet there will always be places that the State bodies have to rescue: between 2003 and 2013 English Heritage saved perhaps six buildings, two industrial, one country house, one rural, one prehistoric and one twentieth-century. But this rate of acquisition is the slowest in its history. So it should be. Acceptance in Lieu of tax, Conditional Exemption, listing and other mechanisms should mean that places can be protected in the market-place rather than in State care.

The Government, in the future, would do well to look closely at these to ensure that they do preserve the best cultural ensembles left in private ownership making them accessible to the public. A sum of £95 million to buy two paintings cannot be sustainable. And the two are linked. In the ten years before 2010 one in eight great house owners sold art to maintain their buildings. Appropriate tax relief in return for public access could staunch art sales, and keep objects on public show in the provinces without the need to find tens of millions to put them in London museums. The stunning success of the Victoria and Albert Museum's ownership of some of the contents of Houghton Hall, Norfolk, is an example of how taxation can be used to maintain a publicly accessible national museum of history in the provinces.

These debates are not new. This book has shown, as so many history books do, that there is little new in the world. Admission charges, tax relief, the cost of acquisition and maintenance, education, public access, conservation principles and more have all been exhaustively discussed since the 1850s. The system in place now is based on the outcome of those discussions. It is not perfect. It may not be sustainable. But up until now, at least, it has done a stunning job. The men from the Ministry did not do it alone, far from it, but without them it would not have been done at all.

NOTES

INTRODUCTION

1 C. R. Peers, 'The Treatment of Old Buildings', *Architectural Journal*, 3rd series, XXXVIII (1931), pp. 311–25; verbatim report of paper read, p. 314.

1 SEEKING THE 'OLDEN TIME'

1 *The Times*, 26 August 1881, p. 10.

2 This is a big subject with a big literature. A good introduction is Rosemary Sweet, *The Discovery of the Past in Eighteenth Century Britain* (London, 2004).

3 Peter Mandler, *History and National Life* (London, 2002); John Henry Raleigh, 'What Scott Meant to the Victorians', *Victorian Studies*, VII (1963), pp. 7–34. During the passage of the Ancient Monuments Bill, which was eventually passed into law in 1882, *The Times* noted that 'Everybody since Sir Walter Scott's days understands the historical interest of an old Abbey or a ruined Castle' (16 April 1874).

4 Adrian Tinniswood, *The Polite Tourist: A History of Country House Visiting* (National Trust, 1998), pp. 132–4; Nicholas Pevsner and Elizabeth Williamson, *The Buildings of England: Leicestershire and Rutland* (London, 2003), pp. 77–85; Richard K. Morris, *Kenilworth Castle* (English Heritage, 2006), pp. 51–2.

5 Patricia Anderson, *The Printed Image and the Transformation of Popular Culture, 1790–1860* (Oxford, 1991); articles on the Tower of London published in the *Penny Magazine* (April 1833; May and June 1836) and the *Saturday Magazine* (August 1833).

6 Peter Mandler, '"In the Olden Time": Romantic History and English National Identity, 1820–50', in *A Union of Multiple Identities: The British Isles, c.1750–c.1850*, ed. Laurence Brockliss and David Eastwood (Manchester, 1997), pp. 82–9; Julia Thomas, *Shakespeare's Shrine: The Bard's Birthplace and the Invention of Stratford upon Avon* (Philadelphia, 2012).

7   William Howitt, *Visits to Remarkable Places: Old Halls, Battle Fields, and Scenes Illustrative of Striking Passages in English History and Poetry*, 2 vols (London, 1840–2).

8   Jack Simmons, *The Victorian Railway* (London, 1991), pp. 270–308.

9   Adrian Tinniswood, *The Polite Tourist: A History of Country House Visiting* (London, 1998), pp. 150–2.

10   Stuart Piggott, *Ruins in a Landscape: Essays in Antiquarianism* (Edinburgh, 1976), pp. 171–95; Kenneth Hudson, *A Social History of Archaeology: The British Experience* (London, 1981), pp. 43–7.

11   Richard Harris Barham, 'The Spectre of Tappington', in *The Ingoldsby Legends; or, Mirth and Marvels by Thomas Ingoldsby Esq.* (New York, 1852), pp. 13–50.

12   Edward Impey, *Castle Acre Priory and Castle* (English Heritage, 2008), pp. 36–9 [guidebook text with footnotes, bibliography and selected documents].

13   Keystone Historic Building Consultants, Exeter, *Cleeve Abbey, Washford, Somerset: Conservation Plan* (English Heritage, October 2000), pp. 62–74.

14   Hazel Fryer et al., *Kenilworth Castle Elizabethan Garden Research Project* (English Heritage, 2006), pp. 167–8.

15   Peter Mandler, *The Fall and Rise of the Stately Home* (New Haven and London, 1997), pp. 97–100.

16   In addition, there were the British Museum (established 1753) and the National Gallery (established 1824), not historic buildings, but publicly owned attractions.

17   H. M. Colvin, ed., *The History of the King's Works*, vol. v: *1660–1782* (London, 1976), p. 384; vol. vi: *1782–1851* (London, 1973), pp. 490–1; A. Keay, *The Crown Jewels* (Historic Royal Palaces, 2002), pp. 62–7.

18   Table of visitor numbers to the Tower of London:

1837	10,408
1838	40,000 [entrance price reduced]
1839	84,000
1840	94,973
1842	107,000
1844	540,000
1850	32,000
1851	233,000 [Great Exhibition]
1856	50,000
1869	107,000
1900	140,000
1901	462,000 [free days introduced]

19   On the Tower of London, see Peter Hammond, 'Epitome of England's History: The Transformation of the Tower of London as a Visitor Attraction in the 19th Century', *Royal*

Armouries Yearbook, 4 (1999), pp. 144–74; Edward Impey, ed., *The White Tower* (New Haven and London, 2008), pp. 203–7. See also Raphael Samuel, 'The Tower of London', in *Island Stories: Unravelling Britain*, vol. II: *Theatres of Memory* (London, 1998), pp. 101–24.

20 Simon Thurley, *Hampton Court: A Social and Architectural History* (New Haven and London, 2003), pp. 317–21.

21 Thurley, *Hampton Court*, pp. 317–21.

22 Nathaniel Hawthorne, *The English Notebooks*, ed. Randall Stewart (New York and London, 1941), p. 284.

23 John Grundy, *A Stranger's Guide to Hampton Court Palace and Gardens* (London, 1865), p. 23; *Gentleman's Magazine* (March 1847), p. 293.

24 Sir John Soane had recommended in 1822 that the round larder be removed as a disfigurement: Soane Museum XII.G.3.2; The National Archives, WORK 1/32, p. 64; WORK 1/34, pp. 48–9; WORK 1/35, pp. 139, 231–2; WORK 1/36, p. 2. pp. 317–21. WORK 1/32 (20 December 1847); WORK 1/36 (6 December 1850, 18 January 1851); WORK 1/66 (19 July 1860).

25 Subsequent editions were dated 1840, 1841 and 1847.

26 J. Bayley, *The History and Antiquities of the Tower of London*, 2 vols (1821–5), I, pp. 668–9.

27 William Harrison Ainsworth, *The Tower of London: A Historical Romance* [1840] (London, 1845), p. v.

28 Charles Knight, ed., *London*, 6 vols (London, 1841–4), II, p. 215.

29 Richard D. Altick, *The Shows of London: A Panoramic History of Exhibitions, 1600–1862* (Harvard, MA, and London, 1978), pp. 434–54; Select Committee on National Monuments and Works of Art, 1841 (416), VI.437, pp. v–vi.

30 Howitt, *Visits to Remarkable Places*, II, p. 234.

31 Howitt, *Visits to Remarkable Places*, I, p. 11; Donald Ulin, 'Seeing the Country: Tourism and Ideology in William Howitt's *Rural Life of England*', *Victorians Institute Journal*, XXX (2002), pp. 41–60.

32 Thomas, *Shakespeare's Shrine*, pp. 40–3.

2 THE OFFICE OF WORKS

1 *The History of the King's Works*, ed. H. M. Colvin, vols I–II: *The Middle Ages* (London, 1963); vol. III, part 1: *1485–1660* (London, 1975); vol. IV, part 2: *1485–1660* (London, 1982); vol. V: *1660–1782* (London, 1976); vol. VI: *1782–1851* (London, 1973).

2 The nearest thing to a history of the Office of Works between 1851 and 1914 is M. H. Port's excellent *Imperial London: Civil Government Building in London, 1850–1915* (New Haven and London, 1995).

3 Port, *Imperial London*, p. 75.

4 Sir Lionel Earle, *Turn Over the Page* (London, 1935), p. 252.

5 Simon Thurley, *Hampton Court: A Social and Architectural History* (New Haven and London, 2003), pp. 294–303.

6   J. Allibone, *Anthony Salvin: Pioneer of Gothic Revival Architecture* (Cambridge, 1988), pp. 97–8. Lanercost Priory was also restored by the Office of Works with Salvin as architect.

7   Salvin's work at the Tower of London is described in William Lennox Lascelles Fitzgerald-de-Ros, *Memorials of the Tower of London* (London, 1866).

8   Geoffrey Parnell, *The English Heritage Book of the Tower of London* (London, 1993), pp. 98–103; Edward Impey and Geoffrey Parnell, *The Tower of London: Official Illustrated History* (London, 2000), p. 118; Allibone, *Anthony Salvin*, pp. 138–43.

9   Stephen Brindle, 'Sir George Gilbert Scott and the Restoration of the Westminster Abbey Chapter House, 1849–1872', in *Westminster Abbey Chapter House: The History, Art and Architecture of 'a Chapter House beyond compare'*, ed. Warwick Rodwell and Richard Mortimer (London, 2010).

10   House of Commons debate, 27 June 1845, *Hansard*, vol. 81, cols 1328–44.

11   Colvin, ed., *The History of the King's Works*, vol. VI: *1782–1851*, pp. 641–5.

12   Note that Westminster Hall was the other disagreement between the Office of Works and the SPAB. For the working of the SPAB committees, see Jenny West's appendices in Chris Miele, ed., *From William Morris: Building Conservation and the Arts and Crafts Cult of Authenticity, 1877–1939*, Yale Studies in British Art 14 (New Haven and London, 2005), pp. 299–335.

13   The background to Mitford's appointment can be found in M. H. Port, 'A Regime for Public Buildings: Experiments in the Office of Works, 1869–75', *Architectural History*, XXVII (1984), pp. 74–85. Also see Algernon Bertram Freeman Mitford, Baron Redesdale, *Memories*, 2 vols (London, 1915), II, p. 703.

14   The Governor's views are in Fitzgerald-de-Ros, *Memorials of the Tower of London*, pp. 18, 7; Mitford's own account is in Lord Redesdale, *A Tragedy in Stone and Other Papers* (London, 1882), pp. 4–5, 29–38.

15   Parnell, *The English Heritage Book of the Tower of London*, pp. 103–8.

16   Ernest Law, *The History of Hampton Court Palace*, 3 vols (London, 1885–9), III, pp. 385–6.

17   I am grateful to David Walker for providing me with a transcript of a history of the Lessels family by Miss Jane Lessels, from which my information about John Lessels derives.

18   Thurley, *Hampton Court*, pp. 303–6.

19   Robert J. Morris, 'The Capitalist, the Professor and the Soldier: The Re-making of Edinburgh Castle, 1850–1900', *Planning Perspectives*, 22 (2007), pp. 55–78; Iain MacIvor, *Edinburgh Castle* (London, 1993), pp. 110–17.

3   THE 'MONUMENTALLY ANCIENT' ACT

1   In 1880 Augustus Henry Lane Fox inherited the estate of his cousin Horace Pitt, 6th Baron Rivers, and gave himself the cognomen Pitt-Rivers.

2   William Chapman, 'The Organisational Context in the History of Archaeology: Pitt-Rivers and Other British Archaeologists in the 1860s', *Antiquaries Journal*, LXIX (1989), pp. 23–32.

3   On Lubbock, see Michael Thompson, *Darwin's Pupil: The Place of Sir John Lubbock, Lord Avebury (1834–1913) in Late Victorian and Edwardian England* (Ely, 2009); Glyn Daniel, *The Origins and Growth of Archaeology* (Harmondsworth, 1967), pp. 118–23.

4   The story of the act is told in a masterly way by Christopher Chippendale in 'The Making of the First Ancient Monuments Act, 1882, and its Administration under General Pitt-Rivers', *Journal of the British Archaeological Association*, CXXXVI (1983), pp. 1–55. Also very useful is Tim Murray, 'The History, Philosophy and Sociology of Archaeology: The Case of the Ancient Monuments Protection Act (1882)', in *Critical Traditions in Contemporary Archaeology: Essays in the Philosophy, History and Socio-Politics of Archaeology*, ed. Valerie Pinsky and Alison Wylie (Albuquerque, NM, 1995), pp. 55–79.

5   Sir John Lubbock, *Addresses Political and Educational* [1877] (London, 1879), pp. 156–7.

6   Described in his own words in Lubbock, *Addresses Political and Educational*, pp. 162–6.

7   *The Times*, 13 and 16 April 1874.

8   Charles Philip Kains-Jackson with a preface by Sir John Lubbock, *Our Ancient Monuments and the Land around Them* (London, 1880).

9   House of Commons debate, 15 April 1874, *Hansard*, vol. 218, col. 589.

10   Horace G. Hutchinson, *Life of Sir John Lubbock, Lord Avebury* (London, 1914), p. 150.

11   M. H. Port, *Imperial London: Civil Government Building in London, 1850–1915* (New Haven and London, 1995), p. 71; L. W. Chubb, rev. Graham Murphy, 'Hunter, Sir Robert (1844–1913)', in *Oxford Dictionary of National Biography* (2004): http://www.oxforddnb.com/view/article/34064?docPos=4 (accessed 29 July 2012).

12   House of Commons debate, 19 February 1878, *Hansard*, vol. 1, cols 1978–80.

13   Lord Eversley, *Commons, Forests and Footpaths: The Story of the Battle during the last Forty Five Years for Public Rights over the Commons, Forests and Footpaths of England and Wales* (London, 1910), p. 303, describes what he did in his own words.

14   Pitt-Rivers file FLO1545, English Heritage Archives, Swindon.

15   Letter from the Treasury to the Secretary at the Office of Works dated 15 May 1883. Contained in Guardianship file AA050517/3 (The National Archives, WORK 14/128).

16   Condition Report of the Bristol and Gloucestershire Archaeological Society sent to Pitt-Rivers on 12 June 1888 (The National Archives, WORK 14/128).

17   Chippendale, 'The Making of the First Ancient Monuments Act, 1882', p. 40.

18   Chippendale, 'The Making of the First Ancient Monuments Act, 1882', p. 23.

19   M. W. Thompson, 'The First Inspector of Ancient Monuments in the Field', *Journal of the Archaeological Association*, XXIII (1960), pp. 103–24.

20   Instructions to Field Examiners and Revisers, December 1884, paragraphs 157–67, pp. 23–5 (referenced in C. Phillips, *Archaeology and the Ordnance Survey, 1791–1965*, London, 1980, p. 17).

21   Pitt-Rivers file FLO1551, English Heritage Archives.

22   Pitt-Rivers file FLO1564, English Heritage Archives.

23   Chippindale, 'The Making of the First Ancient Monuments Act, 1882', p. 28.

24   Pitt-Rivers file FLO1546, English Heritage Archives, containing estimates of expenditure on ancient monuments from 1884 to 1897.

25 As recorded in the preface to Pitt-Rivers, 'Report on the Present Working of the Ancient Monuments Act', contained in Pitt-Rivers file FL01547, English Heritage Archives.

26 Letter to Sir John Lubbock dated 24 January 1891, contained in Pitt-Rivers file FL01551.

27 Letter to Sir John Lubbock dated 24 January 1891, contained in Pitt-Rivers file FL01551.

4 THE OFFICE OF WORKS TAKES CONTROL

1 Peter Fraser, *Lord Esher: A Political Biography* (London, 1973), covers his military interests extensively. For his ceremonial work at the Office of Works, see James Lees-Milne, *The Enigmatic Edwardian: The Life of Reginald, 2nd Viscount Esher* (London, 1986), pp. 96–128; for its long-term impact on the monarchy, see Frank Prochaska, *Royal Bounty: The Making of a Welfare Monarchy* (New Haven, 1995), p. 128.

2 Internal memorandum: Tower of London – Question of charge of Barracks and remarks on design for proposed new Barrack, 13 March 1897 (The National Archives, WORK 14/3001).

3 Letter of reply dated 29 August 1898 (The National Archives, WORK 14/3001).

4 Jonathan Coad, 'Dover Castle, 1898–1963: Preservation of a Monument: A Postscript', in *Studies in History Presented to R. Allen Brown*, ed. C. Harper Bill, C. Holdsworth and J. Nelson (Woodbridge, 1989), pp. 57–62. I am grateful to Jonathan Coad for drawing my attention to this and furnishing me with a copy.

5 The National Archives, WORK 14/114.

6 The National Archives, WORK 19/16/1, f. 734; Ernest Law, *Kensington Palace: The Birthplace of the Queen Illustrated Being an Historical Guide to the State Rooms, Pictures and Gardens* (London, 1899), pp. 41–4.

7 Edward Impey, *Kensington Palace: The Official Illustrated History* (London, 2003), pp. 102–6.

8 Typescript of *circa* 1904 at Osborne House. I am grateful to Michael Hunter for this.

9 'Anniversary Address', *Proceedings of the Society of Antiquaries*, XXI (1907), pp. 431–54.

10 The monument defaced was Castle Rigg stone circle, in 1906.

11 Letter Gen. No. 2/1059, dated 25 August 1903 (The National Archives, WORK 14/2470).

12 Internal memorandum: War Department Historic Buildings dated 22 July 1904 (The National Archives, WORK 14/3001).

13 *The Times*, 24 April 1900.

14 Joan Evans, *A History of the Society of Antiquaries* (Oxford, 1956), pp. 364–5; Christopher Chippendale, 'The Making of the First Ancient Monuments Act, 1882, and its Administration under General Pitt-Rivers', *Journal of the British Archaeological Association*, CXXXVI (1983), p. 31; National Trust Annual Report, 1900 (my thanks to Ben Cowell for providing this reference).

15 The National Archives, LC1/689.

16 Memorandum entitled 'Ancient Monuments Protection Bill'. Sent from the Permanent Secretary, Lord Esher, to the First Commissioner of Works, Aretas Akers-Douglas, on 25 July 1899. Office of Works file AA5489/1 (The National Archives, WORK 14/135).

17 See previous note.

18 Section 5, Ancient Monuments Protection Act [63 & 64 Vict, Ch. 34].

19 Letter from First Commissioner Akers-Douglas to the Treasury, 12 March 1900. Office of Works file AA5489/1 (The National Archives, WORK 14/135).

20 *Nature Notes*, 11 (1900), pp. 107–9. The Selborne Society was a natural history society, but Bryce made clear in this address that they shared common cause with societies campaigning for monuments and buildings.

21 John Ranlett, 'Checking Nature's Desecration: Late-Victorian Environmental Organisation', *Victorian Studies*, XXVI/2 (1983), pp. 218–19.

22 On the influence of these bodies, see also Peter Mandler, '"Against 'Englishness'": English Culture and the Limits to Rural Nostalgia, 1850–1940', *Transactions of the Royal Historical Society*, XII (1997), pp. 169–70.

23 John Earl, 'London Government: A Record of Custodianship', in *Preserving the Past: The Rise of Heritage in Modern Britain*, ed. Michael Hunter (Stroud, 1996), pp. 61–6.

24 Emily Cole, ed., *Lived in London: Blue Plaques and the Stories behind Them* (New Haven and London, 2009), pp. 9–17.

25 Hermione Hobhouse, *London Survey'd: The Work of the Survey of London, 1894–1994* (Swindon, 1994), pp. 2–26; G. Baldwin Brown, *The Care of Ancient Monuments: An Account of the Legislative and Other Measures Adopted in European Countries for Protecting Ancient Monuments and Objects and Scenes of Natural Beauty, and for Preserving the Aspect of Historical Cities* (Cambridge, 1905), p. 157.

26 Brown, *The Care of Ancient Monuments*.

27 Brown, *The Care of Ancient Monuments*, pp. 57–8.

28 Lesley Ferguson, '100 Years of Recording Scotland's Treasured Places', RCAHMS Website: www.rcahms.gov.uk.

29 Grahame Clark in Royal Commission on the Historical Monuments of England: annual report, 1934, English Heritage Archives, p. 421.

30 Paul Readman, 'Landscape Preservation, "Advertising Disfigurement", and English National Identity, *c.*1890–1914', *Rural History*, XII (2001), pp. 61–83.

31 Many accounts of the early history of the National Trust are hagiographic. The founders are normally referred to as 'Saints' or even the 'Trinity'. Robin Fedden, *The Continuing Purpose: A History of the National Trust, its Aims and Work* (London, 1968); John Gaze, *Figures in a Landscape: A History of the National Trust* (London, 1988). Paula Weideger, *Gilding the Acorn: Behind the Façade of the National Trust* (London, 1994), attempts to debunk the myths of the foundation, but goes too far in the other direction. Merlin Waterson, *The National Trust: The First Hundred Years* (London, 1994), is a much more balanced account. The National Trust lacks an authoritative scholarly history.

32 Waterson, *The National Trust*, pp. 52–4.

1 Kate Tiller, 'The VCH: Past, Present and Future', *The Historian*, XLII (1994), pp. 17–19.

2 T. F. Tout, 'The Present State of Medieval Studies in Great Britain', *Proceedings of the British Academy*, VI (1913), p. 154.

3 Nicholas Doggett, 'Peers, Sir Charles Reed (1868–1952)', in *Oxford Dictionary of National Biography* (2004): http://www.oxforddnb.com/view/article/35454 (accessed 29 July 2012); C. A. Ralegh Radford, 'Sir Charles Reed Peers (1868–1952)', *Proceedings of the British Academy*, XXXIX (1953), pp. 363–8.

4 An unscheduled Roman camp at Rispain, Scotland, had been brought into guardianship by Order in Council on 8 February 1890, but that was truly exceptional at the time. The Pharos at Dover also came under the maintenance responsibility of the Office of Works under the War Office Memorandum of 1908, but the land continued to be occupied by the army.

5 Guardianship file AA56224/3 PTI (The National Archives, WORK 14/63).

6 Internal memorandum dated 25 July 1911 (The National Archives, WORK 14/63).

7 Edward Impey, 'A House for Fish or Men? The Structure, Function and Significance of the Fish House at Meare, Somerset', *English Heritage Historical Review*, IV (2009), p. 31; Longleat, Wiltshire, MS 10754 (cook's account, 1529–30). Letter from Richard Harris to the Secretary dated 15 September 1910 as recorded in a letter to the Treasury dated 16 February 1911: Guardianship file AA76207/3 PTI (The National Archives, WORK 14/566).

8 Letter from Major Richard Winstanley to the Secretary dated 7 July 1911; internal memorandum dated 8 November 1911; Sir Frank Baines report dated 2 December 1911. All contained in Guardianship file AA30652/3 PTI (The National Archives, WORK 14/42).

9 Internal memorandum dated 29 February 1912 (The National Archives, WORK 14/42).

10 'Ancient Monuments and Historic Buildings: Report of the Inspector of Ancient Monuments for the Year Ending 31st March 1911. Presented to Both Houses of Parliament by Command of His Majesty', London: HMSO (The National Archives, WORK 14/2470 C442196).

11 The text of this important speech is in *Proceedings of the Society of Antiquaries*, XXIV (1912), pp. 14–32.

12 John Harris, *Moving Rooms: The Trade in Architectural Salvage* (New Haven and London, 2007), pp. 101–17.

13 David Gilmour, 'Curzon, George Nathaniel, Marquess Curzon of Kedleston (1859–1925)', in *Oxford Dictionary of National Biography* (2004): http://www.oxforddnb.com/view/article/32680?docPos=1 (accessed 29 July 2012).

14 John Keay, *To Cherish and Conserve: The Early Years of the Archaeological Survey of India* (New Delhi, 2011), pp. 106–11.

15 *The Preservation of Ancient Monuments and Historic Buildings in Great Britain* (London: Office of Works, 1936) p. 2.

16 *The Times*, 12 October 1911.

17   House of Lords debate, *Hansard*, 30 April 1912, vol. 11, col. 872.

18   *Report from the Joint Select Committee of the House of Lords and the House of Commons on the Ancient Monuments Consolidation Bill ... Together with the Proceedings of the Committee and Minutes of Evidence*, HMSO, 7 November 1912, p. 44, para. 700.

19   The above paragraphs rely almost entirely on David Cannadine, Jenny Keating and Nicola Sheldon, *The Right Kind of History: Teaching the Past in Twentieth-Century England* (London, 2011).

20   Section 6 Subsection 4.

21   Section 12 Subsection 2.

22   Section 19.

23   The full membership was Lord Crawford, Sir Aston Webb, Reginald Bloomfield, Sir Hercules Read, C. P. Trevelyan, Professor Haverfield, Reginald Smith, Charles Peers, Harry Sirr, Lord Burghclere, Lord Beauchamp (First Commissioner) and Professor Lethaby.

24   Ancient Monuments Board for England minutes, 1 April 1914 (The National Archives, WORK 47/1).

25   Philippa Levine, *The Amateur and the Professional: Antiquarians, Historians and Archaeologists in Victorian England, 1838–1886* (Cambridge, 1986), p. 108.

26   *Guide to the Location of Collections Described in the Reports and Calendars Series, 1870–1980* (The Royal Commission on Historical Manuscripts, 1982).

27   William Vaughan, 'God Help the Minister Who Meddles in Art: History Painting in the New Palace of Westminster', in *The Houses of Parliament: History, Art, Architecture*, ed. Christine Riding and Jacqueline Riding (London, 2000), p. 232.

28   David Cannadine, *National Portrait Gallery: A Brief History* (London, 2007).

29   J. Mordaunt Crook, *The British Museum* (London, 1972), pp. 151–93.

30   Francis Sheppard, *The Treasury of London's Past: An Historical Account of the Museum of London and its Predecessors the Guildhall Museum and the London Museum* (London, 1991), pp. 33–66.

31   Ancient Monuments Board for England minutes, 1 April 1914 (The National Archives, WORK 47/1).

32   Ancient Monuments Board for England minutes, 24 March 1915 (The National Archives, WORK 47/1).

33   Letter 5291/7 from Captain J. F. Laycock to Nottinghamshire County Council dated 22 May 1912 (The National Archives, WORK 14/57).

34   The list does not survive; it may merely have been the subject of a verbal agreement discussed by senior staff at the Office of Works in 1912. However, comments on the Guardianship file state, upon taking Rievaulx Abbey into care in 1917, that it was the 'greatest offer' ever received.

6   THE ANCIENT MONUMENTS DEPARTMENT IN INTER-WAR BRITAIN

1   David Cannadine, *The Decline and Fall of the British Aristocracy* (New Haven and London, 1990), pp. 572–81.

2   Eric de Normann, rev. Mark Pottle, 'Earle, Sir Lionel (1866–1948)', in *Oxford Diction-ary of National Biography* (2004): http://www.oxforddnb.com/view/article/32955 (accessed 29 July 2012).

3   'Duff, Sir (Charles) Patrick', in *Who Was Who* (Oxford, 1920–2008): http://www.ukwhoswho.com/view/article/oupww/whowaswho/U154048 (accessed 29 July 2012).

4   Although he had been employed in more junior roles at the Office of Works since 1911.

5   Charles Peers was knighted in 1931, two years before his retirement from the Ancient Monuments Branch.

6   Office of Works Staff List, 1914–15, p. 10; English Heritage Archives, Swindon.

7   Chris Pond, *The Buildings of Loughton and Notable People of the Town* (Loughton and District Historical Society, 2010), pp. 78–9. It is not clear why Baines kept his marriage secret, but he may have thought that he had married beneath him.

8   According to a report dated 25 November 1935 in The National Archives, Treasury file AS129/01; see Office of Works Staff List, 1928 and 1936, English Heritage Archives. I am grateful to Mike Turner for this reference.

9   For instance, W. Ashworth, *The Genesis of British Town Planning* (London, 1993); John Delafons, *Politics and Preservation: A Policy History of the Built Heritage, 1882–1996* (London, 1997); Jukka Jokilehto, *A History of Architectural Conservation* (Oxford, 1999).

10   The crucial text for this section is John Sheail, *Rural Conservation in Inter-War Britain* (Oxford, 1981).

11   Charles Peers to Lionel Earle, 2 December 1919 (The National Archives, WORK 14/1303).

12   Delafons, *Politics and Preservation*, pp. 36–41.

13   Julian Holder, 'Listing by Another Name', paper delivered at English Heritage Staff Conference in 2012.

14   The arguments are set out in Peter Mandler, '"Against 'Englishness'": English Culture and the Limits to Rural Nostalgia, 1850–1940', *Transactions of the Royal Historical Society*, XII (1997), pp. 155–7, where the principal bibliography is also listed.

15   There is much literature on this too, but see D. N. Jones, 'Planning and the Myth of the English Countryside in the Interwar Period', *Rural History*, I (1990), pp. 249–64.

16   Sam Smiles, 'Equivalents for the Megaliths: Prehistory and English Culture, 1920–50', in *The Geographies of Englishness: Landscape and the National Past, 1880–1940*, ed. David Peters Corbett, Ysanne Holt and Fiona Russell (New Haven and London, 2002), pp. 199–223.

17   Letter from Reginald Smith to Charles Peers dated 17 January 1917. Contained in Guardianship file AA46206/3 (The National Archives, WORK 14/692). See Report V for the guardianship story of Grime's Graves.

18   See Alexandra Harris, *Romantic Moderns: English Writers, Artists and the Imagination from Virginia Woolf to John Piper* (London, 2010).

19   Philip Williamson, *Stanley Baldwin: Conservative Leadership and National Values* (Cambridge, 1999), pp. 243–52.

20   Stanley Baldwin, 'Service', in *On England and Other Addresses* (London, 1926), pp. 62–3.

21   Stanley Baldwin, 'Freedom and Discipline', in *This Torch of Freedom: Speeches and Addresses* (London, 1935), pp. 272–5.

22   Baldwin, 'The Love of Country Things', in *This Torch of Freedom*, p. 120.

23   Stanley Baldwin, 'Old Sarum', in *This Torch of Freedom*, p. 132.

24   John Sheail, *Rural Conservation in Inter-war Britain* (Oxford, 1981), p. 61.

25   M. Crinson, 'Architecture and National Projection Between the Wars', in *Cultural Identities and the Aesthetics of Britishness*, ed. D. Arnold (Manchester, 2004), pp. 182–97.

26   Letter from Sir Patrick Duff to Sir James Rae, HM Treasury, 10 December 1934 (The National Archives, Treasury file AS129/01).

7   CREATING A NATIONAL HERITAGE COLLECTION

1   Sir Lionel Earle, *Turn Over the Page* (London, 1935), pp. 131–52.

2   Bridget Cherry and Nikolaus Pevsner, *The Buildings of England: London 2: South* (London, 1983), p. 306.

3   Earle, *Turn Over the Page*, p. 101.

4   Ancient Monuments Board for England minutes, 8 July 1914; contained in Guardianship file AA16284/3 PTI (The National Archives, WORK 14/542). Letter from Charles Peers to H.G.W. D'Almaine dated 20 November 1917; contained in Guardianship file AA71216/3 PTI (The National Archives, WORK 14/547).

5   Guardianship file AA76271/3 PTI (The National Archives, WORK 14/312). Guardianship file AA26267/3 PTI (The National Archives, WORK 14/130).

6   Keith Emerick, 'From Frozen Monuments to Fluid Landscapes: The Conservation and Presentation of Ancient Monuments from 1882 to the Present', unpublished PHD thesis, University of York, 2003, p. 127.

7   Lionel Earle was knighted in 1916.

8   Memorandum entitled 'Rievaulx Abbey, Yorkshire. Offer of Guardianship', dated 2 May 1917. Contained in Guardianship file AA16260/3A PTI (The National Archives, WORK 14/786). A new Deed of Guardianship, cancelling the old one, was drawn up on 13 May 1921, after additional land was added to the guardianship area (Emerick, 'From Frozen Monuments to Fluid Landscapes', p. 127).

9   David Cannadine, *The Decline and Fall of the British Aristocracy* (New Haven and London, 1990), pp. 88–138.

10   Letter from Captain Moseley to the Office of Works dated 26 February 1920 (The National Archives, WORK 14/57).

11   Letter from Lt. Col. Kitson Clark dated 24 March 1920. Letter to Charles Peers from E.W.G. Crossley of Yorkshire Archaeological Society dated 13 January 1912. Contained in Spofforth Caste File AA20141/3 PTI (The National Archives, WORK 14/494).

12 Letter from Charles Romanes to Sir Frank Baines dated 11 November 1921. Contained in Guardianship file AA10928/3A PT1 (The National Archives, WORK 14/394).

13 Letter dated 11 January 1917. Contained in Guardianship file AA10928/3A PT1 (The National Archives, WORK 14/394). The scheduling request was prompted by the imminent sale of the monument that year.

14 Letter from D. M. Harvey to the Assistant Commissioner of the Forestry Commission, 25 May 1926 (The National Archives, WORK 14/394).

15 Note to the Permanent Secretary, Sir Lionel Earle, 20 August 1927 (The National Archives, Grimes Graves file, WORK 14/692).

16 Note by Charles Peers to Sir Lionel Earle, 24 January 1928 (The National Archives, Grimes Graves file, WORK 14/692).

17 As revealed in a letter from Frederick Raby to the Forestry Commission, 8 October 1928 (The National Archives, Grimes Graves file, WORK 14/692).

18 Reply from N. Young, 6 July 1929 (The National Archives, Grimes Graves file, WORK 14/692).

19 Peter Mandler, *The Fall and Rise of the Stately Home* (New Haven and London, 1997), pp. 240 and 447.

20 'Ministry of Works Expenditure on Ancient Monuments Policy' (The National Archives, T218/311).

21 W. G. Clarke FGS, *Our Homeland Prehistoric Antiquities and How To Study Them* (London, 1922), p. 424.

22 A. Saunders, 'A Century of Ancient Monuments Legislation, 1882–1982', *Antiquaries Journal*, LXIII (1983), pp. 11–33.

23 C. Peers, 'A Research Policy for Field Work', *Antiquaries Journal*, IX (1929), pp. 349–53.

24 The Ancient Monuments Act 1931, Section 9 (1).

25 *The Preservation of Ancient Monuments in Britain* (Office of Works, 1936), p. 15.

26 Philip Snowden, *An Autobiography* (London, 1934), p. 760.

27 John Shepherd, *George Lansbury: At The Heart of Old Labour* (Oxford, 2002), p. 267.

28 House of Commons debate, *Hansard*, 23 February 1931, vol. 248, col. 1893.

29 Guardianship file AA10031/3 PT1 (The National Archives, WORK 14/328); Works file AA10031/2 PT1 (The National Archives, WORK 14/1071).

30 Pevensey was gifted to the Nation by the Duke of Devonshire on 7 October 1925. Portchester was taken into care on 23 June 1926.

31 Guardianship file AA66264/3 PT1 (The National Archives, WORK 14/414).

32 As stated in an internal memorandum in Helmsley Castle Works file AA10031/2 PT1 (The National Archives, WORK 14/1071).

33 Goodrich Castle Works file AA96239/2 PT1 (The National Archives, WORK 14/1062). Goodrich was taken into guardianship in 1920.

34 House of Commons debate, *Hansard*, 23 February 1931, vol. 248, cols 1879–94.

35 'Historic Bowes, About Which Nobody Seems to Bother', *Yorkshire Evening Post*,

November 1928. Contained in Guardianship file AA10329/3 PT1 (The National Archives, WORK 14/1025).

36   Letter from A. W. Watts to M. Connolly, 27 November 1928 (The National Archives, WORK 14/1259). In a reply the Office of Works consented to transfer, though this would have to wait until funds were available. The Deed of Guardianship was finally completed on 20 March 1931.

37   Letter from Hugh Corbet to Arthur Heasman, 20 January 1930. Contained in Haughmond Abbey file AA90984/3 PT1 (The National Archives, WORK 14/1223).

38   Guardianship file AA71429/3 PT1 (The National Archives, WORK 14/741).

39   The Deed of Guardianship was signed on 16 July 1926.

40   Letter from Lionel Earle to the owner's land agents dated 13 July 1925. Contained in file AA16278/3 PT1 (The National Archives, WORK 14/386).

41   Note by the Assistant Secretary, 20 April 1937. Contained in Guardianship file AA90127/3 PT1 (The National Archives, WORK 14/2012).

42   His son presented the freehold to the local council in 1958.

43   Minute sheet dated 28 February 1929. Contained in Guardianship file AA36276/3 PT1 (The National Archives, WORK 14/1082).

44   Contained in Office of Works file AM6/1 (The National Archives, WORK 14/2469).

45   Scheduled Ancient Monument Record No. 1019390. Contained in Office of Works file AA71184/3 PT1 (The National Archives, WORK 14/325).

46   Letter from Raby to S. H. Hamer, Secretary of The National Trust, 24 July 1933 (The National Archives, WORK 14/854).

47   Note by the Assistant Secretary dated 18 August 1939. Contained in Office of Works file AA40999/3 PT1 (The National Archives, WORK 14/854).

48   Note from Bushe-Fox to Raby dated 15 December 1937 (The National Archives, WORK 14/854).

49   Note from Sir Patrick Dufff to the First Commissioner, dated 6 July 1938 (The National Archives, WORK 14/854).

50   Letter from Charles Bradshaw & Waterson to Sir Warren Fisher of the Treasury, 14 February 1936. Contained in Office of Works file AA60512/3 PT1 (The National Archives, WORK 14/700).

51   Letter from Raby to Messrs Bradshaw & Waterson, 14 February 1936 (The National Archives, WORK 14/854).

52   Letter from A. Miller to The Treasury dated 14 July 1937 (The National Archives, WORK 14/854).

53   Note to the First Commissioner dated 22 May 1919. Contained in Guardianship file AA105692/3 (The National Archives, WORK 14/1520)

54   Taken into care on 23 July 1929. Note dated 17 December 1928. Contained in Guardianship file AA40055/3 PT1 (The National Archives, WORK 14/1035).

55   There are various ways of calculating this number. By 1939 there had been 168 separate land transactions, but some of these were for additional land against existing sites

and some were for car parks, etc. The figure of 147 represents the core historical and archaeological acquisitions made since 1883.

8 STONEHENGE

1   Christopher Chippindale, *Stonehenge Complete* (4th edition, London, 2012), p. 142.

2   Chippindale, *Stonehenge Complete*, p. 143.

3   Timothy Darvill, *Stonehenge: The Biography of a Landscape* (Stroud, 2006), p. 264.

4   Darvill, *Stonehenge*, p. 265.

5   Andy Worthington, *Stonehenge: Celebration and Subversion* (Loughborough, 2004), p. 57; Stuart Piggott, *The Druids* (London, 1975), p. 181.

6   Christopher Chippindale, 'Stonehenge, General Pitt-Rivers, and the First Ancient Monuments Act', *Archaeological Review from Cambridge*, II/1 (1983), p. 61.

7   John Lubbock, 'On the Preservation of our Ancient Monuments', in *Addresses, Political and Educational* (London, 1879), pp. 160, 163 and 168.

8   House of Commons debate, 15 April 1874, *Hansard*, vol. 218, col. 589.

9   David Souden, *Stonehenge: Mysteries of the Stones and Landscape* (London, 1997), p. 24.

10   House of Commons debate, 15 April 1874, *Hansard*, vol. 218, col. 587. Letter dated 26 May 1883 from Sir Edmund Antrobus to Pitt-Rivers contained in Pitt-Rivers file FL01562, English Heritage Archives, Swindon.

11   Letter by a member of the public sent to the Wiltshire Archaeological and Natural History Society and forwarded on to Pitt-Rivers, 24 September 1884. Contained in Pitt-Rivers file FL01562.

12   Christopher Chippindale, 'The Enclosure of Stonehenge', *Wiltshire Archaeological Magazine*, LXX–LXXI (1978), p. 112.

13   Letter entitled 'on restoration of fallen trilithons', 2 July 1887. Contained in Pitt-Rivers file FL01562, English Heritage Archives. The drafted letter may not have been sanctioned by the Office of Works. The following year Pitt-Rivers was deterred from joining a committee of the British Association on the preservation of Stonehenge. The First Commissioner thought it unfitting for a Government officer to become embroiled in a campaign against Sir Edmund Antrobus.

14   'Stonehenge: Report on the Condition of Stonehenge by the Inspector of Ancient Monuments', Rushmore, Salisbury, 2 October 1893. Contained in Office of Works file AA71786/3C PT1 (The National Archives, WORK 14/213).

15   Letter from Pitt-Rivers to Augustus Franks (Keeper of British and Medieval Antiquities at the British Museum), 20 April 1896. Contained in Pitt-Rivers file FL01545, English Heritage Archives.

16   Chippindale, 'The Enclosure of Stonehenge', p. 112.

17   Mike Pitts, 'Stonehenge', in *Making History: Antiquaries in Britain, 1707–2007*, ed. Sarah McCarthy, Bernard Nurse and David Gaimster (London, 2007), p. 228.

18   Chippindale, 'The Enclosure of Stonehenge', p. 120.

19   Office of Works file AA71786/23B PT I (The National Archives, WORK 14/214).

20   Office of Works file AA71786/3F (English Heritage Archives).

21   Letter from Cecil Chubb to Sir Alfred Mond (First Commissioner of Works), 15 September 1918. Contained in Office of Works file AA71786/3F.

22   'Memorandum: Stonehenge', written by Sir Frank Baines, 2 November 1918. Office of Works file AA71786/100 (The National Archives, WORK 14/2463).

23   'Stonehenge: Report on the Condition of Stones, from Inspection Made from 14th May 1919 to 28th May 1919'. Office of Works file AA71786/100 (The National Archives, WORK 14/2463).

24   'Memorandum: Works of Repair', 29 September 1919. Office of Works file AA71786/2U PT I (The National Archives, WORK 14/485).

25   'Memorandum: Stonehenge, Excavation', written by Charles Peers, 24 January 1919. Office of Works file AA71786/2U PT I (The National Archives, WORK 14/485).

26   Christopher Chippindale, 'What Future for Stonehenge?', *Antiquity*, LVII (1983), p. 174.

27   Chippindale, *Stonehenge Complete*, p. 193.

28   Chippindale, *Stonehenge Complete*, p. 259.

9   AESTHETICS AND PHILOSOPHY

1   Edmund Vale, *Ancient England: A Review of Monuments and Remains in Public Care and Ownership* (London, 1941).

2   Contained in The National Archives, WORK 14/13. Cited in A. Saunders, 'A Century of Ancient Monuments Legislation, 1882–1982', *Antiquaries Journal*, LXIII (1983), p. 18.

3   Jukka Jokilehto, *A History of Architectural Conservation* (Oxford, 1999), pp. 156–63, 181–7.

4   'Ancient monuments and historic buildings: Report of the Inspector of Ancient Monuments for the year ending 31st March 1912. Presented to both Houses of Parliament by Command of His Majesty', London: HMSO (The National Archives, WORK 14/2470).

5   Frank Baines, 'Preservation of Ancient Monuments and Historic Buildings', *Journal of the Royal Institute of British Architects*, XXX/1 (1923), p. 14.

6   C. R. Peers, 'The Treatment of Old Buildings', *Architectural Journal*, 3rd series, XXXVIII (1931), pp. 311–25.

7   Guardianship file AA10342/3 (The National Archives, WORK 14/64).

8   Guardianship file AA10030/3 PT I (The National Archives, WORK 14/34). These Architect's Reports are dated 6 September 1906 and 16 March 1915.

9   Comment on a project at Windsor Castle in 1923. Cited by Alan Cathersides in the English Heritage Seminar Report 'Ivy on Walls', 19 May 2010.

10   D. Robinson, 'The Making of a Monument: The Office of Works and its Successors at Tintern Abbey', *Monmouthshire Antiquary*, XIII (1997), p. 43.

11   Robinson, 'The Making of a Monument', p. 53. Technical report written by Arthur

Heasman; memorandum on Tintern Abbey dated 13 July 1920; both contained in Tintern Abbey Works file AA82074/2 PT4 (The National Archives, WORK 14/1372).

12   Robinson, 'The Making of a Monument', p. 53. Technical report written by Arthur Heasman; memorandum on Tintern Abbey dated 13 July 1920; Ancient Monuments Board for England minutes, 26 January 1921; as recorded in a letter from Lionel Earle to Reginald Blomfield dated 10 June 1921; all contained in Tintern Abbey Works file AA82074/2 PT4 (The National Archives, WORK 14/1372). Peers, 'The Treatment of Old Buildings', p. 316; Robinson, 'The Making of a Monument', p. 48; Keith Emerick, 'From Frozen Monuments to Fluid Landscapes: The Conservation and Presentation of Ancient Monuments from 1882 to the Present', unpublished PHD thesis, University of York, 2003, p. 184. The same approach was used at Rievaulx Abbey, where a ferro-concrete beam was inserted inside the entire length of the south wall. Works file AA16260/2B PT1 (The National Archives, WORK 14/787).

13   Charles Peers in W. Forsyth, 'The Repair of Ancient Buildings', *Architectural Journal*, 3rd series, XXI (1914), pp. 134–5.

14   Richard Percival Graves, *The Brothers Powys* (London, 1983), p. 99.

15   Correspondence from A. R. Powys to the London editor of the *Manchester Guardian*, Professor Rothenstein and various others, 18 February 1922 (SPAB Archive).

16   Speech by Sir Frank Baines and subsequent discussion, 24 February 1922; in press reports, 25 February 1922 (SPAB Archive).

17   Report of the Society for the Protection of Ancient Buildings contained in the Tintern Abbey Works file AA82074/2 PT4 (The National Archives, WORK 14/1372).

18   Sir F. Baines, 'Preservation of Ancient Monuments and Historic Buildings', *Architectural Journal*, 3rd series, XXXI (1924), pp. 104–74.

19   A. R. Powys, *Repair of Ancient Buildings* (London, 1929).

20   Edmund Vale, *Ancient England: A Review of Monuments and Remains in Public Care and Ownership* (London, 1941), pp. 6–7 and 137; Keith Emerick, 'From Frozen Monuments to Fluid Landscapes: The Conservation and Presentation of Ancient Monuments from 1882 to the Present', unpublished PHD thesis, University of York, 2003, p. 137. Rievaulx Abbey Works file AA16260/2B PT1 (The National Archives, WORK 14/787).

21   Note from Peers to the Secretary dated 31 October 1921; memorandum: Bylands Abbey, 24 October 1921. Contained in AA10131/2 PT1 (The National Archives, WORK 14/1032). *Yorkshire Herald*, 31 March 1923.

22   Finchale Priory was not at this time in guardianship, only up for consideration. After being informed of the terms of guardianship in 1906, the Dean and Chapter decided against it. By 1914 there had been a rethink and they now actively offered the site to the Board of Works. It was taken into care on 24 January 1916.

23   Charles Peers, 'The Preservation of Ancient Monuments: A Note on the Exhibition of the Work of the Department of Ancient Monuments and Historic Buildings, HM Office of Works', *Architectural Journal*, XL (1933), p. 436.

24   Arthur Oswald, 'Chiselhampton House Oxfordshire', *Country Life*, CXV (28 January 1954), pp. 216–19, 284–7.

25   Obituary, *Antiquaries Journal*, XXXIII (1953), written by Sir James Mann (with biography).

26   Anna Keay, 'The Presentation of Guardianship Sites', *Transactions of the Ancient Monuments Society*, XLVIII (2004), pp. 7–20.

27   Graham Harvey, *The Forgiveness of Nature: The Story of* Grass (London, 2002), pp. 266–82; Brian Radam, *Lawnmowers and Grasscutters: A Complete Guide* (Marlborough, 2011), pp. 7–16.

28   Note by Paul Baillie Reynolds dated 24 February 1937. Contained in Guardianship file AA66310/3 PT1 (The National Archives, WORK 14/1242).

29   E. Vale. *Ancient England: A Review of Monuments and Remains in Public Care and Ownership* (London, 1941), p. 6.

30   Letter from Jocelyn Bushe-Fox to Paul Ballie Reynolds, 27 April 1937. Contained in Guardianship file AA90127/3 PT1 (The National Archives, WORK 14/2012).

31   Internal memorandum from the First Commissioner to Sir Patrick Duff, 12 September 1933. Contained in Rievaulx Abbey Works file AA16260/2B PT1 (The National Archives, WORK 14/787).

32   In a letter to Lady D'Abernon on 10 September 1934, Ormsby-Gore wrote: 'Rievaulx is unique, not only in its setting but in the wealth of evidence and remains of the Cistercian Order, not merely in Britain but in Europe. Personally I consider it the most important monastic ruin in the guardianship of the Office of Works.'

33   Minute Sheet dated 23 August 1934; contained in Rievaulx Abbey Works file AA16260/2B PT1 (The National Archives, WORK 14/787). Ormsby-Gore visited Rievaulx on 19 August 1934.

34   House of Lords debate, 11 December 1930, *Hansard*, vol. 79, col. 527.

35   Peers, 'The Preservation of Ancient Monuments, p. 436.

10   INVENTING THE HERITAGE INDUSTRY

1   Letter from Sir Patrick Duff to Sir James Rae, 10 December 1934 (The National Archives, Treasury file AS 129/01).

2   Kathryn A. Morrison and John Minnis, *Carscapes: The Motor Car, Architecture and Landscape in England* (New Haven and London, 2012).

3   Kitty Hauser, *Bloody Old Britain: O. G. S. Crawford and the Archaeology of Modern Life* (London, 2008), pp. 70–3.

4   Timothy Mowl, *Stylistic Cold Wars: Betjeman Versus Pevsner* (London, 2000), pp. 55–75.

5   Peter Mandler, *The Fall and Rise of the Stately Home* (New Haven and London, 1997), pp. 193–224.

6   Kirkham Priory Works file AA26282/2 PT1 (The National Archives, WORK 14/357).

7   T. Champion, 'Protecting the Monuments: Archaeological Legislation from the 1882 Act to PPG 16', in *Preserving the Past: The Rise of Heritage in Modern Britain*, ed. M. Hunter (Stroud, 1996), p. 48; Stephen Leach and Alan Whitworth, *Saving the Wall: The Conservation of Hadrian's Wall, 1746–1987* (Stroud, 2011), p. 12.

8   Internal memorandum, 13 April 1905 (The National Archives, WORK 14/85).

9   Office of Works file AA50059/11/1, English Heritage Archives, Swindon.

10   Memorandum entitled 'Recent changes of policy as regards Walmer Castle, the official residence of the Lord Warden'; letter from Schomberg McDonnell to the Treasury, 5 March 1905; memorandum dated 18 January 1912; letter from the Office of Works to HM Treasury dated 22 December 1913. All contained in The National Archives, Treasury file T1/11620. The exact figure is 13,932 adult admissions per year.

11   In 1936 there was a charge of sixpence at eighty monuments and threepence at forty-three monuments.

12   Reply dated 31 October 1918 (The National Archives, Treasury file T1/11620).

13   Letter from Sir Lionel Earle to M. F. Headlam, 15 November 1922. Contained in Guardianship file AA100602/3 (The National Archives, WORK 14/1424).

14   John Hewitt, 'The "Nature" and "Art" of Shell Advertising in the Early 1930s', *Journal of Design History*, V/2 (1992), pp. 121–39. *The Shell Poster Book* (London, 1998).

15   The National Archives, WORK AA16260/2B PT1; WORK 14/787.

16   Published as *Ancient Monuments in the Care of the Office/Ministry of Works: Illustrated Regional Guides*.

17   As noted by John Gotch in *The Growth of the English House* (London, 1909). An extract from the book appears in Guardianship file AA16284/3 PT1 (The National Archives, WORK 14/542).

18   Report entitled 'Warkworth Castle: Appointment of Caretaker' and dated 14 August 1922. Contained in Guardianship file AA16284/3 PT1 (The National Archives, WORK 14/542).

19   Letter from the Chairman, John Cameron, to Sir Patrick Duff dated 24 June 1936. Contained in Guardianship file AA16284/3 PT1 (The National Archives, WORK 14/542).

20   Note from the First Commissioner to Sir Patrick Duff, 12 September 1933. Contained in Rievaulx Abbey Works file AA16260/2B PT1 (The National Archives, WORK 14/787).

21   Whitby Abbey Works file AA10101/2C PT1 (The National Archives, WORK 14/882).

22   Letter from Sir Patrick Duff to Sir James Rae, 10 December 1934 (The National Archives, Treasury file AS129/011).

11   PROTECTION IN ACTION

1   Ancient Monuments Board for England minutes, 28 January 1919 (The National Archives, WORK 47/1).

2   Under section 12 of the 1913 Ancient Monuments Consolidation and Amendment Act the notification letter of intention to schedule a monument by including it in a list required the owner to give notice forthwith to demolish, remove, structurally alter or add to the monument. In effect, the receipt of this letter by the owner meant that the monument became a scheduled ancient monument protected by law.

3 Treasury Report on the Workings of the Ancient Monuments Branch dated 25 November 1935 (The National Archives, Treasury file T218/311).

4 Treasury Report on the Workings of the Ancient Monuments Branch dated 25 November 1935 (The National Archives, Treasury file T218/311).

5 By the Act of 1931 (see pp. 175–6).

6 Ancient Monuments Board for England minutes, 20 May 1936 (The National Archives, WORK 47/2).

7 Ancient Monuments Board for England minutes, 15 February 1939 (The National Archives, WORK 47/2).

8 Ancient Monuments Board for England minutes, 15 February 1939 (The National Archives, WORK 47/2).

9 Ancient Monuments Board for England minutes, 13 November 1947 (The National Archives, WORK 47/3).

10 Ancient Monuments Board for England minutes, 13 November 1947 (The National Archives, WORK 47/3).

11 Office of Works file AA50720/2 PT1 (The National Archives, WORK 14/203).

12 Memorandum: Ancient Monuments Act, 1913; effect of rejection of Preservation Order by House of Lords Committee, dated 26 May 1914. Both contained in Office of Works file AA50720/2 PT1 (The National Archives, WORK 14/203).

13 Ancient Monuments Board for England minutes, 13 November 1947 (The National Archives, WORK 47/3).

14 Keith Emerick, 'From Frozen Monuments to Fluid Landscapes: The Conservation and Presentation of Ancient Monuments from 1882 to the Present', unpublished PhD thesis, University of York, 2003, p. 115); John Harris, *Moving Rooms: The Trade in Architectural Salvage* (New Haven and London, 2007), pp. 242–3.

15 Ancient Monuments Board for England minutes, 1 May 1914 (The National Archives, WORK 47/1). Emerick, 'From Frozen Monuments to Fluid Landscapes'.

16 Ancient Monuments Board for England minutes, 10 June 1914 (The National Archives, WORK 47/1).

17 Ancient Monuments Board for England minutes, 24 March 1915 (The National Archives, WORK 47/1).

18 Guardianship file AA96230/3 PT1 (The National Archives, WORK 14/594). The owner was sent a letter warning that a Preservation Order would be issued on 6 July 1925. By 16 November 1925 the Deed of Guardianship was signed and deposited in the Deed Register.

19 Guardianship file AA66310/3 PT1 (The National Archives, WORK 14/1242). Draft memorandum to the Cabinet entitled 'Preservation of Netley Abbey', undated but written by the First Commissioner in June 1922.

20 English Heritage, 'History and Research: Lexden Earthworks and Bluebottle Grove': http://www.english-heritage.org.uk/daysout/properties/lexden-earthworks-and-bluebottle-grove/history-and-research/ (accessed 2 July 2012).

21 Letter from H. G. Papillion to the Department dated 29 December 1923. Contained in Office of Works file AA40546/3 PT1 (The National Archives, WORK 14/680).

22 An early example of a Government-sanctioned 'rescue excavation', which appears to have been carried out in 1923 or during the first two months of 1924.

23 Note by Charles Peers to the Secretary dated 1 January 1924 (The National Archives, WORK 14/384).

24 Petition submitted to the House of Commons on 19 February 1925.

25 Report of the Ancient Monuments Advisory Committee, 1921, London: HMSO (The National Archives, WORK 14/2470 c442196).

26 The National Archives catalogue information: http://www.nationalarchives.gov. uk/catalogue/displaycataloguedetails.asp?CATID=35&CATLN=1&accessmethod=5&j=1 (accessed 29 July 2012).

12 SAVING HADRIAN'S WALL

1 The most extensive study of the preservation of Hadrian's Wall is Stephen Leach and Alan Whitworth, *Saving the Wall: The Conservation of Hadrian's Wall, 1746–1987* (Stroud, 2011). Their work has to a great extent informed the following.

2 In the year of its foundation the Trust was in correspondence with Pitt-Rivers regarding the protection of the Antonine Wall. These letters are contained in Pitt-Rivers file FL01550, English Heritage Archives, Swindon.

3 The National Archives, WORK 14/2470.

4 'Ancient Monuments and Historic Buildings: Report of the Inspector of Ancient Monuments for the Year Ending 31st March 1911. Presented to Both Houses of Parliament by Command of His Majesty'. London: HMSO (The National Archives, WORK 14/2470).

5 The National Archives, WORK 14/2470.

6 The National Archives, WORK 14/1257. This letter states that Wake was entitled to work within 30 feet of the wall, contrary to the figure of 10 feet given in Leach and Whitworth, *Saving the Wall*, p. 20.

7 Internal memorandum from Charles Peers to the Permanent Secretary, 28 January 1930 (The National Archives, WORK 14/2470).

8 Letter dated 11 February 1930; letter dated 20 February 1930 (The National Archives, WORK 14/2470).

9 Note from Charles Peers to the Secretary, 21 February 1930 (The National Archives, WORK 14/2470).

10 Memorandum dated 26 February 1930 (The National Archives, WORK 14/2470).

11 Newspaper article dated 24 April 1930 (The National Archives, WORK 14/1257).

12 Minutes of the Cabinet, 28 May 1930 and 3 December 1930 (The National Archives, CAB/23/64/7 and CAB/23/65/22).

13 Note for the First Commissioner's use contained in The National Archives, WORK 14/1260.

14 Section 1. Ancient Monuments Act [21 & 22 Geo.5, Ch. 16].

15 First Schedule. Ancient Monuments Act [21 & 22 Geo.5, Ch.16].

16 Note for the First Commissioner's use (The National Archives, WORK 14/1260).

17   A letter from G. M. Trevelyan to Eric Birley dated 11 November 1948 begins: 'Since the Ministry of works has not fulfilled its hope that it would acquire the guardianship of the whole Roman Wall' (contained in English Heritage file AA110014/3 PT1).

13 WHO SAVES COUNTRY HOUSES?

1   Early annual reports of the Historic Buildings Councils highlight the problem of finding domestic staff as a major threat to the survival of great houses.

2   R. Strong, M. Binney and J. Harris, eds, *The Destruction of the Country House* (London, 1974).

3   Roy Strong, *Country Life, 1897–1997: The English Arcadia* (London, 1996), pp. 86–125.

4   Merlin Waterson, *A Noble Thing: The National Trust and its Benefactors* (London, 2011), pp. 39–51.

5   Peter Mandler, *The Fall and Rise of the Stately Home* (New Haven and London, 1997), pp. 311–53.

6   House of Lords debate, 21 November 1945, *Hansard*, vol. 137, col. 1085.

7   File on Brede Place (The National Archives, WORK 14/1201).

8   Diary entry for 4 May 1944 in J. Lees-Milne, *Prophesying Peace: Diaries, 1944–1945* (Norwich, 2003), p. 29.

9   Letter from Sir Eric de Normann to Sir Alan Barlow, 3 October 1946 (The National Archives, T218/418).

10   Letter from Fraser to Sir Eric de Normann, 12 August 1947 (The National Archives, T218/418).

11   Sir Edward Bridges, later Lord Bridges, was the son of the Poet Laureate Robert Bridges. He was Permanent Secretary at the Treasury from 1945 to 1956, and later Chairman of the Royal Fine Art Commission and the Pilgrim Trust, and a member of the Executive Committee of the National Trust. The 'Bridges Report' on redundant churches (1960) led to the creation of the Churches Conservation Trust.

12   Memorandum from Sir Edward Bridges to Mr Trend, HM Treasury, 9 January 1948 (The National Archives, T218/418).

13   Diary entry for 20 February 1948 in J. Lees-Milne, *Midway on the Waves: Diaries, 1948–9* (Norwich, 2005), p. 29.

14   Simon Thurley, *Hampton Court: A Social and Architectural History* (New Haven and London, 2003), pp. 357–70.

15   Edward Hale to Sir Alan Barlow, 20 June 1946 (The National Archives, T227/349).

16   Sir Eric de Normann to Dennis Proctor, 20 March 1948 (The National Archives, WORK 17/177).

17   Diary entry for 9 March 1948 in J. Lees-Milne, *Caves of Ice: Diaries, 1948–49* (Norwich, 2004).

18   Peter Mandler, *The Fall and Rise of the Stately Home* (New Haven and London, 1997), p. 335, quoting a typescript of Dalton's speech.

19 Quoted in Ben Pimlott, *Hugh Dalton* [1985] (London, 1995), p. 456.

20 John Gaze, *Figures in a Landscape: A History of the National Trust* (London, 1988), p. 147.

21 See The National Archives, HLG 126/16.

22 The National Archives, HLG 126/16.

23 Diary entry for 18 April 1947 in Lees-Milne, *Caves of Ice*, pp. 154–5.

24 Memorandum from P. K. Baillie Reynolds to Bryan O'Neil, 21 January 1948 (English Heritage file AA90995/3).

25 Memorandum by Sir Eric de Normann, 6 May 1948 (The National Archives, HLG 126/16).

26 Note of meeting of 8 March 1949 (The National Archives, HLG 126/16).

27 House of Commons debate, 3 July 1953, *Hansard*, vol. 517, col. 755.

28 Proceedings of the Committee on Houses of National Importance, 12 March 1949 (The National Archives, T277/73).

29 *Report of the Committee on Houses of Outstanding Historic or Architectural Interest.* The report and its recommendations have been discussed in some detail elsewhere, e.g., Marcus Binney, 'The Future of the Country House', in *The Destruction of the Country House*, ed. Strong, Binney and Harris, pp. 184–7; Peter Mandler, 'Nationalising the Country House', in *Preserving the Past: The Rise of Heritage in Britain*, ed. M. Hunter (Stroud, 1996), pp. 105–7.

30 Papers relating to the responses of the relevant Government departments are in The National Archives, HLG 126/17.

31 Minutes of a meeting held on 23 October 1950 (The National Archives, HLG 126/17).

32 Instructions to Parliamentary Counsel on the Monuments and Buildings (Protection) Bill, undated but from around June–July 1951 (The National Archives, T218/10).

33 Sir David Eccles, 20 November 1951 (The National Archives, WORK 14/2358).

34 House of Commons debate, 3 July 1953, *Hansard*, vol. 517, col. 755.

35 J. Cornforth, *The Country Houses of England, 1948–1998* (London, 1998), pp. 49–68.

14 WAR AND AFTERMATH

1 *The Spectator*, 18 October 1940.

2 C. M. Kohan, *Works and Buildings* (London, 1952), pp. 386–92.

3 Internal memorandum: 'Ancient Monuments & Historic Buildings, 1945–1952' (The National Archives, WORK 82/10) (Ministry of Works 1949, p. 5).

4 *50 Years of the National Buildings Record, 1941–1991, with an Introduction by Sir John Summerson* (London, 1991).

5 Andrew Saint, 'How Listing Happened', in *Preserving the Past: The Rise of Heritage in Britain*, ed. Michael Hunter (Stroud, 1996), pp. 115–33; Frank Kelsall, 'Not as Ugly as Stonehenge: Architecture and History in the First Lists of Historic Buildings', *Architectural History*, LII (2009), pp. 1–27.

6 Instructions to Parliamentary Counsel on the Monuments and Buildings (Protection) Bill, undated but from around June–July 1951 (The National Archives, T218/10).

7   The proposals in Cabinet Paper CAB 129/45/35 were approved in Cabinet on 23 April 1951 (The National Archives, CAB/128/19).

8   David Kynaston, *Austerity Britain: A World to Build* (London, 2007), p. 24.

9   'Guide to the Ministry of Works Headquarters 1947' (The National Archives, WORK 22/689).

10   E. M. Jope, 'B. H. St J. O'Neil: A Memoir', in *Studies in British History: Essays in Recognition of the Work of B. H. St J. O' Neil*, ed. Jope (London, 1961), p. 9. Memorandum from Bryan O'Neil to Sir Eric de Normann, 9 February 1948 (The National Archives, WORK 14/2199).

11   Sir Harold Emmerson, *The Ministry of Works* (London, 1956).

12   Memorandum from Sir Harold Emmerson to Sir Eric de Normann, 29 October 1947 (The National Archives, WORK 14/2199).

13   Memorandum from Dorothy Johnstone to W.V.Wood, HM Treasury, 19 March 1948 (The National Archives, T218/311).

14   Letter from P. K. Baillie Reynolds to John Fattorini, 18 December 1947 (English Heritage AA20300/3 part 1).

15   Memorandum from P. K. Baillie Reynolds to AS22, 28 August 1947, on AA40523/3 part 1, English Heritage Archives, Swindon.

16   S.4(3) of the 1931 Act stipulated that a copy of the Preservation Order should be 'fixed on some conspicuous part of the monument'.

17   *Evening News*, 30 October 1950. A copy of the article is on English Heritage file AA50508/3 part 1.

18   In 1966 the functions of the Minister of Works under Part I of the Act were transferred to the Minister of Housing and Local Government.

19   Section 3(3) of the 1931 Act and Section 3(2) of the 1913 Act, respectively.

20   Section 4(1) of the 1953 Act.

21   House of Commons debate, 3 July 1953, *Hansard*, vol. 517, cols 753–818.

22   House of Commons debate, 3 July 1953, *Hansard*, vol. 517, cols 753–818.

23   Annual Report, 1953, of the Historic Buildings Council for England, p. 2.

24   Annual Report, 1953, of the Historic Buildings Council for England, p. 6.

25   R. Strong, M. Binney and J. Harris, eds, *The Destruction of the Country House* (London, 1974), p. 8.

15   THE MINISTRY BRANCHES OUT

1   Obituary of Arnold Taylor: www.telegraph.co.uk/news/obituaries/1414922/Arnold -Taylor.html (8 April 2013).

2   Christopher Gerrard, *Medieval Archaeology: Understanding Traditions and Contemporary Approaches* (London, 2003), pp. 95–132.

3   Peter Mandler, *History and National Life* (London, 2002), pp. 93–115.

4   *The Economist*, 24 May 1969.

5   Undated report by Rex Wailes, *circa* 1964 (The National Archives, WORK 14/2926).

6   Minutes of Ancient Monuments Board, 25 May 1951 (The National Archives, WORK 47/3).

7   Memorandum from P. K. Baillie Reynolds to Kenneth Newis, 6 April 1955 (The National Archives, WORK 14/2924).

8   Memorandum from P. K. Baillie Reynolds to S. Rigold, 25 October 1955 (English Heritage file AA30920/3, part 1).

9   See The National Archives, WORK 14/2924.

10   File note by F. C. Withey, 30 October 1959 (The National Archives, WORK 14/2490).

11   The six scheduled sites were the Harwich Crane, Essex, the Old Malt House and Kiln, Stevenage, earthworks of the Surrey Iron Railway, Wortley Top Forge, the pottery at Longton Hall, Stoke-on-Trent, and the Iron Bridge, Shropshire.

12   Marylin Parker, Michael Nevell and Mark Sissons, *Industrial Archaeology: A Handbook*, CBA Practical Handbook 21 (2012), pp. 1–9.

13   House of Commons debate, 26 May 1966, *Hansard*, vol. 729, c.160w.

14   Paper AME/P320 presented to the Ancient Monuments Board meeting of 29 May 1970 (The National Archives, WORK 47/7).

15   Neil Cossons, 'The Conservation of Industrial Monuments', *Museums Journal*, LXXIV (1974), p. 62.

16   P. R. White, 'Stott Park Bobbin Mill, Colton, Cumbria: An Historical Outline, 1835–1971', in *Ancient Monuments and their Interpretation: Essays Presented to A. J. Taylor*, ed. M. R. Apted, R. Gilyard-Beer and A. D. Saunders (Chichester, 1977), p. 346.

17   J. G. Hurst and J. Golson, lecture to the Royal Archaeological Institute, 4 March 1953. A copy of the text is on The National Archives, WORK 14/2476.

18   Annual Report, 1958, of the Deserted Medieval Village Research Group. A copy is on The National Archives, WORK 14/2476.

19   Text of the Memorandum incorporated in the Annual Report, 1965, of the Deserted Medieval Village Research Group. A copy of the report is on The National Archives, WORK 14/2476.

20   Memorandum, 25 March 1950 (The National Archives, WORK 14/2350).

21   Letter from Kenneth Newis to Dorothy Johnstone 3 September 1953 (The National Archives, WORK 14/2350).

22   *Report of the Archbishops' Commission on Redundant Churches, 1958–60*, paras. 163 and 164.

23   Brian Wells to Peter Smith, 23 June 1980 (English Heritage file AA90778/25, part 1).

24   Neil Burton, 'A Cuckoo in the Nest: The Emergence of the Georgian Group', in *From William Morris: Building Conservation and the Arts and Crafts Cult of Authenticity, 1877–1939*, ed. Chris Miele (New Haven and London, 2005), pp. 253–7.

25   *Country Life*, CII (18 July 1947), pp. 126–7.

26   *Country Life*, CII (18 July 1947), pp. 126–7.

27   John Bold, *Greenwich: An Architectural History of the Royal Hospital for Seamen and the Queen's House* (New Haven, 2000), pp. 89–90; *The Queen's House, Greenwich: Fourteenth Monograph of the London Survey Committee* (London, 1937).

1   Kathryn A. Morrison and John Minnis, *Carscapes: The Motor Car, Architecture and Landscape in England* (New Haven and London, 2012).

2   Sophie Andrae, 'From Comprehensive Development to Conservation Areas', in *Preserving the Past: The Rise of Heritage in Modern Britain*, ed. Michael Hunter (Stroud, 1996), p. 141.

3   Richard Crossman, *The Diaries of a Cabinet Minister*, vol. I: *Minister of Housing, 1964–66* (London, 1975), p. 219.

4   Wayland Kennet, *Preservation* (London, 1972), pp. 49–107.

5   The post of Director, equivalent to Under Secretary, was held by three people between 1972 and 1983: Dr Vivian Lipman (1921–1990), Maurice Mendoza (1921–2000) and Peter Rumble (b. 1929). The last took over when Mendoza retired in 1981.

6   A. J. Taylor to G. M. Newton, 18 November 1968 (English Heritage file AA30226/3 part 1).

7   A. J. Taylor to G. M. Newton, 18 November 1968 (English Heritage file AA30226/3 part 1); Sir Osbert Sitwell to Sir Alan Lascelles, Chairman of Historic Buildings Council, 31 July 1959 (English Heritage file AA30226/3 part 1).

8   F.J.E. Raby to Messrs Bradshaw and Waterson, 28 February 1936 (The National Archives, WORK 14/700).

9   Stuart Blaylock, *Bowhill: The Archaeological Study of a Building under Repair in Exeter, Devon, 1977–95* (London, 2005), p. 283.

10   Bushmead Priory (first offered in 1952), Piel Castle (1945), Chisbury Chapel (1938) and Edlingham Castle (1932).

11   Obituary of Andrew Saunders by Henrietta Quinnell: www.cornisharchaeology. org.uk/obituaries.htm (accessed 8 April 2013).

12   A. D. Saunders to Mrs Hewer, 6 April 1977. Contained in AA51560/3 part 1, English Heritage Archives, Swindon.

13   Mendoza to A. R. Head, 5 October 1981. Contained in AA51560/3 part 2, English Heritage Archives.

14   Ancient Monuments Board for England, 1977, 42nd paper, September 1977 meeting (The National Archives, WORK 47/12).

15   Ancient Monuments Board paper AME/P (80)16 (The National Archives, WORK 47/12).

16   *Audley End, Essex: Conservation Plan*, 2 vols (Oxford, 2001), I, p. 18.

17   P. K. Thornton and M. F. Tomlin, *The Furnishing and Decoration of Ham House* (Furniture History Society, 1980), pp. 193–4.

18   Simon Thurley, *Hampton Court: A Social and Architectural History* (New Haven and London, 2003), pp. 370–8.

19   Felldon Clegg Bradley Architects, Conservation Plan: Gloucester Blackfriars, October 2007.

20   Personal communication with Professor Martin Biddle.

21   C. J. Young to A. D. Saunders, 17 April 1980 (English Heritage file AA30602/3 part 1).

22   Derek Sherborn, *An Inspector Recalls: Saving our Heritage* (Lewes, 2003), pp. 165–6; John Delafons, *Politics and Preservation: A Policy History of the Built Heritage, 1882–1996* (London 1997), pp. 133–5.

23   Martin Cherry et al., *Heritage Protection Reform: Statutory Lists: Review of Quality and Coverage, 2010* (English Heritage, July 2010), pp. 14–17.

24   *The Times* (Saturday, 31 January 1981), p. 13 col. F.

25   *The Times* (Saturday, 14 February 1981), p. 15, col. H.

26   Obituary of Maurice Mendoza by Jennie Page in *Conservation Bulletin*, 39 (December 2000).

27   *Organisation of Ancient Monuments* (1981), p. 3.

28   *Organisation of Ancient Monuments* (1981), p. 3.

29   Parliamentary consideration of the bill is summarised in John Delafons, *Politics and Preservation: A Policy History of the Built Heritage, 1882–1996* (London, 1997), pp. 138–41.

30   Elain Harwood and Alan Powers, eds, *The Heroic Period of Conservation*, Twentieth Century Architecture, 7 (The Twentieth Century Society, 2004).

31   For example: Jane Fawcett, ed., *The Future of the Past: Attitudes to Conservation, 1174–1974* (London, 1976); Harwood and Powers, *The Heroic Period of Conservation*.

CONCLUSION

1   Deyan Sudjic, *The Edifice Complex: How the Rich and Powerful Shape the World* (London, 2005), pp. 278–9.

2   Total cost of Historic Scotland and the Royal Commission on Historical Monuments for Scotland divided by the population.

3   Robert Hewison, *The Heritage Industry: Britain in a Climate of Decline* (London, 1987); Sudjic, *The Edifice Complex*, pp. 15–16, 165.

4   *Overseas Visitors to Britain: Understanding Trends, Attitudes and Characteristics* (Visit Britain, September 2010).

5   *Overseas Visitors to Britain: Understanding Trends, Attitudes and Characteristics* (Visit Britain, September 2010), p. 30.

6   Simon Thurley, 'Introduction', in *Building England* (in preparation).